By the Same Author

The Thirsty Muse: Alcohol and the American Writer
Harold Lloyd: The Man on the Clock
Keaton: The Man Who Wouldn't Lie Down
Some Time in the Sun

FIREBRAND

FIREBRAND

The Life of Horace Liveright

TOM DARDIS

RANDOM HOUSE NEW YORK

Portions of the Introduction and Chapter 8 were originally published in somewhat
different form in *The Antioch Review*.

Grateful acknowledgment is made to the following for permission to print both published and
unpublished material:

THE BERTRAND RUSSELL EDITORIAL PROJECT: Excerpts from the Collected Papers of Bertrand
Russell housed at The Bertrand Russell Archives, McMaster University, Hamilton, Ontario.
Used by permission of the Bertrand Russell Archives Copyright Permissions Committee.

COLIN SMYTHE LTD AND THE HOUGHTON LIBRARY, HARVARD UNIVERSITY: Excerpts from
unpublished letters from George Moore to Horace Liveright housed at the Houghton Library,
Harvard University, shelf mark bMS Eng 1066. Copyright © 1995 by the Estate of John
Christopher Medley. Reprinted by permission of Colin Smythe Ltd and the Houghton Library,
Harvard University.

LILLY LIBRARY, INDIANA UNIVERSITY AND JEAN SINCLAIR: Excerpt from two letters dated November
6, 1926 and November 12, 1926 from Upton Sinclair to Horace Liveright. Used by permission
of Lilly Library, Indiana University, Bloomington, Indiana, and Jean Sinclair.

LITTLE, BROWN AND COMPANY: Excerpts from *No Whippings, No Gold Watches* by Louis
Kronenberger. Copyright © 1970 by Louis Kronenberger. Excerpts from *An Unfinished Woman*
by Lillian Hellman. Copyright © 1969 by Lillian Hellman. Reprinted by permission of Little,
Brown and Company.

THE NEWBERRY LIBRARY AND DR. CHARLES MODLIN, LITERARY EXECUTOR FOR THE SHERWOOD
ANDERSON PAPERS AND HAROLD OBER ASSOCIATES: Excerpts from ten letters from Sherwood
Anderson to Horace Liveright housed at The Newberry Library. Used by permission of The
Newberry Library, Dr. Charles Modlin, and Harold Ober Associates.

HAROLD OBER ASSOCIATES: Excerpts from *Memoirs* by Sherwood Anderson. Reprinted by
permission of Harold Ober Associates.

UNIVERSITY OF PENNSYLVANIA: Excerpts from the unpublished writings of Theodore Dreiser from
the Theodore Dreiser Papers housed in the Special Collections at Van Pelt Library, University
of Pennsylvania. Used by permission.

Library of Congress Cataloging-in-Publication Data
Dardis, Tom.
Firebrand: the life of Horace Liveright/Thomas A. Dardis.
p. cm.
Includes bibliographical references and index.
ISBN 0-679-40675-1
1. Liveright, Horace Brisbane, 1884–1933. 2. Publishers and
publishing—United States—Biography. 3. Boni & Liveright—History.
4. Literature publishing—United States—History—20th century.
I. Title.
Z473.L56D37 1995
070.5′092—dc20
[B]   94-41334

Manufactured in the United States of America
24689753
First Edition

Book design by Bernard Klein

Once again for Ellen Ervin

Acknowledgments

Lucy Wilson and Herman Liveright were generous with their time while recalling their father for me; their warm support was invaluable. I am also grateful to them for the loan of the family photos as well as HBL's letters to Lucille Liveright. A second, major source of information about Liveright as a publisher has been Victor Schmalzer, vice president of W. W. Norton Company, the firm that acquired the Liveright properties. Victor's enthusiasm for all things pertaining to HBL was infectious.

Gary Giddins showed me his collection of the Arthur Pell papers. Paul Mayer permitted me to quote from his father's papers in the Billy Rose Collection at the New York Public Library. Mrs. Odette Komroff has allowed me to quote from her husband's unpublished narrative about HBL, and to use some of his photos. Nancy Shawcross of the Van Pelt Library at the University of

Pennsylvania was of great assistance in guiding me through its collection of HBL's papers. Thanks are also extended to the Newberry Library in Chicago, the Firestone Library at Princeton, the Lilly Library at the University of Indiana, the Houghton Library at Harvard, the Beinecke Library at Yale, the McMaster University Library in Hamilton, Ontario, and the Special Collections division of the Columbia University Library. Finally, the staff of the Berg Collection of the New York Public Library was helpful, as was that of its main reference collection, which houses the John Quinn papers.

Ellen Ervin and Benjamin Hellinger have read the manuscript, producing much improvement. Assistance in various forms has been provided by Edward Bernays, Anthony Powell, Edwin Gilcher, Nathan Kroll, Frank Heller, Mary Ellis, Donald Symington, Alex Baskin, William Boni, and Patricia Lambert. Gordon Neavill has graciously shared his knowledge of the history of the Modern Library. Lawrence Rainey's pioneering work on Pound and Eliot was essential, as was Walker Gilmer's earlier account of HBL: *Horace Liveright: Publisher of the Twenties.*

It was John Herman who first suggested that I single out Horace Liveright to write about. My agent, Georges Borchardt, concurred with enthusiasm. Robert Loomis, my editor at Random House, has been steadfast assisting me to improve the quality of this book; his sharp eyes were invaluable.

Contents

Introduction

HORACE Brisbane Liveright, former Wall Street bond salesman and a high school dropout, created the most magnificent yet
messy publishing firm this century has seen. During his thirteen-
year career, Liveright became as notorious for the kinds of books
he published as for the way in which he published them and in so
doing changed forever the methods by which books could be marketed in the United States. A Jew, he entered a field in which Jews
were not welcome. From the outset, Liveright defied convention
by publishing writers whose books were considered obscure, revolutionary, or obscene. Dubbed "The Firebrand," Liveright spent
many days in courtrooms defending his right to publish writers like
Sigmund Freud and Bertrand Russell. He was loathed by the self-
righteous, as much for his books as for the flamboyant lifestyle he
pursued—a style that turned his wildly unorthodox firm into a ten-

year-long party fueled by bootleggers and adorned by chorus girls. Yet his firm, Boni and Liveright, stands for much of what was splendid about the American 1920s.

The handsome man behind it all was tall and bone thin. He possessed an overwhelming personal charm that had much in common with that of his friend the mayor of New York, the Honorable James "Jimmy" Walker. Convinced that he resembled the great lover of the day, the actor John Barrymore, Liveright acted out the part of the Great Profile in his own hectic love life. Something of a mesmerist, Liveright used his charm to have his way with literary agents, writers, booksellers, and reviewers. He was, first and last, a born showman, whose business methods earned him envy, scorn and hatred.

Always unconventional, he placed his business in an obscure brownstone residence just off Sixth Avenue on West Forty-eighth Street, deep in the heart of Manhattan's speakeasy district. Casual visitors to the offices might well have believed they had entered not a place where books were the main concern but rather a rehearsal hall, because the offices were often filled with theatrical agents, singers and dancers waiting to be auditioned and there were always beautiful girls galore. From 1924 onward Liveright became an active Broadway producer, best remembered for his famous production of *Dracula,* starring Bela Lugosi. Liveright's critics considered a book publisher's involvement with Broadway as beneath contempt. They were equally outraged by Horace's constant Wall Street speculations that bled the firm of its money on a regular basis. In July 1928, his company achieved the peculiar distinction of having six out of the ten best-selling books in the United States on its list yet having no ready cash with which to pay its bills. With sales exceeding a million dollars a year, the firm produced only paper-thin profits of a few thousand or none at all. Horace was the most generous publisher of his time—almost any writer of talent could obtain a Liveright advance. He spent incoming money as fast as it arrived. When his sales manager informed him that Hart Crane's first volume, *White Buildings,* was out of print and had sold only 350 copies, Horace ordered the book to be reprinted immediately and gave Crane an advance for *The Bridge.* He was, as Ezra Pound observed, "a pearl among publishers."

From the beginning Liveright operated as a gambler might, basing his enterprise on taking chances on the new and startling literary talents emerging all over the world after the war. Because he thought it would be fun, Liveright took up Ezra Pound's famous war cry, "Make it New!" with a vengeance. Pound himself was on Horace's list as early as 1920, thereby attracting other innovative writers to the firm, among them T. S. Eliot, whose *The Waste Land* was published by Liveright when the firm was only in its fifth year. He had begun publishing the plays of Eugene O'Neill in 1919, a year before O'Neill's first Broadway success. In the previous year, Horace had reissued Theodore Dreiser's *Sister Carrie* and then brought out all of that writer's later books. When Sherwood Anderson first encountered the work of William Faulkner, he had no doubt that *Soldiers' Pay* should appear on the list he shared with Dreiser and O'Neill. Ernest Hemingway thought that the correct place for his friend Gertrude Stein was with the ever-bountiful Horace, who nevertheless rejected her. He was surely right, though, when he published Hemingway's first book, *In Our Time,* as well as the first efforts of e. e. cummings, Djuna Barnes, Dorothy Parker, Lewis Mumford, and Hart Crane.

Liveright became famous for the lavish parties he threw at the brownstone. His guests knew they would drink the best bootleg liquor in town and that they might meet prominent figures like Theodore Dreiser, Dorothy Parker, Paul Robeson, Carl Van Vechten, Ben Hecht, Ira and George Gershwin, and many attractive young women from the chorus line of the *Follies.* The chief tastemakers of the day, Alexander Woollcott, George Jean Nathan, Ernest Boyd, and Burton Rascoe, were often in attendance at these affairs, discussing the latest juicy bits of literary gossip. Probably the most listened-to of all the regular guests was the redoubtable financier Otto Kahn, reputed to be the wise man of Wall Street. There were so many parties that Horace's severest critics thought of the Liveright years as a decade-long party that ended only when the market crashed in 1929 and all the soap bubbles burst at once.

Despite the party atmosphere prevailing at Boni and Liveright, a torrent of notable books kept appearing, all adorned with the oddly inappropriate logo of a cowled monk. In addition to his impressive list of American writers, Horace had the distinction of bringing out the novels of Stendhal for the first time in America, as well as the first novels of two French Nobel Prize winners, Roger Martin du Gard and François Mauriac. In all, seven of Liveright's authors went on to win the Nobel Prize.

Liveright's forays against traditional thinking were not confined to literature. Besides popularizing the work of Sigmund Freud (*A General Introduction to Psychoanalysis*) the firm also published two of his main disciples, Sándor Ferenczi and Wilhelm Stekel. Many American booksellers kept all three of these writers' works "under the counter," out of fear of prosecution by the authorities or by representatives of the vice societies. Liveright fought censorship more vigorously than any other publisher of his time.

U.S. book publishing was never the same after Horace Liveright's arrival. He was largely responsible for the idea, now commonplace, that books constituted news and should be treated accordingly, a practice quite contrary to that prevailing among his competitors, who ran their firms like conservative banking houses. With his gaudy showmanship and genius for publicity, Liveright created new and hitherto unknown audiences for books.

Always in the limelight of publicity or scandal, Liveright craved recognition for himself just as much as for the amazing books he published. Despite his tireless ebullience and the self-confidence he seemed to radiate, it is clear that he was often a man working against his own interests. For Horace, success was never enough. There was always something new and challenging for him to take up, some wrong of the past to right, some outrageous act to dare the lightning.

People could not hold neutral feelings about Horace Liveright. Ben Hecht, who regarded him as "The Scoundrel," wrote, produced and directed a satirical film about his publisher. Lillian Hellman found in Horace a figure of unforgettable grandeur. His short, brilliant career resembles that of a meteor streaking across the heavens and crashing with a roar which echoed for decades. He was surely emblematic of the "Golden Twenties," and, as F. Scott Fitzgerald said of himself, he was "never disposed to accept the present but always striving to change it, better it, or even sometimes destroy it. There were always far horizons that were more golden, bluer skies somewhere."

FIREBRAND

New York Bound

Dear God, bless Horace too and make him a good boy.
—Liveright family prayers

WHEN Horace Liveright told people his life story, he usually began with the origin of his name. What he related was longer on imagination than fact, but in time the tale took on a life of its own, and he may have begun to believe the yarn about his Sephardic Jewish ancestry. His version of history chronicled a time in four-teenth-century Spain when the family name was "Labrengo." At the height of Torquemada's power and the Spanish Inquisition, the family had fled to Portugal, then to Holland and finally to Würzburg, Germany. New names were routinely given to Jewish immigrants there, and Horace's ancestors, he believed, were handed the name "Leibrecht" (for "courage and forthrightness.") When Horace's father came through the gates of Ellis Island in the mid–nineteenth century, he decided to make life easier for himself by anglicizing this name to "Liveright." Most Americans mispronounce it as Liver-right; the correct way sounds like a command: *Live-right!*

The ascertainable truth is that the Liveright family can be traced back to Würzburg but no further—anything prior is pure speculation. Horace's father, Henry, was born in Würzburg in 1841 and came to the United States in 1857 as part of the huge German immigration wave of the midcentury. He settled first in Lewistown, Pennsylvania, before establishing himself in the dry goods business in Pittsburgh. After the end of the Civil War he moved again, this time to Philadelphia, where he met Henrietta Fleisher, another child of German-Jewish immigrants. They married in 1872. The young couple tried their luck in various enterprises in Davenport, Iowa, before returning to Pennsylvania, where Henry took up his principal life's work: the operation of several coal mines in the area around Osceola Mills, in the western part of the state. He mined the Moshannon soft coal, highly prized for its combustive qualities. Not so highly prized was the productivity of the somewhat broken-down mines he had purchased. They only showed a profit during the period of the anthracite coal mine strikes in the eastern part of the state. The strikes created a sudden surge of demand for Henry's coal, and, as long as the disputes continued, the Osceola mines operated at a profit.

Henry ran a company store for his workers, but here his basic kindness worked against his business judgment. As the baby of the family, Horace was allowed the special privilege of sitting for hours on end, watching the miners making their various purchases while he consumed vast amounts of ginger cookies and candy. There were few cash transactions at Henry's store, as Horace recalled it:

> The company deducted at the end of every month . . . from the miners' pay what had been purchased. . . . I know that people continually criticized Father for not charging more for his merchandise than he did, allowing the miners to pile up big debits on the com-

pany's books . . . he could never be happy when the men who
worked for him were poor and unhappy. He would always rather
face wholesale grocers with no funds to meet their demands than
turn away a poor Slavic miner or an Irish wife of one of his mule-
team drivers, without bacon or molasses or flour, or whatever they
needed and could not pay for.

Horace was convinced that his father's company store always operated at a loss.

Tall and bearded, Henry Liveright looked very much a patri-
arch; he was forty-four when Horace was born on December 10,
1884.* He was, by any standard, an extraordinarily well read man.
His home library in the Osceola Mills days was considered the best
in town. Henry purchased the collected works of the standard
British and American writers. Those were the days when people
bought sets from traveling book dealers who went from door to
door in the more affluent areas to peddle their wares. Besides
Thackeray and Dickens, Henry went in for the poets, especially the
German ones, Goethe, Schiller, and Heine; Shakespeare was his
passion. Horace later thought that his urge to produce a modern-
dress *Hamlet* in New York in the mid-twenties was inspired by his
father's love for the play. Horace read it repeatedly in his boyhood.
The Liveright household was decidedly a bookish one.

A largely self-educated man of high culture, Henry was famous
for his fairness in business as well as for his numerous charities. He
was outgoing and had a wide variety of friends. Horace clearly
admired his father for his wisdom and probity. His feelings about
his mother were nowhere near as positive. She was the real head of
the Liveright family, and had no reluctance to discipline her children and to assume control in her husband's absence. This was
especially true after the family moved to Philadelphia when Horace

*Like many "boy wonders," Horace wasn't satisfied with his real age and usually gave his birth
date as 1886.

was in grammar school and Henry remained in Osceola Mills for weeks at a time.

Henrietta Liveright, or "Henny" as she was known to nearly everyone all her life, was as remarkable in her own way as her husband. As her youngest son recalled, she was considered beautiful in her youth. Standing a little over five feet tall and never weighing more than a hundred pounds, Henny had a will to power, a wish to dominate her surroundings. Besides her tasks as the mother of six children, Henny became the center of Osceola Mills's social life, tirelessly organizing charity benefits, dances, and cultural events. Despite the fact that there were only two Jewish families in the town, Henny was undisputed in her social leadership. Her energy was enormous. She took all her organizational skills with her when the family moved to Philadelphia, where they flourished on a far grander scale; she was still exercising them when she died at the age of ninety-eight.

Although Jewish, the Liveright family was not Orthodox and neither of Horace's parents had any particularly strong religious feelings. However, when Alfred, Horace's eldest brother, married a Christian girl, Henny refused to speak to either her son or his bride for several years. In this area Henny was adamant: religion *did* matter.

It is clear from his autobiography, where he wrote that "She ruled her family, with the possible exception of myself," that Horace had reservations about Henny. Indeed, he had good reason to mistrust his mother. When hospitalized for some childhood illness at age twelve or so, he misbehaved so badly that the nurses and doctors told his mother that she would have to do something to curb her son's high spirits. Henny did just that: She promised to give Horace a gold watch if he adjusted his conduct to conform to hospital regulations. When he did, Henny brought the fine watch she had purchased and mounted it on the wall next to his bed. On the day of his discharge, she demanded its return. It had served its purpose and it was now time for the watch to perform another function unconnected with Horace Liveright. Horace never forgot the experience, often recalling the details for his children.

From the very beginning, Horace saw himself as the family rebel, as someone endowed with extraordinary powers, destined to perform heroic deeds far beyond mastering the humdrum routine required merely to earn a living in the world. Along with this was his feeling that he belonged to some sort of aristocracy. His socially prominent godmother, Sue Brisbane Lowry, had bestowed her middle name on young Horace, who used it on all his business cards and correspondence; once he became a national figure he dropped the Brisbane.

The new home in Philadelphia, where Horace lived from his ninth to his eighteenth year, was a large one at 718 North Twentieth Street. The house was large enough to contain his parents and their six children as well as two or three servants. Horace, the youngest, had two sisters and three brothers. Alfred, the oldest, was fourteen years older than Horace. After obtaining a law degree, he went to work for his father at the mines. Horace's favorite brother, Lewis, died in the influenza epidemic of 1918. The third brother, Otto, became a well-known literary agent ("O. K. Liveright") in New York during the 1920s; his clients included Sherwood Anderson.

Caroline Liveright, or Carrie as she was known to the family, has been described as a "Cinderella" type of girl, who remained at home all her life, essentially becoming a family domestic. Ada Liveright, however, his favorite sister, possessed a goodly share of her mother's dynamism. Although she never attended college, she became the chief librarian of the Philadelphia Pedagogical Library. Horace regarded her as a second mother. He trusted her without reservation, especially her taste in books, often relying on her opinions when he doubted his own.

In 1898, the war year, when torches flared in the streets of

Horace at ten.
Lucy Wilson collection

America to rally citizens against the shaky might of Spain, Henry Liveright's mines suffered a harsh series of economic blows, so sharp that it was necessary to send young Horace not to the esteemed Penn Charter School, where three of his cousins were enrolled, but to the public Central High School. His family had become, as he later put it, "just poor relations" in a Philadelphia where nearly all his Fleisher relatives had achieved unqualified success in medicine, law, and the other esteemed professions. It wasn't so much that the public school was just that but that Penn Charter was regarded as a college preparatory school. Horace had suffered what he then regarded as a tragedy: the loss of several of his closest friends, the ignominy of his family's financial plight, and the knowledge that he wasn't likely to be attending college.

The reduced circumstances of the Liveright family were felt strongly by Henny, who had to fight hard to retain her place in the social pecking order of the richer Jewish families in their neighborhood. Years later, Horace attempted to convey some of the hurt he had felt, choosing to recall the apparent silliness of worrying about where his family bought their desserts:

> If the . . . Green Street Fleishers . . . got their ice cream at Mason's and ours at Kuhn's on Fairmount Avenue, what difference should it have made? But I not dimly but clearly remember that when we were able to buy our desserts at Mason's that it *did* make a big difference.

Horace's ever-increasing curiosity about sexual matters took the form of looking up some unfamiliar words in the family's unabridged *Webster's*. One day Henny discovered him completely engrossed in his researches and asked him just what words he was searching for. When he told her without hesitation, she became both distressed and furious. Henny knew of no way to answer his questions, and Horace was marched off to bed without supper. Neither of his parents was capable of conducting any discussion of sex with their children; this form of Puritanism was almost universal in that time and has changed but little in our own. Education in human sexuality became an important issue for Horace, whose early and upsetting encounter with it certainly left its mark on the future publisher of Freud, Stekel, and Bertrand Russell.

Horace read voraciously in his early teens. Although he liked

Dickens and read all of the novels, he prided himself especially on his thorough knowledge of Thackeray. It gave him a great sense of superiority to unfold his Thackeray lore in the presence of his aunts and uncles. Love of this author caused some trouble for Horace at school. Enamored of a Thackeray satire on Goethe—

> *And when Charlotte saw him carried*
> *Past her window on a shutter*
> *She proceeded, Oh, so calmly*
> *With her cutting bread and butter.*

—Horace passed the last two lines off as his own. Unfortunately, his English teacher knew her Thackeray, too, and Horace underwent a brief period of disgrace with his classmates, family, and friends.

Coming down from the heights, Horace devoured all the Alexandre Dumas and G. A. Henty adventure novels, plus all of Kipling. When it came to Mark Twain, interestingly enough, Horace preferred Tom Sawyer to Huck Finn, a choice perhaps determined by his feeling that Tom had a talent for using his worldly potential far more than his more deeply divided comrade. The most important literary influence on young Horace, however, was W. S. Gilbert, the librettist for the Gilbert and Sullivan operettas. Gilbert's work set the style for a play of his that was almost produced on Broadway while he was still in his teens.

When Horace began public high school, he had scored the highest entrance examination grade; his closest rival in the test scores was also Jewish. When this fact became known to their fellow students, they were not pleased, and Horace remembered a fight in the school yard with a boy who called him a "sheenie." Horace engaged in a number of such battles; his only drawback as a fighter was his extreme thinness. When he gained his full height of five feet ten inches (tall at the time), his weight was barely 110 pounds. Whether he was a lightweight or not, "sheenie" was a fighting word, and he never avoided these brawls. He later believed that he had encountered more anti-Semitism in his school years than he ever did in Wall Street.

At school, Horace was sensitive to the fact that he was competing against his fellow students. As a result, he was determined to be first at all costs, but sometimes the cost became excessive. In his last year at elementary school his general average was 87.5; he'd been told that he was the number one boy in his graduating class. But what if somebody from one of the other public schools had a higher average? He had to find out and did so by bicycling all over town to pick up the news. His worst imagining came true: A good friend at another school had received an average of 88.2. What to do? When he arrived home, Horace carefully changed the grade on his report card to 88.5, thus ensuring his coming out on top. This became a short-lived, hollow victory, for the fear of discovery began to haunt him. He scanned the papers feverishly for weeks, searching for the incriminating list of the honor boys and their scores. The list was never published, but Horace was deeply affected by the event. In the unfinished autobiography, he crossed out a phrase that read "how greatly my dishonest act influenced my whole after life." It is obvious that its removal indicated that Horace did not want his readers to think that he took his "little prank" all that seriously, but he clearly did.

From the time he entered his early teens, Horace possessed unusually strong sexual appeal. Although he knew this, he was often convinced that he was ugly and that his ears, in particular, were the chief offenders. It was their size that concerned him; at age nine he'd gone to a doctor's office to see if he could have "something done about them." The doctor joshed him, but Horace brooded for years about his huge appendages. Later on, it was his nose that bothered him; all his life his thinness depressed him. But many young women found Horace very attractive. At fifteen he began dating Helen, a young woman three years older, who believed he was sixteen. Together they read Shakespeare's sonnets and discussed the problems of life and love. When she kissed him, he quickly pulled himself from her arms and then ran all the way home. He'd heard that good girls did not kiss; Helen must clearly be very bad indeed. Horace never did resolve the good girl/bad girl dilemma.

His first year of high school was successful, but by the halfway point in his sophomore year Horace found that he could no longer concentrate on his studies. He began to fall farther and farther behind in all his subjects. The competing attraction was the real world of work. It wasn't the work itself so much as the *freedom* it would give him—the freedom eventually to leave home. His brother Alfred had graduated from high school at fourteen and from college *cum laude* at eighteen. What was the use of even thinking about college, when Alfred had already beaten him in this area by at least three years? But it was his brother Otto who would give him the freedom he craved.

Otto was then the chief margin clerk for the banking and brokerage firm of Sinclair and Chester, at that time one of the leading financial organizations in Philadelphia. Its head, George Sinclair, was a member of both the Philadelphia and New York stock exchanges. Otto greatly admired Sinclair, and was able to convince him to hire his younger brother as an office boy at three dollars per week.

For a boy as bright as Horace to have college ripped from his future must have been a severe blow to his parents. In later years Horace told several conflicting versions of the event—one of them concentrating on a quarrel with a history teacher whose views on the American past did not agree with his own. It may be that, even when he was fifteen, Henry and Henny knew they couldn't budge him once he'd made up his mind. If it seemed to be a matter of principle, Horace became as adamant as his mother was in her own affairs. It was of little importance which was the decisive event: the fact was that Horace at sixteen was through with school forever.

At Sinclair and Chester, Horace distributed the mail, ran errands and posted the day's figures on the big board. He performed all his functions with extraordinary speed. Before the days of postal meters it was the task of office boys, at the conclusion of the day's work, to send customers some sort of reckoning of their accounts. These documents had to be placed in envelopes and the postage affixed by hand. Here Horace excelled with his speed; in later life he compared himself with the famous philanthropist Otto Kahn, who also began his career by stamping envelopes rapidly.

He quickly became cynical about working for Sinclair and Chester. Both partners were friends of his parents, but Horace distrusted Sinclair. Despite his great social charm and apparent warmth, Horace found him "intensely egocentric and a snob." As Horace saw it, working for Sinclair and Chester was essentially working for a gambling house with greater pretensions than the notorious "bucket shops" that conducted their businesses just down the street. These were just barely legal enterprises in which the shops covered themselves against possible losses from their customers' transactions by charging them heavier commissions than did the legitimate exchanges. Horace began to patronize the bucket shops by placing his money on almost anything, and using the money he made to bet on things like the outcome of the Penn-Harvard football game. But he lost that bet in particular and before very long he nearly lost his job.

At sixteen, now earning eighteen dollars a week, Horace was drinking regularly. He would occasionally have lunch with his father, whose office was just around the corner. One day, after consuming his usual potion of two beers with Henry, Horace visited one of his favorite bucket shops; on leaving, he walked into the arms of Sinclair's partner, Mr. Chester, who marched his young employee back to the office for a straight talk about drinking and gambling. Chester told Horace that it would break his parents' hearts if he lost his job through gambling. Horace responded with a tearful determination to change his wicked ways. Later, Horace claimed that his tears were strictly of the crocodile variety: He had, by then, obtained ample proof that the partners were swindling many of their customers, and this gave him an excuse to continue his dangerous behavior.

Horace's interest really lay elsewhere: music had always been a strong presence in his life. Henry was a steady opera-goer who took his last born to all the repertory favorites. But it was the words, not so much the music, that fascinated Horace. He and his friends, especially Marcus Lewin, read and reread the lyrics of W. S. Gilbert, the lyricist of the Savoy operas that had just conquered the English-speaking world. *H.M.S. Pinafore, The Gondoliers,* and *The Mikado* were being performed wherever English could be sung. Not until the advent of Cole Porter at the end of the 1920s would song lyrics display such extraordinary cleverness, topical wit, and humor. Besides Gilbert and Sullivan, Horace was devouring hundreds of plays, mostly modern ones by G. B. Shaw, Arthur Pinero, and Oscar Wilde. But it was those W. S. Gilbert lyrics that became the model for all his own literary efforts at this time.

A year and a half after the end of the Spanish-American War, at the time of the Dewey Jubilee Parade, people were still singing songs about the *Maine:*

> *You ought to be ashamed*
> *For doing such a thing*
> *As blowing up the* Maine
> *One two three and*
> *Cuba will be free*
> *There'll be a hot time*
> *In the old town tonight!*

The hot town for Horace was, of course, New York, the center of the U.S. music publishing industry. He went there to sell what he considered to be his first really salable tune. He called it "Mammy Gwine to Buy de Moon," the type of song then called a "coon song" or "darky lullaby." The song's chorus concluded with

> *Don't you fret*
> *Mammy won't forget*
> *When he's not f—u—l—l*
> *She's gwine to buy dat moon.*

Horace was accompanied on his selling trip by a tiny eighteen-year-old young girl named Isobel D'Armond, who served as his accompanist on the rounds of the Tin Pan Alley merchants. After spending several days sightseeing in glorious Manhattan, young Isobel and Horace began their trek from door to door in hopes of a buyer. To buy a song, a publisher must hear it played; pretty Isobel was welcome, but Horace presented a problem because he couldn't sing very well. Nevertheless, the owner of the Von Tilzer Music Company found the young couple so fetching that he took them out to lunch. Delightful, but they would have to wait for a final decision about the song. The wait was endless, and it was the far more famous firm of Witmark that bought all rights to "Mammy" in a contract dated October 23, 1900. Horace and Marcus Lewin, now his composer, were each to receive two cents on every copy sold; at the end of the first year the total royalties earned by Horace were $3.66, a figure that would never increase.

The intoxicating effect of selling this work encouraged the two boys to begin writing an operetta they called *John Smith*. After making some progress on the first act, Lewin had to leave for Heilanstalt Falkenstein in Switzerland, for treatment of an undefined illness. Weeks passed, and Horace became desperate for his collaborator. His cable produced bad news from Lewin:

Your cablegram came to hand yesterday afternoon, and found me in bed where I had been for the last 12 days suffering from

influenza. . . . I have been feeling unwell, terribly nervous and have
had severe annoyance from an operation which was performed on
my nose and at present am in a considerably weakened condition.
. . . I feel it must be a great disappointment to you in my not having anything ready. . . . I think that you had better consider me and
my music uncertain factors in connection with our operetta, and go
ahead and do the best you can without me. So good luck to you,
old man, and here's wishing you all the good things that your hard
work and exceeding talent merit. . . .

Cables from places with comic-opera names like Heilanstalt
Falkenstein possess a sense of the absurd that Horace may have
failed to notice in his now desperate need to find a new composer
as fast as possible. He chose Herbert Haessler, a young Philadelphia
musician who, unfortunately, made his living by working nights;
Horace was rarely able to see his collaborator in the flesh.
Nevertheless, the libretto for *John Smith* was completed in just a
few months. Horace immediately sent off copies to several of the
leading Broadway production firms. He received a quick response
from one Edward E. Rice, who wrote Horace that

There is much good material in it. The lyrics are better than usual.
The second act needs a good deal of work but we think you can
take care of that. We would like to hear the music very soon. . . .
As I already told you we figure it would take about $30,000 to put
it on and you would have to raise at least half of it. Let me hear
from you.

Most of *John Smith* is now lost, but remaining fragments make it
clear that it dealt very broadly with the comic aspects of the initial
encounter between the English explorer and the Indians he found
in the Virginia Colony. The comic opera began with a stirring invo-
cation:

The chief, the chief, the chief!
Good morning chief,
We might use many adjectives
descriptive of your merit,
Or tell in split infinitives
the virtues you inherit,
But common sense and lack of time
compel us to defer it—
In brief—you are our chief.

Horace had left not the slightest doubt in the minds of his audience that his fealty to the spirit of Gilbert and Sullivan was absolute—their influence can be detected in the few pages that survive. It may have been imitative, but obviously some admired it, for Rice was willing to invest in at least half the production costs. The news from New York was joyous indeed, but it left Horace pondering where he'd obtain the necessary $15,000 in order to proceed. His friend Milt Appel suggested that they form a partnership in which they would pool their respective recent winnings in the bucket shop and at the racetrack. If they pooled their winnings for the next few months, they surely could convince their families to come up with the remainder. The results were disappointing: the partners saw their original $4,000 dwindle away to only $500—Milt's system of betting at the track hadn't included things like pulled tendons, crooked jockeys, or any of the other vagaries of the turf.

Horace was forced to start all over again by convincing his various friends to agree to put up $5,000 if he could raise an equal amount by himself. The final $5,000 would presumably come from wealthy family members who surely would be glad to participate in the launching of a notable theatrical career. While all these various fund-raising activities dragged on, Edward Rice appeared to show no particular degree of impatience. When several months had passed, Horace decided to return to Manhattan and apprise Rice of the current situation.

When he reached Rice's office for his appointment on a Friday afternoon, Horace was told that Rice was busy rehearsing a new play out at the Manhattan Beach Club in Brooklyn. Rice's message gave Horace a choice: Come on down today to Manhattan Beach or wait to see him on the following Monday morning. Horace elected to wait out the weekend by himself in New York and would have done so had he not just then luckily encountered on Broadway Isobel, his young accompanist of the previous year. When she heard about Horace's project, Isobel urged Horace to take her along to meet Rice, whom she felt might be able to do something for her own career.

Rice's first question when he encountered Horace in Manhattan Beach was brutally direct: "Well, Liveright, did you bring the money along?" Horace told him that he now had five thousand dollars pledged by his friends and that the final ten would become available when Rice deposited *his* fifteen in the bank. Rice's reply indicated that he was not to be intimidated by a skinny sixteen-year-old kid from Philadelphia: "Don't worry about my money, get yours first. I'm putting up not only money, but scenery, costumes, booking the best theater in New York and how about my brains and experience?" He then invited Isobel and Horace out to dinner, where he discussed the idea of commencing rehearsals of *John Smith* on the following day, while Horace was still in New York. Later, he brought his guests back to the hotel to introduce them to the company rehearsing his play *Show Girl*—it was this company that would soon be performing *John Smith*. When Horace went to bed that night he was transfixed with the idea that he would soon be making his Broadway debut while still in his teens:

[it] brought more joy and hope to me than future meetings and hours spent with Presidents, Prime Ministers, or royalty. Never

again in my life have I been so dazzled. . . . I was an author, an artist coming into his own.

The following day Rice's orchestra leader conducted what amounted to a first run-through of some of Horace's best material to the admiring comments of the chorus girls, who listened avidly to the words of the young rival of Gilbert and Sullivan:

> *Hooray, hooray, hooray,*
> *Let the chief now have his say*
> *For he's bound to speak*
> *Some time this week*
> *So let it be today.*

During the following week Horace returned with Rice to New York, where the contracts were to be drawn up. Horace had promised to have his uncle, Ben Fleisher, bring a $5,000 check from Philadelphia to the scheduled meeting. As for the boys in Philadelphia, they agreed to send a check for $500 "for starters": they would send the rest when they knew surely that Uncle Ben had contributed his share. On the day of Horace's return to Manhattan, he stopped off at the Herald Square Hotel to change his clothes. There he found a telegram from his uncle:

RICE IS NO GOOD I WOULD HAVE NOTHING TO DO WITH HIM

B. FLEISHER

Faced with this news, Horace's immediate reaction was to consume several shots of his favorite whiskey, Carstairs.

When he'd calmed down, he phoned Rice and read him the telegram. Strangely enough, Rice appeared to be "singularly undisturbed" by the bad news. He assured Horace that he was still willing to invest in the show, perhaps not as much as he'd intended to originally, but that he had not misrepresented himself

to Horace nor had Horace to his uncle. Two days later he wrote
Horace:

> I am pleased to note that your uncle's withdrawal has not damp-
> ened your ardor. Go ahead and get your syndicate organized and
> when completed, count on me to take hold of the show. . . . Let
> me hear from you as often as possible and with lots of luck to you
> and hoping, kid, that you're not taking it too hard, always yours
> truly.

But Horace did just that: He later stated that he took the remain-
der of a quart of scotch to bed with him and stayed drunk for the
next two days. The combined efforts of Isobel and a friend were
required to get the crestfallen Horace ready for the sad ride back to
Philadelphia. It had become clear that Rice was not going to put a
penny into the production without the cash in hand contributions
of Uncle Ben and the family. The young author was not going to
have his maiden effort performed on Broadway; he was, in his eyes,
a failure before reaching his seventeenth birthday.

Somewhere about this time, Horace completed the sexual education that he'd begun years earlier when he consulted the pages of
the unabridged Webster's. The advanced lessons were given at
Kitty Weigel's famous establishment in the red-light district of
Philadelphia. Horace thought of Kitty as a combination of Guy de
Maupassant's Madame Tellier and Diamond Lil; he liked to patronize her place strictly as an observer, ordering a few drinks while
talking to the girls as they awaited their customers. One night, as
he told the story, Horace passed the demarcation line between
being, as he named it, "high" and "tight." The friends who had
accompanied him to Kitty's Place kept urging him to sample the
merchandise with one of the girls who appeared to be extremely
shy, the young olive-skinned Gladys. With mixed feelings of ner-

vousness combined with simple lust, Horace followed Gladys up the wide stairway to the rooms upstairs.

When Gladys discovered that she had a virginal patron, she was amused. She quickly abandoned her former shyness and used her powers to entertain her uncertain young guest. She was technically successful, but this first experience of sexual activity was not pleasing to Horace—he found it "horrible, sordid and a physical disappointment to both of us, I am sure, and a psychic shock which happily re-established romance in my soul." His protest is not particularly convincing (he was writing these words, in part, to convince his readers of his virtues), especially the part about Gladys, who probably took it all in her stride. Horace asserted that the bordello experience at Kitty's was his first and last such adventure; he claimed that the effect of it had made him skip the peep shows of Paris and the live sexual circuses of Berlin.

In later years Horace appeared to blame this initiation in the brothel as one factor contributing to the somewhat tangled sex life of his maturity. Horace also blamed his parents for his winding up "twisted and torn" by their not having supplied him with a better sexual education, but this seems patently unfair. At that time, and for decades to come, many young American males received their sexual initiation at the hands of prostitutes, with widely varying aftereffects. Nice girls didn't do it; society deplored the business of sex for sale but looked the other way in practice. Horace's introduction to sex was similar, for example, to that of his friend Eugene O'Neill, who lost his virginity while drunk in a brothel, but under far more adverse conditions, for he was forced into going through with the act by his drunken brother Jamie.

As a result of his reading and his observation of his father's miners, Horace embraced socialism as his basic political stance in life. The future publisher of John Reed's *Ten Days That Shook the World* and Mike Gold's *Jews Without Money,* as well as works by Leon Trotsky and Upton Sinclair, would often attempt to convince his father about the merits of the socialist cause. During his frequent long visits to the mines in Osceola, Henry Liveright continued to keep in close touch with his youngest son by means of letters. On one occasion, while hailing Horace as a fellow Thackerayite, Henry answered his son's concerns by taking on the characteristics of one of the novelist's memorable creations:

> Col Newcombe [sic] presents his compliments to his son but he hopes that his vagaries will not land him in the final abode of that fine hero of fiction . . . I was surprised to find in perusing the contents of your letter, dear Horace, that you are considering joining the ranks of the Socialists. . . .

Henry went on to produce various "proofs" that socialism would never work, but Horace was convinced that the American workingman required protection from the capitalist masters. He set out his convictions in some verses that may have been written for a show:

> *A working man is the nation's pride*
> *The bulwark of its strength*
> *This chariot should ride on a mighty rising tide*
> *That has no breadth or length.*
> *There should be no boss at the forge or shop*
> *Who would dictate when to start or stop*
> *And those Freeman's friends—Referendum and*
> *Recall*
> *Should be his only statutes, if he have a law at all.*

Horace may have thought like a socialist but he did not dress the part. With the ever-increasing income he derived from his various financial transactions at the bucket shops, Horace became something of a juvenile dandy—he dressed in the latest fashions, wore a flower in the lapel of his coat and began the lifelong habit of carrying a walking stick. He soon became a vital part of a group of younger men who made their living by the dips and turns of the stock market—Horace joined them in their parties and dinners at the principal hotels in downtown Philadelphia.

Arising partly from his new socialist convictions but more likely from a sense of justice, Horace began to brood about some of the more flagrant business policies of Sinclair and Chester's brokerage firm. He had become slowly aware that there were considerable irregularities concerning certain "discretionary" accounts—Sinclair and his associates would often manipulate the allocation of that day's losers and winners so that the "discretionary" accounts (his own and those of his friends) received an unwarranted benefit from the transactions. If certain stocks were bought in the morning and went up in the next day or so, the profits were allocated to the discretionary accounts; if these stocks went down, the losses were debited against the other accounts. All of this was done in complete secrecy, but Horace could not have failed to discover the operation. When he confronted Sinclair with his knowledge of the scheme, Sinclair told him that it might be a good idea if he concentrated his efforts on his job. But Horace was not to be silenced.

Besides his father and his brother Otto, who had moved to New York to work for Sinclair and Chester, Horace also informed his Uncle Morris, a man of power and influence in the Philadelphia financial world, about the situation. Years later, Horace liked to describe the scene in which he (at seventeen) confronted the guilty partners in the billiard room of Sinclair's mansion. After consuming enough alcohol to make him tipsy, Horace told the partners what he thought of them and that they could go to hell: He was quitting their filthy business forever. That some confrontation occurred is beyond doubt, but the scene may not have been so melodramatic. Horace's flair for self-dramatization was as powerful as that of some of the novelists he later published.

The upshot of the confrontation was curious. Horace was

offered his brother Otto's job in the firm's New York office; Otto was glad to return to Philadelphia to be reunited with his many friends there. For Horace the offer would contain the prospect of working in New York at a salary of forty dollars a week, a small fortune then. In New York he would not be concerned with the speculative side of the business—he would be employed strictly as a bond salesman. It was probable that the influence of Horace's family—particularly his Uncle Morris with his wide network of friends in the market—persuaded Sinclair and Chester to make their offer. And, with Horace in New York, the partners might have felt themselves out of danger from any threat posed by Horace to their shady business activities. If Horace felt that he was selling out by accepting the offer, he could reflect on his father's advice to stop tilting at windmills, telling him that the behavior of his employers was indeed the way of the American business world and he must accept that fact to survive in it. But Horace may have had the last word: he cynically demanded forty-five dollars a week and the partners agreed.

Leaving Philadelphia was, for Horace, a decisive step. As he once put it, "Freedom! . . . No one waiting for me on a stair-landing when I came home at two or three in the morning, a bit worse for wear. No one to ask . . . where I was going, what I did and how I did it." Almost frighteningly thin, intensely bright, affable and witty and with an immense shrewdness about his fellowman, Horace Liveright began in 1902 what he may well have thought of as the conquest of New York. He was eighteen.

"I Believe in My Destiny"

I usually wore a flower in my button hole and sported a
heavy crooked walking stick; habits which have clung to me
for life.

—HBL, 1933

HORACE began living in New York humbly enough by moving
in with his cousin Tessa, who was renting a large apartment on
West Seventy-first Street with her husband, Arthur Wolfson, and
their two young daughters. Mr. Wolfson encouraged Horace to
continue with his reading and was delighted when Horace
devoured Flaubert's *Salammbô*, Gibbon, Villon, Ibsen, and anything
else he recommended. Wolfson deplored, however, his young
guest's habit of chewing cloves, the aroma of which filled the
house. Horace used the cloves to disguise the alcohol that was frequently on his breath. His hosts might have been alarmed had they
realized how much he was drinking.

He began his career as a bond salesman by taking a training
course in Newark, New Jersey, in the offices of Lansing Brothers

and Coe,* where he worked under the direction of a man called
Ben Stroube. Horace was a natural salesman, whose sheer force
and charm of personality were matched by his persistence. Early on
he realized that the bonds he was selling were in no way superior to
other bonds on the market; the personality factor was indeed going
to be central to his future success.

Horace put his new skills to the test through his attempts to sell
bonds to the Fidelity Trust Company of Newark. The young secretary and treasurer of the company, Frederick Egner, told Horace
immediately that he had not one good reason to buy his bonds. Not
at all dismayed, Horace searched for common conversational
ground. He began by asking Egner about his theatrical interests—
would he like to go to something with him one night? He discovered a common interest in music; Puccini was one of Egner's major
passions. Horace was able to sustain an enthusiastic conversation
about the works of the popular operatic composer, whom he really
didn't like very much, and he was invited to lunch in the dining
room at the Fidelity the next day. The dining room was in the
Prudential Building, and Egner introduced him to several officials
of the Prudential Life Insurance Company as well as the president
of his own company:

> "This is my good friend, Horace B. Liveright," he said, "who is mis-
> representing Lansing of New York. He doesn't know anything
> about bonds but he's a nice kid and his cousin, Frank, helps to run
> Bamberger." We sat together at lunch, talking not about bonds but
> about books and music.

Before long, Horace was taking Egner on book-hunting trips to
the shops along Fourth Avenue in Manhattan. He also attempted to

*When Horace attempted to set down the events of his life, he began to dictate a narrative that is
frequently contradictory. For reasons best known to himself, the firm of Sinclair and Chester
ceases to exist after Horace's departure from Philadelphia and is replaced by Lansing Brothers
and Coe.

persuade Egner to desert his wife and children for a bachelor evening at the theater.

His salary at Lansing Brothers and Coe rose to $60 a week—this amount plus the $40 or so he made on his own in various curb stock dealings enabled him to afford the luxury of a bachelor flat at the Beverwick Hotel on West Twenty-seventh Street. Here it was not necessary to chew cloves, and there was nothing to remind him of home. His old friend Isobel, always ready to help, chose to furnish the apartment with the type of furniture known as Mission Oak, noted mainly for its durability. In time, Horace threw it all out and started again. At the Beverwick, Horace entertained a growing number of friends; he was very much a young man about town, amassing a wide knowledge of the city's restaurants, theaters and hotels.

He finally did persuade Egner to join him in a theatrical evening, beginning at his apartment. When Egner arrived, he was introduced to two beautiful young sisters named Edna and Sadie, who were there to fill out the foursome Horace had planned. After dinner and the play there was dancing and champagne at the famous Haymarket. The evening was a huge success; Fred Egner spent the night at Horace's place, and a few days later Horace sold the Fidelity $250,000 worth of railroad bonds on which he made a commission of $1,200—almost half a year's salary. This was the beginning of what proved to be not only a firm business relationship but an equally strong friendship. Horace's "personality business" had paid off handsomely and continued to do so.

Horace liked to boast about his amatory triumphs. One story concerned an affair he'd been having with a beautiful woman called Effie, the twenty-six-year-old wife of one of his older customers on Wall Street. Effie took a proprietary interest in Horace's career— not as a bond salesman but as a future writer of operettas. As Horace told it, her interest brought her to his rooms at the Beverwick, where the couple was discovered by the husband, who promptly shot Horace in the leg. Or at least Horace claimed he did; in his account of the incident, he drops the matter almost immediately after bringing it up but makes a peculiar point about it: "I did not feel that I was betraying him in any sense of the word, and it was only his vast wealth that made it possible for him to have shot me in the right leg when he found her in my arms."* Horace wrote that only his magnificent constitution had enabled him to recover from the wound in such an amazingly short time.

If they learned about it, the effect of the alleged shooting on his employers at Lansing was apparently nil. They were far more concerned about a matter they regarded with genuine dread: Horace's openly proclaimed socialism. He had even had the audacity to discuss his views with the president of the firm, old Mr. Lansing, at lunch. The following day Horace was summoned to the office of his immediate boss, Mr. Stroube, who told him that despite his status as their star salesman, he would either have to change his socialist views—at least stop talking about them—or risk losing his job. In his account of this episode, Horace mentions that he "had had a couple of stiff hookers" before going in to see Stroube. It may have been with the aid of those hookers that Horace resisted the temptation being offered him: give up his convictions and become, in time, a wealthy man at Lansing. In a rage, he told Stroube that "I don't need Lansing any more than he needs me." Stroube responded by firing Horace, with the good-natured advice that he start his own bond business. How could he fail?

At nineteen, Horace again saw himself as a failure. He had to leave his apartment in New York and go back home again to Henny, Ada, and Carrie. Once there, he began to think about rewriting *John Smith* but had no enthusiasm for it—the writing seemed derivative. To stave off boredom, he accepted the reading suggestions of his sister Ada, who introduced him to the work of

*Horace's logic here is mind-boggling.

HBL in his
early twenties.
UPI/Bettman

John Dewey and Thorstein Veblen. Henny gave parties at which she introduced several eligible young women, but none had any of the qualities he desired in a woman: physical beauty and superior intelligence. Months passed while he marked time at home.

He had not long to wait. His friend Fred Egner, aware of his plight, put in a good word for him to George Day, president of Day, Adams and Company—a major New York brokerage firm—who sent Horace an invitation for lunch at the University Club in New York. Day, a bookish man who eventually left the investment business to become a teacher, recognized a kinship with Horace. That feeling, plus Horace's excellent customer contacts, resulted in an unexpectedly good job offer. He would receive a base pay of $5,000 a year plus 10 percent on all his sales. This sum, in 1990s dollars, would amount to more than $100,000 a year. Horace accepted the offer. He was to begin his career as a big-time bond salesman working for one of the most stable firms on Wall Street. What more could he want?

The answer was, of course, something else. Horace would never be happy working for other people—he had to have the freedom to exercise the gambling talents that distinguished so many of his decisions. His first supervisor, Ben Stroube, had cautioned him against this early on:

> You're a gambler and gamblers don't make money in the long run. Quit gambling, young man, and build up your personality business, as you call it, and you'll be making ten thousand a year if my guess is right before you're twenty-five.

After only one year with Day, Adams, Horace refused to renew his contract. Instead, he ordered some new stationery that read:

Horace Brisbane Liveright

Investments

Securities

His success was huge, for within just a year or so he had built up his capital to the amount of $40,000, more than three-quarters of a million in mid-1990s money. But even on his own, selling bonds was still a bore. His charm made selling them an effortless task; buying them was just another lesson in familiar gambling techniques. With a future that seemed to contain nothing but success, Horace began to yearn to escape the daily grind for something exotic—perhaps foreign travel was the answer. His old Philadelphia friend Len Goldsmith urged Horace to join him on an extended trip to England. But Horace was reluctant to leave the security his little business gave him, thinking it wiser to hold on until he really could afford to get out of the bond business entirely.

In the meantime, he began to work on a new operetta; he was not going to give up on his writing career.

Isobel D'Armond kept turning up in Horace's early life as if she were some genie who was there whenever he needed her special services. Suddenly, here she was again, back in New York and determined to find a career in newspaper journalism—daring in those days when most males chose to defend journalism from the inroads of "chattering women." Isobel was not alone. She had brought along a beautiful young friend from Philadelphia named Eleanor Bennett, with whom Horace fell in love the moment they were introduced. She, too, had come to New York to get a job on a New York paper; she succeeded in landing one, first on *The New York Herald* and then on *The Evening Sun*. Shortly after beginning his three-year affair with Eleanor, Horace moved out of his rooms at the Beverwick and rented a far more expensive apartment in the area.

Portraying their life together, Horace paints an overly idyllic picture of a devoted couple spending their evenings at home: Eleanor playing Chopin or Schubert and Horace reading philosophy—Josiah Royce and William James. In the same account, he describes almost nightly high-stakes poker games, for Horace's passion for gambling intensified during the time of his romance with Eleanor. Al Ziemer's gambling establishment at Forty-sixth and Broadway, located in what was a glorified theatrical boarding house, had three or four rooms set aside for straight poker games "with the pot always open. . . . There were no fancy stud games, no crazy deuces-wild, no complicated combinations or variations." Ziemer encouraged the players to bring along their girl friends; the presence of the girls, who were thought of as mascots, was almost guaranteed to make the players come more frequently. Horace rarely lost at Ziemer's, and he became enchanted with his prowess:

I bragged about it on Wall Street. I bragged about it at Rector's and Martin's and the Café Madrid. When my host [Ziemer] complimented me on my skill, it meant more to me than selling a hundred thousand dollars worth of bonds the next day. It gave me and dear, hospitable Al, too, great pleasure to bring my rich Wall Street friends to his place. Somehow or other, most of them lost and lost steadily. In the time we went there, I remember when my brother, Otto, lost about a thousand dollars, which was a good deal for him at that time, but very light for the game they played. . . . David Posner of the stock exchange firm of Posner and Company, where I was now carrying a large account, lost about fifteen thousand, to add to Al's winnings. After any exceptionally disastrous losing, we had meetings at my rooms where I would give learned dissertations to these losers on the art of playing poker.

It took some time for Horace to realize that at least one or two of Ziemer's employees took a hand in every game—so-called house players—who were there to make sure the house came out ahead. He was even slower to understand that Ziemer had been using him as a decoy to lure his rich Wall Street friends to the tables. His friends stopped coming after they lost, but this did not deter Horace; he felt that he was invincible.

At Ziemer's he and Eleanor had become friendly with a black waiter called Webster, whose job was to serve drinks and oversee the buffet supper. When the last of Horace's friends had been "taken," Webster passed them the word that Horace would be next—Ziemer was planning to clean him out of five thousand dollars in the next few games. After an evening of Wagner at the Metropolitan Opera, Eleanor begged Horace not to visit Ziemer's. Webster had told her that this was to be the night when a marked deck would be put into play whenever a player asked for a new deck of cards. Despite this certain knowledge that he would be cheated, Horace insisted on going on to Ziemer's as usual. Ziemer allowed him to win two or three hands before he began dealing with the marked deck. With the limit increased to $200 and a pot of $14,000 on the table, Horace was dealt a king, queen, jack and ten of spades and one low card—a tempting hand that would encourage any gambler to play aggressively. But the forewarned Horace threw down his cards. "For the first time since I'd known him, Al lost his composure. His face grew white with anger or disappointment, or maybe just shocked surprise . . . he blurted out, 'My God, Horace, you're not throwing down that hand!' "

This was Horace's final appearance at Ziemer's. The following day one of Ziemer's players told him that the hands against him that night would have been a royal flush in diamonds, four eights, and a full house. Ziemer figured that this combination would have cost Horace at least $10,000.

In addition to managing his bond business, Horace was also engaged in stock market trading, which he approached in the same high-stakes spirit he showed at Ziemer's. He developed a fanatical belief in the shares of the Hocking Coal and Iron Company, a firm that no one seemed to know much about. He became convinced that the erratic flurries exhibited by the Hocking stock demonstrated that its value was severely underrated and that it was merely a matter of time before it went through the roof. So he kept buying more and more of the stock, awaiting vindication for taking such a huge chance on a dark horse.

Eleanor attempted to dissuade Horace from any further stock market activities, particularly the Hocking stock:

If you sold Hocking now you would be worth about $160,000, and you're only twenty-five. You hate Wall Street. . . . Let us go to Europe for a few months where you can think things over calmly and decide what you want to do with your life. You're too young, and too nice to continue your cheap gambling and drinking without their killing you or, what is worse, killing your soul.

Horace agreed to go to Europe with Eleanor, and he even proposed marriage. But only two weeks before their scheduled departure, Eleanor was stricken with pneumonia; she was dead in only a few days. Horace was devastated by the shock of losing the first woman he'd loved.

With the death of Eleanor, Horace gave up on his promises to her, returning to the stock market, determined this time to invest wisely. He placed a great deal of his money in Union Pacific stock, seemingly stable at the time but made anything but that because of the unexpected death of the railroad's president, E. H. Harriman. Horace lost at least half of his capital; once again he swore off Wall Street. Only briefly, however, for he was still infatuated with the possibilities of his beloved Hocking stock. He began putting everything he possessed into buying blocks of the stock. This was just before the chimerical bubble burst: Hocking fell from 80 to $12\frac{1}{2}$ — Horace had lost virtually all the assets he had built up in the past three years. Not until 1925 would Horace again venture into the temptations of Wall Street.

Had it not been for his marriage to Lucille Elsas in 1910, Horace would most likely never have entered the world of book publishing. Family memories have it that Horace met Lucille at a party in New York and that he began courting her immediately. The oldest child of a wealthy businessman, Hermann Elsas, Lucille was intelligent and beautiful, with a cascade of brilliant Titian red hair down her back. Although raised in New York, Lucille and her sister, Mary, had spent months at a time in Paris, London, Zurich, St. Moritz and Munich. The Elsas family loved to travel, and Lucille's mother regularly "took the cure" in Bavaria. Lucille was, in fact, something of an American princess who was courted by a number of eligible young men from the time she entered her teens.

It became apparent early on that Horace's most serious rival for Lucille's hand was young Walter Lippmann, then still at Harvard,

Lucille Elsas before her marriage to HBL.
Lucy Wilson collection

who was to become the famous political pundit whose words were read by millions of Americans on the front pages of their daily papers. Like both her suitors, Lucille had become convinced of the merits of the socialist cause and took a strong interest in the political concerns of the day. She and Lippmann had been corresponding regularly for some time, but now she began a steady, intense period of letter writing with Horace. This was the day when many people still sat down and filled page after page addressed to people whom they had last encountered only hours earlier.

Walter Lippmann thought very highly of Lucille and felt that she was not sufficiently aware of her talents. He kept urging her to have more faith in herself by proclaiming it to the world at large. Lucille resisted his entreaties by telling him, "You believe that I should stand and sing on mountain peaks . . . it is not true! The altitude would prove to be too strong and bright!" Horace also tried to boost Lucille's self-confidence, but his efforts did not move her any more than did Lippmann's. The one talent she had confidence in was her singing voice, which was outstanding, but here she had the misfortune to be surpassed by her younger sister, who became world famous as Mary Ellis at the Metropolitan Opera in New York and at Paramount Pictures in mid-thirties Hollywood.

While courting Lucille, Horace exercised his writing talents by means of mock birth announcements:

> Mr. and Mrs. Hermann Elsas . . . called it Lucille and discovered immediately that it was gifted with a voice which would cost a fortune to cultivate, for six hours after her appearance Miss Elsas was humming the Wedding March. This beautiful melody has been on her mind ever since, also her . . . tresses which by the way are directly responsible for her first meeting with her fiancé.

Horace's rivalry with Lippmann was not a real contest. Horace's children maintain that Lucille never quite believed in Walter's feeling for her. She only found out after she had made her choice between the ever witty Horace with his brilliant smile and the staid and far less demonstrative Walter, how much he had cared for her. Lippmann's biographer relates how bad Walter felt when Lucille finally decided to marry Horace. He was "furious" about her choice and broke off their correspondence. Although he was persuaded to attend the wedding, Lippmann "refused to kiss the bride, turning from her with the remark 'It's too late now.' "

In his jocular spoofing of their courtship, Horace once pretended to have misunderstood a friend's remark which he claimed to have heard as "her *père* is streaked with gold and [he] asked for an immediate introduction." From the beginning money was to play an important role in the marriage: her *père* was indeed streaked with gold. Born in Germany, Hermann Elsas was a wealthy self-made Jew who had made his fortune in cotton and paper products in Atlanta, Georgia toward the end of the century. The story of the Elsas family is reputed to be the one used, in part, by Alfred Uhry in his play *Driving Miss Daisy*.

The Elsas clan had taken a new name, not at Ellis Island but in Europe at the time of the Franco-Prussian War in 1870. Someone in the family, Lucille's sister, Mary Ellis, reports, "had been living on the German border of what was then Alsace-Lorraine. When the German Army came, he quickly changed his name to Elsas [Alsace]."

By 1910 Mr. Elsas had concentrated his manufacturing activities in the paper products area by creating the International Paper Company, which became one of the major forces in the industry. Perhaps their best-known product was the Lily Cup, a paper cup that could once be found in nearly every business office in the United States. The conservative Mr. Elsas was very unlike his young son-in-law, who always referred to him as "The President," usually sarcastically but occasionally with respect for his financial achievements. In addition to his paper mills, Mr. Elsas also owned vast stretches of forest in Canada that fed them.

When Horace married Lucille, Mr. Elsas found that he had acquired a most unusual son-in-law—a man of ferocious energies who, while having no clear idea of what field might best serve him, knew that great personal success must lie in the immediate future: NOW.

In the years before his marriage, Horace had continued working for himself selling bonds and other securities. He alternated this with full-time employment at some of the leading houses in New York, among them Sutro and Brothers. But it had become an increasingly boring situation for him; the connection with the Elsas family promised to be a form of liberation from the tedium he'd grown to hate. He welcomed the opportunity to join his rich father-in-law in his various business ventures. Horace was given, in the next three or four years, a series of jobs in the major divisions of the Elsas companies; all of them carried the title of either junior or senior vice president. Most of them involved selling, always Horace's strong point; all involved a considerable amount of travel.

Selling Mr. Elsas's products from coast to coast produced for Horace a fund of funny stories that he loved to relate, some of them patently untrue. The most outrageous (and famous) of the stories is Horace's single-handed effort to corner the toilet paper market in North America. To accomplish this, Horace bought up millions upon millions of rolls of the stuff while at the same time renting enormous amounts of warehouse space in order to house his immense pile. He wound up with a lot of toilet paper housed in warehouses all over New England. As he told the story to the novelist Manuel Komroff, the attempt failed. The project had been doomed from the start. Komroff records the details of the story, evidently believing it, but it is doubtful that Mr. Elsas would have countenanced such gambles with his money. There is something here that resembles Faulkner's famous "inflatable mule" stories: no one would seriously attempt to corner the toilet paper market.

The Liverights lived in a series of "apartment hotels" in mid-Manhattan in the early years of their marriage. When their first child, Herman, was born in 1911, followed by Lucy in 1913, larger quarters were required, and the couple moved to the Walton Hotel at Seventieth Street and Columbus Avenue. Horace and

Lucille were still devoted to letter writing, a practice they took up vigorously again when Horace's travels for the Grand Lake Company (one of Mr. Elsas's subsidiaries) took him all over the country. Horace wrote to Lucille while on the run—when and wherever he could find the time—even on the railway coaches and sleepers that delivered him to his selling territories. The correspondence shows clearly how seriously he took his new career, as in this letter of 1914, which also indicates that he sometimes acted in a managerial role:

I believe in my destiny—in the Grand Lake Company's destiny—they are inseparable, because *I am* the GL Co. . . . I fired half the help yesterday, got busy on the long distance phone, got a *real* foreman here this morning, who got things in some shape.

and again in October of the same year, on board the Southwestern Limited:

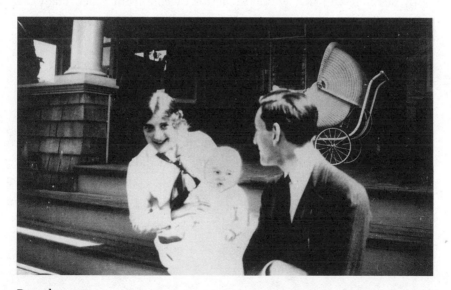

Proud parents, 1911.
Lucy Wilson collection

—all I need for big success is two years of fair business and fair prices. My gamble has been a good one so far, in two years we'll be a second Continental or I'll have to start all over again. . . . First call for dinner and I'm hungry!

Unfortunately, we have only Horace's side of this extensive correspondence; Lucille's letters have not survived.

Some early strains in the marriage were beginning to show. One theme that recurs frequently is the state of Lucille's health; Horace worries about whether she is really suffering from specific ailments or from hypochondria. He also resents Lucille's criticism of his lifestyle, as when he tells her that "I reiterate that 99% of our unhappiness is caused by your dissatisfaction with me & my ways & ideas & actions."

There is no doubt that he missed her on these trips:

By this time you have gotten the letter I wrote from Schenectady, and it hardly seems real that I am way out on the Mississippi, instead of having just kissed you and baby [Herman] as I stepped out to take the ten minutes to eight trolley so *don't* worry about my comfort, health and spirits. If you are only feeling better and Herman is feeling himself again . . . I will spend the week in a happy frame of mind. . . . I long for the time when you and I can motor through America and visit lots of the places I have been on these long trips . . . goodby dearest, be good and *happy.*—Livey.

One of his letters from this period concludes with the stark sentence "I am terribly lonely."

Lucille's general unhappiness was a constant in many of these letters, as in one of August 1912:

As you know, I'm going to give you bulletins from this trip—long letters tire me too much, because I would try to say everything I felt, thought or might think and really to what purpose? We would still have our little misunderstandings, my letters would make you no happier a week after you got them, if I happened to be with you then and I begin to believe that more normal letters, and more normal conversation—less vivisection, less self in every way will help you more than anything could.

Another undated letter from Horace during this period, written in Cincinnati, presses Lucille to reveal the cause of her concerns:

Hope you slept well last night, my darling. I certainly did and didn't get up until ten o'clock. I am terribly worried about you and your sleeplessness & nervousness. Something *must* be done. You must have the solution for me when I get back. Don't you realize my dear, that it isn't fair that I should have to work and worry at both ends—office and home?

It would appear that Lucille's unhappiness arose from a variety of things she found objectionable in her life with Horace. The most obvious was her sudden assumption of the role of mother of two children as well as housekeeper for a man who spent weeks at a time on the road. Previously the hostess at frequent parties, Lucille now spent her days coping with servants and children while worrying about her absent husband, who, she felt, was not always faithful to her:

You upset me all the time by inferring that I am anything but a loving, loyal husband, sweetheart & father. You don't think I *enjoy* being alone, do you? Your lack of absolute faith in me is anything but an inspiration.

Sometimes Horace tackled this issue with a saucy, mischievous tone, as in this letter written on board the Southwestern Limited in October 1914:

I feel well but I'm getting pretty tired of being away from you and the baby & New York. . . . I am now flirting a little bit with the two girls in the seats ahead of me. Both like me & if St. Joseph weren't only ten minutes away (it is now 2:40 P.M.) I'd talk to them & maybe hold their hands. They are the first girls I've noticed since I left N.Y. I've honestly been too busy to notice anything—

Lucille also felt (correctly) that Horace did not take care of himself: he smoked and drank far too much, forgot to eat, and neglected his sleep. Under her direction, he was habitually undertaking new regimens to change these unhealthy patterns and to improve his spiritual life as well:

Starting my new life today, as I am—a new life that values correctly the real things—love, peace, joy, fine thoughts, work—not merely making money—thrift, but not meanness—friendship, for all mankind, not just a chosen few. . . . I intend to do everything reasonably possible to value as highly as she that one thing that my dearest wife and companion prizes before everything as the real source of life's life—and that is health. In the past I have endeavored to take care of my body but from now on my wife shall be my nurse and doctor, not when I am sick but when I am well and the care I have always taken shall be as nothing to the vigilance, perspicacity & conscientious concern I shall exercise for the rest of my days. . . .

So far, so good, but Horace could not resist ridiculing the entire concept as he concludes his letter:

—then if I die young I can lie on my last earthly resting place, look upon my dear wife's face and murmur as the angel of death sneaks up to snatch me "—darling, it can't be helped, I didn't drink enough."

One of the first schemes that Horace undertook for the Elsas companies was Pick-Quick toilet paper, a merchandising gimmick that misfired badly; there was no market for Dickensian toilet paper.

Horace was becoming more convinced that working for "The President" was impossible: he had to be on his own. In 1915 his letters to Lucille begin to refer to the forthcoming creation of what he calls "The Liveright Company," a firm that was apparently to be funded by Elsas; what the firm would be dealing with is not mentioned in this letter of July 15:

> I have to take a flying trip to Chicago and then get back here so that too much does not accumulate. . . . I must go & I think this necessity will make it easier to stay with the Grand Lake Co. until the Liveright Company gets started. Good lord, I have so much to say & so little time to say it! To finish the business, assure the President that I will do nothing *rash* but that I *had* to do something & that I'm sure, up to date, what's been done is all for the best.

Nothing came of these plans, and the only "Liveright" company that materialized was, of course, Boni and Liveright. But that event was still two years away.

After leaving the Grand Lake Paper Company in 1916, Horace pursued a number of small manufacturing ventures, all of them capitalized by Mr. Elsas. They were mainly of the "helping the busy housewife" variety; one of them, for example, was a self-sealing jar. None of these efforts got off the ground, and Mr. Elsas began to be impatient with the seemingly endless funding required by Horace's projects.

In the fall of that year he first met young Albert Boni, then unemployed, at the advertising agency owned by Horace's second cousin and good friend, Alfred Wallerstein. Horace and Albert were both given free desk space at the agency, but it was only after a few months had passed that they became aware of each other. The encounter was to be decisive in both men's lives; it led to their partnership and the firm of Boni and Liveright, the firm that changed American book publishing forever.

"Let's Call It the Modern Library!"

[Liveright] was a tall, handsome, dark-eyed man with the
persuasive powers of a Svengali and the forensic qualities and
attractive appearance of a Sir Henry Irving.
—Lawrence Langner, 1951

(1)

THE intellectual and literary fireworks that we know as the
American Twenties really began in New York and Chicago in the
years just following the outbreak of war in Europe in 1914. A spirit
of change was in the air: sexual and political change, as well as literary. In New York the place to find the new politics, the new literature—especially the new theater—was Greenwich Village,
where the rents were still cheap enough to attract young artists and
writers. Here, on the tree-lined streets, were bars and cafés where
women smoked and drank openly, where young women bobbed
their hair at least five years before most other American women
had themselves shorn. Sexual freedom had only recently become a
permissible subject for discussion; Freud's views on the psyche
were just beginning to be heard as a faint whisper drifting across
the Atlantic. In the Village you could see plays that could be per-

formed in no other city in America; you could buy books and magazines that weren't available elsewhere. This was the heyday of the
new American Bohemia—the world of Edna St. Vincent Millay,
John Reed, Djuna Barnes, Waldo Frank, and Theodore Dreiser.
Collectively, they were all committed to some form of change in
what they regarded as the prevailing complacency and dullness of
life in America.

Horace found the Village fascinating, spending many evenings
there after work, making friends with writers whom he would
later publish. At no time then did he have the slightest notion that
he would be entering book publishing in less than a year; his agreement with Albert Boni was the first sign that he might be amenable
to his cousin Alfred's suggestion: "If you can't write books, publish
them!"

Albert and Charles Boni were the sons of a well-to-do German
Jewish family who sent Charles for a year to Cornell University and
then on to Harvard, where he completed his degree in 1913. Their
father gave Albert the money to enroll in Harvard Law School, but
he and his brother were mad about literature. Not seeing himself as
a writer, Albert opened the Washington Square Bookshop in New
York with the money intended for his law school fees. The store,
located at 137 MacDougal Street, became part of a complex that
included Polly Holliday's restaurant and the Liberal Club. Regular
patrons included Max Eastman, John Reed, and Emma Goldman,
as well as all the people associated with the early years of the
Theatre Guild.

The Bonis were committed socialists, and their store became a
center for Villagers in the movement, who made the store a port of
call where they met their friends. The brothers began to do a little
publishing on the side, by starting a verse magazine, *The Glebe*,
edited by the poet Alfred Kreymborg. Although work by important poets such as H.D. and William Carlos Williams appeared

Albert Boni.
Manuel Komroff collection

there, it only lasted a year. By 1915 the store was thriving, but a little package that arrived there one day changed everything for the Boni brothers.

The little package was a tiny volume of scenes from Shakespeare; it was distributed by a tobacco manufacturer who wished to drum up trade for the sale of cigars and cigarettes by placing the little volumes in the packages. Albert Boni found the idea of "little books" intriguing; he and his brother discussed the possibilities of merchandising some of them. Their many friends in the Village were happy to assist. Among them was Horace's erstwhile rival for Lucille, Walter Lippmann, as well as Harry Scherman (later to create the Book-of-the-Month Club) and Lawrence Langner, a founder with Albert Boni of the Washington

Square Players, a precursor of the Theatre Guild. After listening to their collective wisdom, Albert decided that a somewhat larger volume, to be retailed at a quarter, might just be successful. Accordingly, he had a dummy made up that contained the text of *Romeo and Juliet.* It was dispatched to the Whitman Chocolate Company in Philadelphia along with a list of fourteen other titles supposedly available. These little imitation leather books were supposed to be inserted in the more popular boxes of chocolate sold by Whitman; lovers liked candy in those days. The Bonis were shocked to receive an immediate, firm order for 15,000 books. Great news—but they didn't have any books to ship. To fulfill the order, money had to be raised overnight by the Bonis, Harry Scherman, and two other friends. They called their product the Little Leather Library.

After the Whitman sales had run their course, the Bonis began to sell to the Woolworth chain of five-and-ten-cent stores; the bookshops had refused to handle their little volumes because of the low profit margin. In the first year of their enterprise, over a million books were sold. Albert's hunch had been right; the only thing wrong was the price.

No one seems to know why the Bonis sold their "LLL" line, as well as their bookstore, but by 1916 the brothers were entirely out of the publishing world, and it was at this critical time that Albert encountered Horace Liveright at the offices of Alfred Wallerstein's advertising agency. Wallerstein, a shrewd Wall Street investor, had offered Horace free desk space to use as a base for merchandising one or more of the household gadgets that he had been offered. Months passed before Horace finally met Albert, who was also using Wallerstein's office as he planned his next move. At their first meeting, Horace produced a few of the gadgets and asked Albert's opinion; Albert responded by showing him several of the Little Leather books he had in his desk. Horace was fascinated by the little volumes and asked Albert if he could take home a few to show his father-in-law, who was close to making his very last investment in Horace's future. Boni had explained his idea; wouldn't it be possible to duplicate the previous success of the LLL books in a larger format at a higher price? The new series would constitute a library, a *modern* library of recognized classics and books that were close to becoming such.

In a 1972 interview, Boni recalled that he had also told Alfred Wallerstein all about the Little Leather Library and his plans. Wallerstein was so taken with the idea that he asked Boni if he would like a partner to supply the necessary funds to get the project started. Boni was delighted with his employer's offer, and the two partners shook hands on the deal. As he told the story, Boni then left the office for a few hours to sell some advertising. When he returned that afternoon, he found that some dramatic changes had occurred in his absence:

> When I go to see him he [Wallerstein] says, Albert, I thought you and I were going to go into publishing together. I look at him in amazement and say, well, we are unless you change your mind. He says, Horace says he's going in with you. I said, he never told me that and I didn't accept him. Then Wallerstein told me that Horace . . . [had] speculated with his wife's money . . . and then the father-in-law had told him, I'll give you a chance to get going. I'll give you one more chance. Wallerstein said I think that what you're proposing is the last chance for him. I honestly believe today that all along he was thinking of Horace Liveright as my partner and not of himself.

Boni accepted the situation with as much grace as he could muster, especially since it appeared that Horace was not only enthusiastic but also had some money to invest. But before anything could be decided, a serious question had to be answered: what were the prospects of the two men getting along in a partnership? Boni approached his close friend Lawrence Langner and

received a disturbing answer: "No, Horace Liveright is a great pro-
moter, but you need someone with an editorial background and
who will work 15 hours per day." When Horace, not aware of
Albert's talk with Langner, approached him with the same question, he received an equally negative answer: Boni was simply not
the man to go into business with. Nevertheless, the two men
agreed to undertake a six-month partnership, with Horace contributing $12,500 of Mr. Elsas's money and Albert $4,000 to the
firm of Boni & Liveright. Perhaps one reason for Langner's feeling
that Horace didn't really belong in publishing is revealed in the
description he wrote many years later (the epigraph for this chapter), comparing Horace to Svengali and to the famous actor Sir
Henry Irving. The stage, yes, but hardly publishing.

The presence of Jews in American book publishing was an anomaly
in the pre–World War I years. When Horace and Albert Boni created their firm in the late spring of 1917, they were entering a
Christian industry—owned by Christians and staffed by them.
Anti-Semitism was the main factor, but there were other causes
working to keep book publishing a WASP business from top to
bottom, especially the top. The vast majority of the prominent
New York firms had their roots in the mid- and late nineteenth
centuries: Harper & Brothers, Charles Scribner's Sons, G. P.
Putnam's Sons, and Doubleday. In Boston, the past ruled
supreme: Houghton Mifflin and Little, Brown. All these old firms
were controlled by the heirs of the original founders, a fact that left
its mark on the books they published. Max Schuster, the Jewish
cofounder of Simon and Schuster, observed that before the war,
"Publishing had the position of being a closed universe, for the elite
and the Brahmins in Boston, and for the high and mighty publishers
in New York." Nearly all the editors of these firms had been educated at Yale, Harvard, or Princeton. In short, American book
publishing was something of a gentlemen's club, which rigorously

rejected outsiders. But by 1917 the outsiders included several young Jews who had decided to be included by creating their own houses.

Before 1917, most American book publishers had certain editorial traits in common. Politically speaking, their choices were on the conservative side; an exception to this would be Macmillan's publishing of Jack London. The basic conservatism was reflected in the kinds of literary books they published. Most U.S. firms ignored the feverish wave of literary experimentation taking place in Europe. It is for this reason that so many of the major works of the twentieth-century modernists were published by Jewish firms in the late teens and twenties. This was to be true of all Joyce's works, including *Dubliners* and *A Portrait of the Artist as a Young Man* (Huebsch) and *Ulysses* (Random House), D. H. Lawrence's *Women in Love* and *The Rainbow* (Seltzer), all of Ezra Pound, Eliot's *The Waste Land* (B&L), Sherwood Anderson's *Winesburg, Ohio* (Huebsch), and the first two works of two men Anderson helped get published, Ernest Hemingway's *In Our Time* and William Faulkner's *Soldiers' Pay* (B&L). Finally, it was Horace who published all of Eugene O'Neill's plays, all of Hart Crane, Djuna Barnes, and e. e. cummings.

H. L. Mencken, in a piece published in *The Smart Set* in May 1917—the month when Horace began his business—denounced the current situation in U.S. book publishing:

> Most of the older and richer houses are run by old women in pantaloons; there is no great trade in America, indeed, which shows a vaster imbecility. Reflection and discrimination seem to have been almost completely divorced from publishing; books are printed for any and all reasons save the reason that they are worth printing. Some of the largest houses in the country devote themselves chiefly to merchanting garbage that should make any self-respecting publisher blush.

If Horace read this piece (it is likely that he did) he may have considered it to be a challenge, especially in view of the fact that Mencken's article went out of its way to praise the recently created firm of Alfred A. Knopf, whose list he strongly admired.

Ben Huebsch, then located in 1911 down on Union Square on the East Side of Manhattan, had been the first to break down the barrier, by publishing serious works such as Joyce's *Dubliners* and *A Portrait of the Artist as a Young Man,* as well as a wide range of books on socialist topics. Four years later, Alfred A. Knopf started his firm in small offices on West Forty-second Street, with a 1915 list that consisted of eleven titles, ten of them German, French, or Italian translations. These were the only books he could afford to buy or that agents were willing to sell to him. Boni and Liveright would be the third Jewish firm to challenge the old order. Within just a few years, Boni and Liveright, located in a nondescript office building at 105 West Fortieth Street, close to the old Metropolitan Opera House, would produce lists that quickly equaled in quality those of Huebsch and Knopf. Before finding its own voice, however, the new firm used as an opening wedge the reprint series that the partners called the Modern Library.

For those born after 1950, it is difficult to describe the immense effect of the Modern Library on at least two and perhaps three generations of readers. The Modern Library was a kind of insurance policy guaranteeing that if a book was included in the series it *had* to be good, whether it was a recognized classic or a book dating back only a year or two. Besides the series' reflection of prevailing taste, people used it as a tool for self-education. Many American writers of the day developed a strongly sentimental feeling about their early devotion to the Modern Library. For example, in 1951, when Charles Scribner III told Hemingway that he was going to cancel the reprint contracts for the Modern Library editions of *The Sun Also Rises* and *A Farewell to Arms,* the decision made their author very unhappy. He felt that the series had been part of his growing up. In addition, when Bennett Cerf and Donald Klopfer had included his books in the Modern Library at the beginning of the thirties, Hemingway was grateful; his stock as a writer then was nowhere near as high as it would become in later decades. The mere fact of being included in the Modern Library became (for young writers) the ultimate accolade: your books might not be selling, but you had really made it if you had a title or two in the Modern Library. This was true of writers as diverse as e. e. cummings (*The Enormous Room*), Faulkner (*Sanctuary*), and Dashiell Hammett (*The Maltese Falcon*). In the midst of his own depression in 1934, one good piece of news for Scott Fitzgerald was Bennett Cerf's decision to include *The Great Gatsby,* although Fitzgerald lived long enough to see it remaindered because of its low rate of sale (700 copies a year) in the late thirties.

The first twelve Modern Library titles, at a retail price of sixty cents, appeared in May 1917, just a month after America's entry into the war against the Central Powers. From the moment they became available it was clear that a new and significant presence had entered the publishing scene; their debut was greeted with a wave of praise. *The New York Times* and the *New York Evening Mail* both hailed the event with favorable editorials; the *Evening Post* spoke of "these delightful volumes"; the chief voice of the American book trade, *Publishers Weekly,* said, "The bookseller looking for a quick turnover will do well to look out for the Modern Library." *The Philadelphia Evening Telegram* observed, "I have four of the admirable little volumes and think them a remarkable piece of workmanship for the price asked." Several critics referred to the line's launching as "the most important publishing event of 1917." This may have been hype, but history has confirmed its basic truth. Many of the titles were adopted for college courses by professors who wanted books for their students at the lowest possible cost— the Modern Library supplied that need with the added factor of giving readers the best available texts. Booksellers fell in love with these low-priced items that moved off their shelves with amazing speed. The Modern Library was a huge success on all counts except for one problem that Horace and Boni could not have anticipated.

Despite the overwhelming praise the initial titles received, there were some justified complaints—oddly enough, they concerned smell. When the warmer days of summer arrived, the books began to give off an unmistakably fishy odor, which was traced to the fish oil used in the bindings—probably cod liver oil. The situation was eventually corrected, but the irony of binding great works of the imagination between covers reeking of fish oil haunted the firm for years.

The first Modern Library list of twelve titles was a varied one; all twelve books are still in print (in one edition or another) after seventy-five years. Here are the titles:

Oscar Wilde	*The Picture of Dorian Gray*
August Strindberg	*Married*
Rudyard Kipling	*Soldiers Three*
Robert Louis Stevenson	*Treasure Island*
H. G. Wells	*The War in the Air*
Henrik Ibsen	*A Doll's House*
Anatole France	*The Red Lily*
Guy de Maupassant	*Mlle. Fifi*
Friedrich Nietzsche	*Thus Spake Zarathustra*
Fedor [*sic*] Dostoyevsky	*Poor People*
Maurice Maeterlinck	*St. Antony*
Arthur Schopenhauer	*Pessimism*

Four of these authors (Kipling, Wells, Maeterlinck, and France) were still alive in 1917. Most of the books were not in copyright in the United States; the list could be fairly said to represent the best in contemporary English and Continental literature. Wilde's novel added a bit of spice to the list, as his work was widely regarded as a threat to society, while Maupassant was thought to be "French naughty."

In later years Boni claimed that he alone had selected all the early Modern Library titles, but there is reason to doubt this. Why wouldn't Horace have contributed his share of knowledge to the enterprise? He certainly knew as much or more about modern literature as Boni. Besides slighting Horace, Boni had not a word to say about his uncle, Thomas Seltzer, who became a third partner in the firm in late 1917. There is no doubt that Boni depended greatly upon the advice of his uncle, who was widely known as an editor and translator. When Seltzer joined Boni and Liveright, he brought

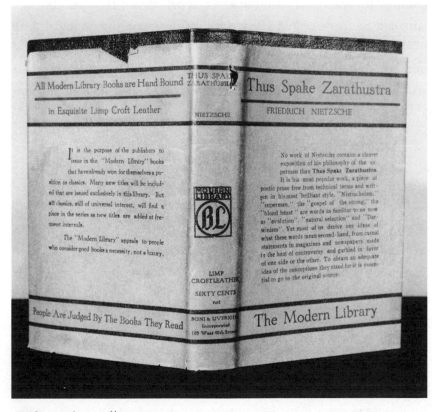

Modern Library #9, 1917.

Gordon A. Neavill collection

with him some much needed capital to a firm that, despite its huge initial success, had a severe cash flow problem. Although he maintained a strong influence on the taste of his nephew, Seltzer had little or no interest in American literature; D. H. Lawrence excepted, his entire attention was turned to modern German and Russian books.

Recalling their visits to New York in the early twenties, D. H. and Frieda Lawrence spoke fondly of their stays with Toby Seltzer and his wife, who lived in an incredibly crowded apartment on the Upper West Side, just off Broadway. Seltzer was a tiny man, just under five feet, who had an encyclopedic knowledge about everything literary in all the modern languages; he demonstrated his abilities by translating a number of works from the German and Russian. Seltzer exerted a powerful influence on the editorial taste of the Modern Library in its formative years, probably as great, if not greater, than Albert Boni. As for Horace's contribution, it would seem unlikely that he would not have made suggestions about the titles to be included in the series.

(2)

> Ten years later the Boni and Liveright group of intellectual radicals would spend an hour or so almost every afternoon drinking toasts to Lenin and Trotsky, and make plans for the Union of Soviet Republics of America.
> —HBL, 1927

IT was not surprising that the new firm of Boni and Liveright would have on its list a goodly share of what used to be referred to as "socially significant" books or, more accurately, left-wing writing. Boni and Horace published a number of such works in 1918, just as the war was ending. One was a now-long-forgotten antiwar novel,

Men in War, by the Hungarian writer Andreas Latzko. Although the book had a sale of fewer than 4,000 copies (this was the United States of "Over There" and *Over the Top*), Horace was forced to withdraw the book from circulation because the government felt that it was a book calculated to be "injurious to the morale of our armies, or detrimental to the proper conduct of the war." The ban was lifted in 1919, but it did not affect the sales picture; the war had become, for the moment at least, passé.

The partners had far more luck with Leon Trotsky's little volume about the situation in Russia, which became their first best seller. The credit for it goes to Horace, who in the early days following the October Revolution of 1917 shouted at his partner: "Albert, what the hell is the matter with you? So many of your friends and relatives are in the Russian Revolution . . . why can't you get us a book from Lenin? *Why don't you get us a book from Lenin?*" Boni made the attempt, but discovered that all of Vladimir Lenin's books were solid tomes about the economic history of Russia, and of little interest to American readers. Horace then settled for second best by asking about Leon Trotsky, the much-publicized leader of the Red Army. Boni later recalled that someone had told him that Trotsky had written an extended pamphlet while he was in exile in Switzerland. The title was mouthwatering: *The Bolsheviki and World Peace.* The main problem was locating a copy of the work. Toby Seltzer thought he might just have a copy in his huge library at home, but he failed to locate it. Albert Boni, convinced that it *must* be there, went through every inch of Seltzer's apartment, which closely resembled a used-book store, finally locating it after digging his way through the thousands of volumes that Seltzer had acquired. The little book was a German version of the Russian original. A translator began work immediately; the book was in the stores in just a few weeks, selling 20,000 copies in its first year.

Trotsky's views on the United States' place in the war were not appealing to the Wilson administration. Within a few months of publication, Horace received a letter from the director of public information, the infamous George Creel, who did not care for Horace's taste:

> In view of the fact of changed relations, and with regard to the attitude of Military Intelligence and various other branches of the Government, I would advise you to discontinue the sale and distribution of Trotsky's book. Personally, I regard Trotsky, and have always regarded him, as an implacable enemy of America, opposed at every point to our democratic ideals.

Many booksellers withdrew the book from sale, but not before it had sold enough copies to justify its publication. Horace did not feel that his integrity was threatened by trafficking with Creel if that traffic could be used to his advantage; he had the gall to ask Creel if he could use his letter for promotional purposes. Strangely enough, Creel agreed: "use my letter . . . in any manner you see fit."

The publication of the Latzko and Trotsky books established Boni and Liveright as a house that dared to take chances, and it was, therefore, no surprise that John Reed's famous study of the Russian Revolution, *Ten Days That Shook the World*,* appeared under that imprint. Horace had become friendly with both Reed and his companion, Louise Bryant, at the time he'd been coming down to the Village to associate with those young people who wanted to change the pattern of American society. *Ten Days* did not fare as well as Trotsky's book (who was John Reed?); it sold only 6,000 copies in its first year. Many of the reviews were scorching, and B&L was taken to task by many critics for publishing such a "Bolshy" book. Reed wrote to Louise from Moscow, telling her that Lenin had read the volume and that she should "tell Horace that the big chief

---

*Horace's lawyer, Arthur Garfield Hays, supplied Reed with his title.

thinks my book the best." Reed's book became perhaps the best-known account of the revolution; it continued to be successful in the Modern Library for decades, especially in the 1930s and 1940s, when many Americans wanted to read a short, clear-cut survey of the events that had altered the world so drastically. The title itself caught on to such an extent that when Sergei Eisenstein's film *October* was released here in 1928 the American distributor used Reed's title rather than Eisenstein's.

Publishing Reed in 1919 encouraged other young Americans to come to the B&L offices with their manuscripts; many of them were friends of Reed and Bryant. The most important was Eugene O'Neill, whose appearance on Horace's list that year began a four-teen-year association with the firm. The little book, for which Horace advanced $125, was *The Moon of the Caribbees and Six Other Plays of the Sea*. It is possible that Horace first met O'Neill through his brother Otto, who played several leading roles in the early Provincetown plays, or it may have been John Reed who brought the two men together. A third possibility is that Frank Shay of the Washington Square Bookshop was the connecting link—he had actually published a small pamphlet of O'Neill's earliest plays in a series devoted to the efforts of the Provincetown Players. It makes little difference who it was, for Horace did not always take the advice given him; in the case of O'Neill he was playing one of the longest shots in his career. It was Horace's intuition at work here, the same intuition that determined so many of his choices. In O'Neill's case the gamble was overwhelmingly against the odds: publishing produced plays is hard, very hard, but attempting to sell largely unproduced ones was (and still is) an action that some would deem suicidal.

Horace was proved to have been right when O'Neill achieved his first big commercial success only a year later with *Beyond the Horizon,* which won the Pulitzer Prize for 1920. Despite his faith in O'Neill, Horace did not like *Horizon* and was convinced that it would fail. When Lucille was away, he wrote her that he "as well as . . . Julian . . . T. R. Smith . . . Edna Millay" all thought the play to be a bad one despite the magnificent reviews. In another letter he told Lucille that *Horizon* "was a terrible frost & I was sorely disappointed. The book will be a [failure?] too." After the success of the play Horace told Lucille that he had been in error: "—hell, I'm glad I'm wrong but where, oh where is my critical faculty?"

Despite many competitive offers, O'Neill was loyal to Horace and remained with the firm until its bankruptcy in 1933. Horace's technique of marketing O'Neill as the one playwright whose work deserved a large audience was exemplary. O'Neill was probably the only American dramatist to sell more than a hundred thousand copies of a new play—*Strange Interlude* of 1928—in its very first year.

To say that Eugene O'Neill was shy falls far short of the mark; he was averse to the noise and occasional frenzy of some of Horace's famous parties. Although he was invited to all of them, O'Neill rarely appeared. He never became particularly close to Horace—partly from worry about his loss of control over his drinking in the early twenties. When O'Neill gave up drinking for good in 1925, he saw less and less of Horace, whom he now considered to be a threat to his sobriety—it was hard to be around Horace and *not* drink.

With John Reed on his list, it was not surprising that Horace would also publish Upton Sinclair, an avowed socialist who became, with the exception of Jack London, the most widely read American writer outside the United States. When he died in his ninetieth year in 1962, Sinclair had published more than a hundred books. Only one of them is still widely read—*The Jungle* (1906), which begins with a Chicago meatpacking plant worker falling to his death from a high catwalk into a huge, boiling cauldron of meat; in seconds, the body of the worker becomes a part of that day's production of sausage. *The Jungle* made Sinclair famous; President Theodore Roosevelt was so stirred by the novel that he immediately began a campaign for Congress to create the first Pure Food and Drug Act. Through the teens and twenties, Sinclair published a steady stream of novels, exposé books, and treatises about the need for a socialist America.

Some have wondered why a hard-drinking, "libertine" publisher like Horace should have become involved with an old-fashioned writer like Sinclair, who, he believed, would never find a large audience, a writer who possessed few of the literary graces common to most B&L authors. The unifying bond between Horace and Sinclair was their belief in socialism and a devotion to the truth. Otherwise, they were about as far apart as they could be. The abstemious Sinclair was a life-long advocate of temperance (he wrote a book about the subject, *The Cup of Fury,* in 1955) and extraordinarily prudish about sexual matters; many of the titles on Horace's lists must surely have distressed him.

In his own way, Sinclair was as bad a writer as Theodore Dreiser. He was essentially a writer of polemics about the major social issues of the day: education, capital and labor, organized religion, and political corruption. His work was devoid of humor, and he had severe difficulties in creating believable fictional characters—they were nearly always merely mouthpieces for Sinclair's ideas. Because of his undeviating socialist convictions, by 1918 Sinclair had become a pariah in the New York publishing community. Almost no one wished to publish a writer considered to be dangerous and who did not sell particularly well. To overcome this resistance, Sinclair (like Mark Twain and Dostoevsky before him) took on the role of publisher by establishing a mail-order business operated from his home in Pasadena, California. When he approached Horace with the manuscript of his new book, a pacifist novel he called *Jimmy Higgins,* he proposed what amounted to a cooperative publishing venture that had Sinclair typesetting the book in California and Horace printing both the trade edition and the mail-order volumes in the East. They would clearly divide their selling territories and share in the profits—if there were any. It was going to be a hard job getting *Jimmy Higgins* into the bookstores.

Few publishers would have entered into such a deal, especially in the climate of fear and trembling that swept over America through 1919 and on into the following year. This was the time of the infamous U.S. government–led "Palmer Raids," named for A. Mitchell Palmer, the attorney general. Any deviation from the accepted political norms of the day was harshly treated. The main victims were those who had opposed the war effort, communists, and socialists. Part of the fear emanating from Washington was due to the recent triumph of Lenin and Trotsky in the USSR. The rallying cry against all "subversives" was "Down with the Bolsheviki!" Sinclair's *Jimmy Higgins*—an openly pacifist novel written by a notorious socialist—was sure to attract the wrath of the government. Horace became worried enough to consult with Sinclair about toning the book down a bit, but it was published pretty much the way it had been written. Horace's concern was justified, because Palmer's people were ruthless once they had decided to take action; they thought nothing of smashing into the newsrooms of deviant papers and magazines, destroying everything in their path. One aspect of the novel that particularly concerned Horace was placing the hero among the U.S. armed forces who had gone to Vladivostok and Arkhangelsk along with British, French, and Japanese troops in an interventionist move to attack the Red Army at the end of 1918. Their presence had failed to weaken the power of the Soviets, and their forces had been quietly withdrawn the following year, but in the months just preceding publication of *Jimmy Higgins,* the issue of the American presence in Russia was volatile. Horace discovered just how unwelcome Sinclair's book was in some quarters when the American News Company canceled its order of 400 copies, while the Union News Company decided it didn't want the 250 copies it had ordered.

Jimmy Higgins wound up selling fewer than 3,000 copies in the United States. The low sales can be explained partly by poor reviews; the New York evening *Sun* epitomized them, calling the book "rot." But the real reason for its failure would appear to be the American public's weariness with the war and everything connected with it. Sinclair was touched by Horace's willingness to proceed with a book he knew to be a loser from the start: "I do admire your courage in publishing the book and it is gratifying to have your faith and interest."

Throughout the early twenties Sinclair kept testing Horace's courage by giving him books that had but little chance of commercial success. His next novel, *They Call Me Carpenter* (1922), was essentially a book of dialogues between Christ returned to Earth and a rich businessman who embodies everything that is wrong with American life. This was again a co-op deal, but with *Carpenter* the partners fared better than with *Jimmy Higgins*—the book sold about six thousand copies. It was Sinclair's next work of fiction, *Oil!* of 1927, an exposé of the Harding administration and the Teapot Dome Scandal, that cost Horace a national best-seller and an author. Despite some misgivings about the didactic aspects of the book, Horace was more than willing to take on *Oil!* It was the immense length of the manuscript that troubled him. He felt that if Sinclair

> could bring it down to 160,000 words, I think it would have a bigger chance in the market place. No one will object to the $2.50 price because everyone is used to that figure now for a novel even written by an unknown author. . . . Let's hear more from you . . . and tell me when I may expect to get another installment of it.

Sinclair continued to work on *Oil!* for the next eight months of 1926, but instead of decreasing in size, it grew to become a book of 230,000 words, or "five hundred and twenty pages of the size I am making." (Again, Sinclair was doing his own typesetting in California.) To pack this many words into the confines of a five-hundred-page book would indicate that he was using a tiny, scarcely readable typeface that would surely doom the novel despite all its author's good intentions:

> I have been working very hard on this book, and I think it is the best thing I have ever done. The reason it is so long is because I have taken the trouble to invent sufficient story to carry my ideas.

It became clear that Sinclair was offering Horace his book on a "take-it-or-leave-it" basis when he told him,

> Let me say I would rather you did not take the book unless you believe in it with all your heart and will advertise and boost it. It is the first full length novel that I have published in eight years. I think it is my best novel and stands a good chance of popular success. I hope you will feel the same way. If you don't there will be no feelings hurt.

Apparently unable to agree with Horace over the length, Sinclair offered his book to Charles Boni, who by 1927 was running his own firm of Albert and Charles Boni and who accepted it at once. Under ordinary circumstances *Oil!* would probably have sold about five or six thousand copies, but inexplicably for such a prudish writer, the Boston censors decided that at least one page in the novel offended them enough to warrant its suppression in that city. In 1927 the words "Banned in Boston" indicated that the work must surely contain considerable salacious material. Those who rushed the stores for Upton Sinclair's treatment of sexual situations were severely disappointed, but *Oil!* was a huge success, as was Sinclair's next book, *Boston,* a novel about Sacco and Vanzetti.

With the exception of these two books of the late 1920s, it was not until the 1940s and early 1950s that Sinclair found immense success. His Lanny Budd series of eleven novels about a stalwart young American who is entrusted by FDR to become his "eyes and ears" in prewar Europe became huge best-sellers, and Sinclair regained the national fame won in 1934 when he narrowly missed being elected governor of California in his EPIC (End Poverty in California) campaign. He met his defeat through the efforts of Irving Thalberg and Louis B. Mayer of MGM, who manufactured phony newsreels showing hobos from all over America descending on California to take their places in Sinclair's socialist paradise. In addition to their publishing ventures, Horace and Sinclair were later, in the 1930s, to become involved with the career of Sergei Eisenstein in Hollywood when both the Russian director and Horace were working at Paramount. Sinclair supplied Eisenstein with the $100,000 he needed to make his ill-fated film *Que Viva Mexico!* on location in Mexico after Horace and the director had both been fired by Paramount.

Horace's loss of Sinclair as a B&L author did nothing to diminish their friendship, which ripened during Horace's dealings with Eisenstein. At the bitter end, it was Upton Sinclair who delivered Horace's funeral eulogy.

In the summer of 1918 Horace found himself with two partners with whom he had in common their shared enthusiasm for socialism and little else. His partners appeared uninterested in the kinds of books that were being written all around them, especially those by Greenwich Village people like Waldo Frank, Djuna Barnes, and Theodore Dreiser. In general, both Boni and his uncle favored Continental books, especially serious volumes about current trends in economics and sociology—difficult subjects for a trade publisher. When both Boni and Seltzer agreed on something, Horace, as part of their agreement, was forced to go along. Occasionally he was allied with Seltzer against Boni, but this was infrequent. This situation was obviously hard to bear; although he was the president of the firm, he could easily be outvoted in deciding what the firm published. But there were even stronger reasons for his dissatisfaction.

Besides managing the firm's finances, Horace went on regular selling trips to bookstores throughout the country; so, too, did Boni, while his younger brother, Charles, covered the New York stores. In 1918, when Horace had just returned from a trip, he discovered that affairs had gone badly in his absence. He told Lucille in an angry May letter that

> Albert is positively immoral in his attitude towards business. I just found out this morning that instead of 1000 of each of the next 15 titles, only 500 or 600 of them had been bound & then I found a lot of mistakes . . . in the way both Toby [Seltzer] and Albert had edited and manufactured the new titles—but Toby is not so bad. But the worst part is Albert's indifference . . . If he doesn't tend to selling the books properly, Toby had promised me to advocate kicking him out, so we'll wait and see.

As Horace had become increasingly impatient with the carelessness of the Bonis, he looked forward to the day when he could hire an old friend from his Wall Street days—the only such link to his past as a stock and bond trader. Julian Messner was as constant a reader as Horace; he was "a couple of inches shorter than I, thirty or more pounds heavier, swarthy, with deep-set black eyes, straight nose and full lips." Julian had a Sephardic background and decided at the beginning of their friendship that Horace must surely be a distant cousin. In May 1918 Horace wrote Lucille, "We have offered my dear Julian the manufacturing end of the business at $40.00 per week. . . . I pray that he accepts—it will greatly help our business & will be such a happy arrangement." Julian accepted, and hiring him proved to be one of Horace's best decisions: Messner became sales manager and general factotum as well. Since Albert Boni left the firm in July 1918, only a few weeks after Julian's arrival, it would seem likely that Horace was really hiring him as a replacement for Albert and his brother, Charles. In the long run, it was the Boni brothers' indifference to the running of the business that had infuriated Horace; "I will thank God when Julian gets here & shares some of the responsibilities with me." For reasons that remain obscure, Messner always addressed Horace as "Mr. Liveright," despite their friendship of more than a decade. Over the years Julian developed a fierce loyalty to Horace that prevailed long past the day when Liveright left the company.

What the firm had needed was a controlling voice, which it found in Horace after he and Boni used an age-old method of choice: they threw a coin and Horace won the toss; he became the majority stockholder. Another version of the coin-tossing episode has Boni winning the toss, with the apparently sure knowledge that he would be able to obtain the financial backing he'd require to go it alone. At the very last moment the funds became unavailable, and Boni then decided to allow Horace to continue the business on his own with the help of Uncle Toby Seltzer. By late 1918 Boni had sold his interest to Horace and departed for an inspection visit to the land of the Great Experiment, where he was arrested as a suspected spy for foreign interests. He spent several months imprisoned in a Russian jail before returning to America.

Once Julian Messner had begun taking over many of the tasks that Horace was saddled with, it was time for him to seek an editor in chief who might replace Toby, uneasily filling the role after Albert Boni's departure. Horace's first choice was the young American poet Jeanne Robert Foster. Besides her literary credentials, Mrs. Foster was a beautiful woman. Married to an older, disabled man, she was also the companion of the wealthy Irish-American lawyer and art patron John Quinn. Quinn represented Joyce, Eliot, and Pound in all their literary dealings in America. He was the creator of one of the greatest private collections of modern art in the United States. Mrs. Foster's wit and charm endeared her to the publishing worlds of New York, Paris, and London; Ford Madox Ford thought so highly of her that he appointed her the New York editor of his *Transatlantic Review,* an undersubsidized magazine that required the cash infusions of John Quinn to keep it alive. He called her a "ravishingly beautiful lady" and "an admirable business woman."

Horace offered her the job of editor-in-chief as well as a contract to publish her second collection of verse. Mrs. Foster signed the book contract but rejected the job offer for reasons that can be surmised. A probable one is that her closeness to John Quinn (an extreme anti-Semite) would have made working for Horace difficult. Or Quinn may have been jealous, fearing that Horace would take more than a professional interest in his editor. He would have been right: Horace found the combination of beauty and intelligence to be irresistible (it was at about this time that he reputedly had a brief affair with Djuna Barnes just before she gave up on the male sex). Perhaps to throw Lucille off the track about his feelings for Mrs. Foster, Horace teased her in a 1919 letter: "It's funny how much everybody seems to like me—all except you—I believe Mrs. Foster fell for me pretty hard last night." This method of joshing Lucille about his possible affairs with women was almost guaranteed to produce the opposite of the effect intended—Lucille became increasingly suspicious about Horace's interest in the many beautiful women he encountered in his work.

The man Horace finally hired was Thomas R. Smith—known to everyone as Tommy Smith—perhaps the most colorful New York editor of the twenties. Smith was passionate about collecting rare books, especially the kind that booksellers used to identify as

Tommy Smith.
Warder Collection, W. W. Norton Co.

"curiosa" in catalogs. Today we call such books erotica or pornography, depending on our point of view. Smith was also very fond of drinking, a difficult task after the enforcement of the Prohibition Act of 1920. Smith was as enthusiastic about publishing books as Horace. Short, cherubic, usually wearing a pince-nez, Tommy Smith knew as much about the book world as anyone has ever known: He could summon up on demand the sales figures of books published twenty years previously; he knew the author-publisher relationships of all the notable writers in American and England, useful knowledge about writers who might be persuaded to come over to Liveright. He could work with writers as different as Gertrude Atherton and Hart Crane.

Smith knew everybody who was worth knowing in New York at the beginning of the twenties. Among his friends were the

Barrymores (all three), Booth Tarkington, Wilson Mizner, Anita Loos, "Diamond Jim" Brady, James Huneker, F. Scott Fitzgerald, Frank Crowninshield (of *Vanity Fair*), and Dorothy Parker. He drank incessantly, and in his years of triumph at Liveright he fairly earned the equivalent of praise that Lincoln bestowed on Grant when his best general was accused of being a drunk: "Would that I had ten more like him!" A giver of lavish parties, he was a welcome visitor at nearly every literary household in New York. He was rumored to know the madams of all the fashionable brothels in town on a first-name basis and could give you expert advice about what you might find there. In no way did this indicate that Smith patronized these places—his own sex life seems to have been almost nonexistent—there was a wife from whom he was separated and a daughter in the distant past. Besides socializing, Smith directed most of his energies to his love for literature and writers. He was a man of far greater literary sophistication than Maxwell Perkins of Scribner's.

Although American born, Smith had been educated in England and had served his editorial apprenticeship with Moffat, Yard and Company before becoming the managing editor of *The Century,* a high-toned literary periodical. It was during this period of his life (1915 through 1920) that he became acquainted with so many of the leading writers in London and New York. He was a regular guest of Scott and Zelda Fitzgerald in Great Neck. H. L. Mencken counted Smith among his three or four intimates in the early twenties despite his friend's "certain English intonations and mannerisms." On his frequent New York visits, Mencken was often at Smith's apartment up on West 105th Street, which contained a library characterized by Mencken as "curious." Outside of a collection of volumes on British history, the entire library consisted of elegant pornography, most of it the illustrated kind. Smith might be said to have taken his erotica seriously, for in 1922 he compiled a huge two-volume anthology entitled *Poetica Erotica.* Horace published it at a very high price—$15.00—to keep it from the attention of the law. It sold only about 2,700 copies then but has been in print for most of the past seventy years.

But it is likely that Smith's deeper interests lay in alcohol, because after the passage of the Volstead Act he had his large kitchen ripped out to make way for case after case of choice liquors and wines piled up to the ceiling. It is now hard to appreciate the deep shock serious drinkers felt when they realized that they could never again purchase liquor legitimately. Some dedicated drinkers, like Smith, bought up everything they could afford to store for the dark days of privation that lay ahead.

Before joining Horace, Smith became a literary agent with only one client, the feisty Irishman George Moore, whose exacting terms drove publishers wild with rage and also made them fear the censors—in this case a more cultivated form of Dreiser's problems. Soon after Smith's arrival at B&L in 1918, Moore's books, new and old, began appearing on the list of the firm that had as its logo a small picture of a cowled monk at his writing desk—perhaps the most inappropriate one possible for a publisher determined to offend public taste. The firm's monk logo was invariably accompanied by the words "Good Books," a description that was often accurate.

In 1919 Seltzer also sold his stock to Horace to go into business under his own name with the publication that year of a limited edition of D. H. Lawrence's *Women in Love*. Seltzer remained Lawrence's chief U.S. publisher until 1926, when he finally rejoined his nephews in the firm they had created in 1922, A. and C. Boni. In the 1920s the Bonis published a number of important books, including all of Marcel Proust and many D. H. Lawrence titles; their greatest success was Thornton Wilder's *The Bridge of San Luis Rey*.

Horace was undoubtedly glad to see them depart; his only reservation might have been their use of the name Boni in their firm's name. He, of course, could abandon their name, but by 1920 the firm of B&L was widely known, and changing it might prove to be dangerous. The Boni brothers' perfectly legitimate use of their name caused confusion in the minds of book buyers and reviewers, who constantly conflated the two firms. Whatever the name, Horace was now on his own to publish whatever he wanted and could express his interest in new American writers. As early as the summer of 1917 in the very first days of B&L's existence he had established contact with Theodore Dreiser, the great white bull elephant of American prose—the writer who always seemed to generate difficulties for his publishers. In time Horace thought his relationship with Dreiser was perhaps the most important one in his publishing career—but perhaps the most unpleasant, as well.

Putting Up with Dreiser

I sometimes think that my desire is for expression that is
entirely too frank for this time—hence that I must pay the
price of being unpalatable.
    —Theodore Dreiser to H. L. Mencken, March 10, 1911

(1)

Theodore Dreiser might have become a forgotten, failed
writer of the early years of this century had he not obtained the
energetic backing of two men: H. L. Mencken and Horace
Liveright. Beginning in the early teens and continuing for the next
decade, the sage of Baltimore conducted a one-man campaign to
convince the American reading public that a great American writer
was being seriously neglected. Mencken's campaign affected few
ordinary readers, but had a lasting effect on critics and reviewers all
over the country who looked on Mencken as their beacon in the
cultural darkness he so vividly described in his polemics. In his
immensely long and detailed study of Dreiser in *A Book of Prefaces,*
plus odd reviews and press statements, Mencken beat the drum for
Dreiser as the harbinger of a new voice in American letters—the
voice of unadorned truth.

Mencken's recently published memoirs indicate that he made no bones about why he campaigned so vigorously for Dreiser:

> Ever since . . . 1909, I had been on the lookout for an author who would serve me as a sort of tank in my war upon the frauds and dolts who still reigned in American letters. It was not enough to ridicule and revile the fakers they admired and whooped up, though I did this with great enthusiasm; it was also necessary, if only for the sake of the dramatic contest, to fight for writers, and especially for newcomers, they sniffed at. . . . What I needed was some American, preferably young, to mass my artillery behind, and I gave a good deal of diligence to the search for him.

When Dreiser published *Jennie Gerhardt* in 1911, Mencken's review hailed it as "the best American novel I have ever read, with the lonesome but Himalayan exception of *Huckleberry Finn*." By 1911 Mencken had known Dreiser for three years and wrote him at the time of *Jennie*'s publication that "My second reading . . . has increased my enthusiasm for it . . . you have written the best American novel ever done." Thoughtful American readers paid closer attention to Mencken than they did to any other living critic; his review of *Jennie* established Dreiser's reputation virtually overnight. Besides his praise, Mencken made no effort to conceal the facts about Dreiser's supreme gracelessness, as well as his frequent dip into the sentimentality found in the mass circulation magazines of the day. But Mencken told his audience that Dreiser was, nevertheless, the single most important living American writer and that they should honor his books by reading them. Achieving this aim was to be Horace's role in the creation of an audience for Dreiser.

It is more than likely that Horace had read some of Mencken's preachments about Dreiser. Even if he hadn't, he could have discovered much about him by reading the daily papers throughout

1916. Dreiser's fifth novel, *The "Genius,"* had been removed from bookstores by its publisher through the pressure exerted by the man who was to be Horace's continuing enemy through the twenties, John S. Sumner of the New York Society for the Suppression of Vice. Sumner had found *The "Genius"* to contain seventy-five "lewd" passages in addition to seventeen examples of profanity in its 736 densely printed pages. Sumner's ultimatum was simple: Remove the offending passages or face criminal prosecution. Terrified by Sumner's power, Dreiser's publisher (the American branch of the British firm John Lane) recalled all the books from the stores pending a decision from the courts. Eventually, no action was ever taken by Sumner, but thousands of copies of *The "Genius"* continued to rot in Lane's warehouse for the next seven years. Before its suppression the book had sold about eight thousand copies; Horace was convinced that many times this number could be moved if the book were reissued.

With his ears open to the literary gossip of the Village, Horace had heard that Frank Shay, the new owner of the Washington Square Bookshop, had contracted to reissue *Sister Carrie*. By 1917 *Carrie* had acquired a literary reputation as a book that had been suppressed by its publisher, Doubleday, Page, in 1900. While this was not strictly true, Dreiser's first novel had been given minimum attention by the firm, and it sold only a few hundred copies of the thousand they printed. It is doubtful if many more would have been sold even if Doubleday had been more aggressive; most critics hated the novel—the American public was not yet ready for *Sister Carrie*. The problem was the sad, uncompromising story of the decline of George Hurstwood, who leaves his prosperous life and marriage and eventually kills himself, while Carrie, in contrast, who breaks the moral code of the day by having sex outside of marriage, becomes a successful actress. Many critics hated Dreiser for not punishing Carrie as a "fallen woman."

Dreiser was so discouraged by the book's failure that he gave up novel writing for the best part of a decade. He returned to the dreary business of editing various women's magazines, not writing another novel until the 1911 *Jennie Gerhardt*. Seven years after *Sister Carrie*'s first appearance in 1900, Dreiser invested several thousand dollars in a small publishing firm, B. W. Dodge, that reissued *Carrie* and sold several thousand copies before it went bankrupt. When Frank Shay agreed in 1917 to republish the book, Dreiser was overjoyed, but just as quickly disappointed, when Shay discovered that he was about to be drafted and would have to abandon the plans. It was at this point that Horace approached Dreiser with an offer to take over the Shay contract as well as a commitment to reissue all his earlier books, including the suppressed *"Genius."* Anticipating that Dreiser might be difficult to deal with, Horace offered him a 25 percent royalty, more than twice the going rate.

The personal relationship between the young publisher (Horace was thirty-two) and the forty-eight-year-old novelist who became, in literary terms at least, his star author, was strained from the beginning. In all their thirteen-year correspondence they were never on a first-name basis. Dreiser was frequently convinced that Horace was cheating him of his royalties, while Horace had ample evidence that Dreiser was secretly negotiating behind his back with other publishers to take over the publication of his books. As for Horace, whatever Dreiser did had to be expected: if you were going to be the publisher of America's greatest living novelist, you must expect trouble. And that is what he received from Theodore Dreiser.

Both of Dreiser's major biographers have demonstrated that their subject's ordinary social demeanor was on the lugubrious side; he was glum most of the time and socially ill at ease. He had a lifelong habit of taking a handkerchief from his pocket and folding and unfolding it meticulously with maddening regularity while he spoke to you. If he wasn't in his "how *awful* things are" manner, he might become arrogant and rude; in time, he alienated many of his friends. Horace's charm proved unavailing; the anti-Semitic Dreiser resented the fact that he was being published by a Jew and perhaps a crooked one at that.

In his various dealings with Dreiser while editor of *The Smart Set*, Mencken discovered how his friend regarded his publishers. At the time of *Jennie Gerhardt*'s publication by Harper, Dreiser became dissatisfied,

> and I was to learn that this was his habitual attitude towards publishers. He had rows with every one that ever published him, and on his side, at least, those rows were often extraordinarily bitter and raucous. More than once I have heard him allege with perfect seriousness that his publisher of the moment was cheating him on royalties—and keeping two sets of books to conceal the fact.

Dreiser was steadfast about the cheating, but employees of B&L found it hard to take him seriously in this area. Bennett Cerf, one of Horace's young vice presidents, recalled that Dreiser was "always thinking that everybody was cheating. He'd come in about every three months to examine the ledger to see whether his royalty statements were correct. . . . He'd made little marks against all the items he'd examined and then he'd go out to lunch and we'd rub all the marks off, and when he came back he wouldn't even notice."

The difficulties with Dreiser even extended to the mechanics of getting his books published. He habitually rewrote them while they were already in galleys, a practice that is costly to either author or publisher. To placate Dreiser, Horace nearly always went along with accepting the expenses incurred by a writer who often delivered manuscripts not yet ready for the printer. When Horace wrote Dreiser about the proofs of his play *The Hand of the Potter* (a work he had not wished to publish), he pointed out that:

Our printers advise me that from their reading of the play they are under the impression that you refer to many things in this last act that do not appear in any part of the play as it is at present, for example the box and oil cloth that you brought in in Act Three as you revised it. . . . I just got the corrected proofs of "Free and Other Stories" and find that you have practically rewritten the whole book. Not only will it probably be cheaper to reset this whole book, but on account of the poor copy . . . extra charges will be made for composition. Of course, you are the doctor so far as costs are concerned . . . but I must ask you to give us clean copy at the start.

When Dreiser chose to interpret this plea as an example of Horace's raging at him, Horace was prudently fair:

Where on earth do you get the impression that I was in a rage when I wrote you about your corrections? My wife tells me that I never lose my temper with anyone excepting her and I think she is right. I look forward to seeing you Monday to go over everything.

Trying to placate this consistently unhappy writer was useless; each time Horace gave in on something, Dreiser would ask for something else—he never changed in all their years together.

Dreiser was a man filled with distrust of his fellowman—especially if that man had anything to do with book publishing. After his disasters with Doubleday and John Lane, Dreiser harbored what became a lifelong resentment against the entire publishing trade. In the next thirteen years he directed his suspicion and hatred against the man who was most determined to make him a national figure—Horace Liveright. Characteristically, Dreiser made it clear in this very first contract with Horace that he was only *lending* him the plates to print *Sister Carrie* for an edition of a thousand copies; if Dreiser wanted to contract with someone else later, he would be free to take the plates back.* Horace agreed to all his new author's terms, which would be the first in an unending series of such concessions. As Dreiser's fame increased in the following decade, Horace gave in to his demands as a matter of course. He had concluded that to be Dreiser's publisher was a guarantee that his firm would quickly be identified as the house most vitally concerned with the new spirit in American writing that he sensed was boiling up all around him.

(2)

> I was always in doubt about your alliance with [Liveright]. He now has a great deal of money, obtaining same from some new Jew backer. Confidentially, he is forever approaching [George Jean] Nathan and me, and lately he offered us a blank contract, including even 50% royalty. But we are too comfortable with Knopf.
> —H. L. Mencken to Dreiser, September 2, 1920

IN the early years, it was H. L. Mencken who kept urging Dreiser to leave Horace for another publisher. Their correspondence on the subject is strewn with anti-Semitic remarks, with Mencken filling Dreiser's receptive ears with his prejudice against Horace, strange considering that Mencken's only publisher was another Jew, Alfred A. Knopf. This is a commonplace, of course, in anti-Semitic feeling that Jews are a worthless race, but I know a particular one unlike all the others.

Besides suspecting Horace of cheating him on his royalties, Dreiser constantly reviled Horace for what he thought were the abnormally low sales figures that B&L produced for him. Many

---

*Dreiser had bought his plates from Doubleday; he was still renting them as late as 1935.

Theodore Dreiser: almost a smile.
Warder Collection, W. W. Norton Co.

writers feel their publishers let them down, but with Dreiser this feeling became a mania. He appeared to believe that Horace was simply not doing his job well. This attitude may have been a studied one, simply to obtain from Horace greater attention than he actually deserved. Horace would reply, in letter after letter, that greater sales figures could only be produced if Dreiser delivered a major new novel. For the first five years of their association, the only Dreiser titles Horace had to sell were either old books like *Sister Carrie* or new volumes of short stories, plays, or essays. Some of the things that Dreiser complained about were the figures for his play, *The Hand of the Potter* (2,312 copies), and a collection of short stories, *Twelve Men* (1,725 copies). Horace had agreed to publish the play solely to retain Dreiser as an author; he had but little enthusiasm for the stories, either. The fact was that Dreiser had delusions of grandeur about the market for his work: even when he did produce major novels their sales were not very impressive:

Jennie Gerhardt (1911)	7,700 copies
The Financier (1912)	1,727 copies
The Titan (1914)	8,000 copies
The "Genius" (1915)	8,000 copies

However, with critical interest in Dreiser rising steadily, Horace was convinced that a new Dreiser novel would rescue him from the sales of *Hey Rub-a-Dub Dub: A Book of the Mystery and Terror and Wonder of Life* (essays, 1920, 3,164 copies) and the autobiographical *A Book About Myself* (1922, 3,806 copies). For a brief time, both men appeared to know what that book would be.

In 1919 Dreiser indicated that he was, in fact, writing a big novel and that Horace would surely be its publisher. This was *The Bulwark,* a book in which Horace made his first investment by putting Dreiser on the B&L payroll in the amount of $333 a month for a total $4,000 advance. Neither Dreiser nor Horace lived long enough to see the publication of *The Bulwark*. It was published posthumously in 1946, more than a quarter of a century after Horace's initial contract.

Over the next few years, Dreiser used the unfinished *Bulwark* as a carrot for Horace's desire to produce a best seller. Delivery dates came and went, but Horace's hopes were hard to quench. When Dreiser failed to produce the manuscript, Horace wrote a number of letters to his new home in California, reminding him that it was an absolute necessity for his reputation to have a new novel before the public. Dreiser was not happy with this news, telling Mencken that "Liveright . . . is insane on the subject of publishing a new novel by me." He wrote Horace expressing his anger about the letters he kept receiving from New York:

> The burden of their song . . . has been that it is so important for me to do another novel, that the public expects it of me, that my reputation as a writer somehow hangs not on anything I have done in the past but on what I may hope to do in the future, that I must have a *new* and smashing success in order to restore or at least retain my waning reputation. . . . If I have not already written the Great American Novel then I never will, for I have already written as good a novel as I will ever write. . . . Quite frankly, I am not running a race with anyone.

Horace did not give up on *The Bulwark* for another year or so, while Dreiser earned out his advance for it by applying the monies earned by his other B&L titles to the contract—a procedure that most publishers would have found unacceptable. But Dreiser was Dreiser. At first unknown to Horace, but increasingly harder for him to ignore, was the discovery that Dreiser was seeking out other publishers to take on *The Bulwark*. There were no takers, and the troubled relationship between them continued. In a curious way, Horace and Dreiser, despite their profound differences, were right for each other. In Horace, Dreiser found a publisher who believed in his work to the point of being willing to fight for it in the courts, as well as someone willing to pay handsome advances for works that Dreiser found he couldn't finish. Horace had the satisfaction of knowing that, in the long run, Dreiser would be regarded as the major American novelist of the era and that, no matter how much trouble he might make, he was worth every bit of it. To make B&L credible as an emerging house in American publishing, Dreiser was the ideal writer to have on their list. This relationship had nothing personal about it; each man distrusted the other—it was a matter of need on both sides.

(3)

> [I] called him up and told him [HBL] to go to hell and then he came down to my place and literally—not figuratively— wept—and agreed to do anything within reason if I would stay.
> —Dreiser to H. L. Mencken, September 20, 1920

WE may doubt that Horace wept on this occasion, but knowing his fierce pride, it may now seem strange that he would take so much abuse from a writer who was consistently rude, challenging, and boorish in the extreme. What did he see in Dreiser's work that made it all worthwhile?

Only three of Dreiser's novels are still read; *Sister Carrie* leads them all, largely because of the book's intrinsic merit, but also due to its public domain status—a fact that has resulted in half a dozen editions currently in print. *Jennie Gerhardt* and *An American Tragedy* are less read; the length of the second has curtailed its use in class-rooms. The rest of Dreiser's books are largely ignored—perhaps wisely so—but it is extraordinary how Dreiser has maintained his literary eminence, considering how badly he wrote. Everything negative his critics have said about him is painfully true. Even Horace was fully aware of the sheer clumsiness of his major author—the kind of terrible writing that all the editing and cutting in the world can't help. Few deny that Dreiser's writing is slovenly, graceless and ponderous beyond belief. Despite knowing the truth about Dreiser's literary weaknesses, both Horace and Mencken were convinced that establishing him as a major figure was essential. As a critic Mencken risked little, but Horace wound up spending more time and money on Dreiser than on any other writer he published.

When Dreiser sat back to read the praise of his foremost defender, he may well have recalled the old saying "With friends like these, who needs enemies?"

> "The Genius," coming after "The Titan," marks the high tide of his bad writing. There are passages in it so clumsy, so inept, so irritating that seem almost unbelievable; nothing worse is to be found in the newspapers. . . . It is flaccid, elephantine, doltish, coarse, dismal, flatulent, sophomoric, ignorant, unconvincing, wearisome. . . . The book is an endless emission of the obvious, with touches of the scandalous to light up its killing monotony. It runs to 736 pages of small type; its reading is an unbearable weariness to the flesh; in the midst of it one has forgotten the beginning and is unconcerned about the end.

Nevertheless, Mencken concluded his famous essay by saying that Dreiser must be forgiven these affronts to the language because he alone on the literary landscape dares speak the truth, a "groping toward a light but dimly seen":

> He is driving at nothing, he is merely trying to represent what he sees and feels. His moving impulse is no flabby yearning to teach, to expound, to make simple; it is that "obscure inner necessity" of

which Conrad tells us, the irresistible creative passion of a genuine artist, standing spellbound before the impenetrable enigma that is life, enamored by the strange beauty that plays over its sordidness, challenged to a wondering and half-terrified sort of representation of what passes for understanding.

Horace may have comforted himself by rereading passages like this whenever Dreiser barged into the office, demanding an immediate inspection of the books, or wrote still another letter vilifying Horace and his firm. All through the early twenties he continued to have Horace reissue his older titles, while supplying him with travel books and collections of short stories. The only bright spot in these early years with Dreiser was the reissue of The "Genius," which quickly sold more than forty thousand copies. It was not until 1925, however, that Horace's faith in Dreiser was justified by the publication of An American Tragedy, but even that event was to have its dark side.

"Going Toward the Light"
with Pound and Eliot

Horace . . . is a pearl among publishers.
—Ezra Pound to John Quinn, June 20, 1920

I have written, mostly when I was at Lausanne for treatment
last winter, a long poem of about 450 [lines] . . . I think it is
the best I have ever done, and Pound thinks so too. Pound
introduced me to Liveright in Paris, and Liveright made me
the offer . . .
—T. S. Eliot to John Quinn, June 25, 1922

(1)

IT was not until the end of 1921 that Horace felt he could afford
to take time away from daily business routines to carry out his first
extended buying trip to Europe. His visit was to last for a month;
the results would not be visible for another year or so but the long-
term benefits would be remarkable. He established first-time contacts with writers, publishers, and agents that would guarantee the
greatness of the firm in the years that followed.

The results of Liveright's furiously busy six days in Paris at the
beginning of 1922, with Ezra Pound as his guide and mentor,
surely constitute proof that Horace was determined to produce the
most advanced and daring list of any U.S. publisher. He had looked
forward to meeting the man who was "making everything new" in

Paris: "I have a hunch that I'll like the five days in Paris with Ezra Pound, who will welcome me warmly, best of all." It was to be his first meeting with Pound, whom he had been publishing for the past two years: *Instigations* (1919) and *Poems 1909–1921* (1921). The little books sold only about five hundred copies, but Horace's faith in Pound never wavered. As for Pound, he thought of his publisher only in the highest terms, telling his New York lawyer and feeless agent John Quinn that Liveright was "much more of a man than most publishers" and that he was "going toward the light not from it." (Pound may have been laying on the praise here with a heavy hand because of his certain knowledge that Quinn, to whom he owed much, could not abide Jews.)

Pound believed that Horace could become the main publisher of his brand of literary modernism. In this sense Pound can be regarded as the ringmaster whose task was to move his friends Eliot, Joyce, and Yeats away from the scarcely read avant-garde journals or the staid publishing houses like Macmillan (Yeats) and establish them at B&L in the new and friendly stream of contemporary writing. By this time Pound knew how much Horace relied on publicity and advertising to make his books known in the marketplace. Besides that, he knew that B&L was just about to publish e. e. cummings's *The Enormous Room* and that it was dickering with Djuna Barnes for a collection of her stories. Finally, there was the burgeoning Modern Library. All signs indicated that Liveright was the coming man.

Aside from business, Pound got along with Horace so well in post-Christmas Paris that the poet became the publisher's daily guide to the sights of the town. Forty years later, in one of the later *Cantos,* Pound recalled going to a bar with Horace in which a man with a wooden leg and his female companion entertained:

> *while the 60 year old bat did a hoolah*
> *to the great applause of that bistro*

"Entrez donc, mais entrez,
c'est la maison de tout le monde"
(This to me and H. Liveright vers le Noël)

Pound took Horace to lots of parties, where he met Stravinsky, Constantin Brancusi, Erik Satie, and Picasso—to no avail since Horace spoke not a word of French. He met one of his future authors, Paul Morand, with whom he got along very well—Morand spoke fluent English. He encountered his old friend from the Village days, Djuna Barnes, and danced with her. He was amazed how many people Pound knew at all these parties, as Pound introduced him to dozens of guests.

On the night of January 4, Pound arranged a little dinner party in order for Horace to meet two of his closest friends, James Joyce and T. S. Eliot. Both men had been hearing much about the man from New York who might prove to make them famous. They found him charming, terribly well informed about almost every-thing, and absolutely unlike any other publisher they had met before. Liveright appeared to be interested in *what* he was publish-ing; it also seemed apparent that he published what he liked and that he would publish things he knew couldn't possibly make him a dime. Liveright also seemed to be in the publishing business for *fun.* The fact that Horace was Jewish appeared to be of no conse-quence to them—surely remarkable when one thinks about the degree of Eliot's current and Pound's later anti-Semitism. Strangely enough, it was Eliot who later struck the anti-Semitic note against Horace; Pound never changed his mind about Liveright.

Eliot had arrived in Paris from Lausanne on the second of January, bearing with him his untitled but still not completed "long poem of 435 lines." In the following two weeks he and Pound would wrestle back and forth over the text of *The Waste Land,* the poem that has remained the most influential in twentieth-century

English poetry, and with James Joyce's *Ulysses* one of the two ultimate touchstones of literary modernism. Pound had become determined to find a publisher for Eliot's work even before they had
concluded their joint editing task. Now, here was Horace Liveright
in Paris, just the right man to talk about how to publish what Pound
believed was the summing up of "our modern experiment."

James Joyce had recently completed his seven-year labor on
Ulysses, and he, too, was interested in obtaining an American publisher who might dare the prevailing American laws against obscenity by presenting the book to a wide audience. His current New
York publisher, Ben Huebsch, was sympathetic, but it was also
clear that he feared criminal prosecution. *Dubliners* and *A Portrait of
the Artist as a Young Man* were daring books, but not at all comparable to a work that had already been declared obscene in the courts
of New York City, despite the efforts of John Quinn, who
defended it. Even in this climate, Horace was more than inclined
seriously to consider publishing a book that he'd been reading,
chapter by chapter, in the pages of *The Little Review*.

By the time they finished their dinner on that January 4, 1922,
Horace had made agreements with all three writers.

Pound: B&L would retain the services of Pound as their
European scout at an annual salary of $500. This sum was to be
applied as his fee for translating whatever French books he discovered and that were purchased by Horace. Pound produced the
agreement that very night for Liveright's signature. He characteristically added a final paragraph: "Mr. Liveright agrees not to
demand Mr. Pound's signature on the translation of any work that
Mr. Pound considers a disgrace to humanity or too imbecile to be
borne."

Joyce: B&L would publish the unexpurgated text of *Ulysses* for an
advance of $1,000 as early as was feasible—a reference here to the
sure difficulty of publishing a work that had already run afoul of the
law. Joyce did not sign Horace's contract that night or in the days

that followed—both men stepped back to consider the possible outcome of B&L's proceeding with publication in the immediate future. Horace wrote to John Quinn in New York for advice on the matter—an unwise decision considering his negative view of Horace—and eventually received a discouraging reply. As for Joyce's refusal to sign, Pound expressed his puzzlement in a letter to Quinn:

> Liveright . . . offered to bring out Ulysses in the U.S. and hand over 1000 bones to J.J. Why the hell he didn't nail it AT once I don't know. The terms were O.K. 1000 dollars for first edition rt. However, Joyce is off my hands, free, white, 21, etc.

Eliot: B&L would publish the "long poem" (*The Waste Land*) before the end of 1922 for an advance of $150. The question of periodical publication was mentioned but not resolved. Nor was the question that Horace raised that night—wasn't the poem "as is" going to make an awfully *small* book? Couldn't Eliot do something about this matter? Eliot assured Horace that he could and would.

The names of the guests at dinner that night resonate strongly today, but they were actually little-known young men. Eliot was thirty-three, Pound thirty-six, and Joyce thirty-nine. Horace, at thirty-six, was just the right age to be publishing these three assaulters of literary tradition. Of the three, only Joyce had any reputation in America—the serialization of *Ulysses* and the resulting court trial over the book's alleged obscenity had given him a certain notoriety. Pound and Eliot had each had small volumes of their early work published by Knopf, but their names were virtually unknown in the United States. Had Horace any notion that he was dining that night with the "Holy Trinity" of literary modernism? Had he any inkling that Pound, Eliot, and Joyce were to become, within a decade, the chief lions of the modern movement, the three writers who did more than any others in this century to change our

Ezra Pound and John Quinn, Paris, 1923.
Poetry Society of America

taste about literary values, whose attitude to tradition was Pound's famous rallying cry, "Make it New"? Liveright may have had some such feeling on his own, but it was clearly the power of Pound's convictions about Eliot and Joyce that persuaded him to publish them.

Perhaps the most remarkable aspect of Horace's offer for *The Waste Land* was the fact that he had not read a single word of it—Pound's assurances were good enough for him. They were also good enough for a number of other individuals who were quite eager to undertake publication without even a glimpse of the manuscript— such were Pound's persuasive powers. Back in America, two radically different periodicals began laying plans to acquire what was rumored to be the poem of the century; again, both magazines relied on Pound alone. *Vanity Fair* was then under the editorial direction of the poet John Peale Bishop, who was just about to give up the job to his Princeton classmate Edmund Wilson. Bishop had been advised about the poem by Jeanne Foster, who had received the word from *il miglior fabbro* (the better maker) himself: "What would *Vanity Fair* pay Eliot for 'Waste Land.' Cd. yr. friend there [Bishop] get in touch with T.S.E." With the full support of Edmund Wilson, Bishop set sail for London in August, but long before he arrived, several new factors had been introduced.

Vanity Fair was then, as now, a mass-market journal, with a circulation of 90,000 copies. Its chief rival for Eliot's work was to be the prestigious *Dial,* a highbrow literary journal with a circulation of 6,500 copies. It was subsidized by two wealthy Americans, Scofield Thayer and James Sibley Watson Jr., and Gilbert Seldes was the chief editor. Earlier in the year, Thayer had been in London and offered Eliot $150 for *The Waste Land*—an offer which Eliot felt was an insult for a work that had taken him a year to complete. Negotiations were broken off with *The Dial* at this point, but

Thayer did not give up that easily. He remained in touch with his copublisher, Watson, who was currently being psychoanalyzed in Vienna by Freud. Both men continued to express strong interest as the poem advanced toward completion.

In reading through the surviving documents, it seems clear that Pound was using *Vanity Fair* as a stalking horse to obtain better terms from *The Dial*. In addition, Pound (and probably Eliot) thought that a work of such importance as *The Waste Land* belonged in the dignified pages of the subsidized journal, rather than the flashier ones of *Vanity Fair*. It was at this point that Pound hit upon the idea of having *The Dial* augment its original offer of $150 by writing to Thayer a letter that contained a broad hint of what he had in mind: "I wish to Christ he [Eliot] had the December award." The award was the prestigious Dial Award for distinguished service to literature which had only been created in the previous year— Sherwood Anderson had been the first winner. The recipient was paid the sum of $2,000, a huge sum at the time. By putting this idea into Thayer's head, Pound hoped to make him aware that he could still hope to procure the poem for the magazine even after Eliot's disdainful rejection of the original offer. If that offer were added to the $2,000 of the award, Eliot would be paid a total of $2,150, or about $35,000 today.

Pound's hint worked. After consulting with his partner Watson in Vienna, Thayer made his combined offer, which was accepted. As Thayer and Pound worked out the details of how and when the poem would appear in *The Dial,* Horace and Eliot (in London) ran into trouble that summer over the contract for the little book. Eliot, then a banker, did not care for Horace's standard B&L one-page "letter of agreement," feeling that this form of contract was a one-way street in which the publisher grabbed everything for himself. This, at least, is what Eliot told John Quinn, his lawyer/patron/friend in New York:

DISSATISFIED LIVERIGHT CONTRACT POEM I ASK YOU
FOR YOUR ASSISTANCE. APOLOGIES. WRITING.

By 1922 John Quinn found himself in the uncomfortable position of handling the literary affairs in America of the three most
unconventional writers then writing in English—perhaps in line
with the taste of the man who possessed the largest American collection of Matisses, Picassos, Derains, and Légers. It wasn't that
Quinn had any trouble comprehending their work—it was rather
the type of publisher willing to bring it out in the United States that
made him contemptuous whenever he was forced to refer to these
publishers in correspondence with Eliot, Joyce, and Pound. Quinn
hated all Jews, but it never seems to have crossed his mind why *only*
Jews (Liveright, Huebsch, and Knopf) were willing to invest
money in writers who appeared to have no sales possibilities whatever, thus challenging his notions that Jews were only interested in
the pursuit of money. Horace was not only Jewish, he was thought
by Quinn to be vulgar because of the way he sought publicity for
his books.

Starting a new publishing firm in 1917 was a dangerous risk; the
fact that Horace was a Jew only increased that risk. Many literary
agents were not at all happy to be dealing with Jews, thus effectively cutting them off from much of the best available American or
British material. It was not by choice that ten of the first eleven
titles published by Alfred Knopf were translations from the French
and German—books whose sheets had been printed abroad. The
literary agents were not about to rally round the new young Jewish
publishers until they had proved themselves by success. Reading
through Quinn's correspondence indicates some of the difficulties
experienced by Horace in this era of discrimination.

In the United States of 1922, Quinn was not singular in his
loathing for Jews. From Quinn's point of view, Horace was a
cheap, lying, vulgar charlatan whose main occupation was to cheat

his authors of the royalties they might have earned. He indicated to both Eliot and Pound that this is what they must expect if they persisted in placing their works with Jewish firms.

Quinn's animus against Jews in general and Horace in particular was extreme. When Pound was raising funds for the purpose of liberating Eliot from his bank job in London, calling the enterprise "Bel Esprit," Horace was eager to make a contribution. But when Quinn heard about his offer back in New York he exploded in rage, writing Pound that "[Liveright] is vulgarity personified. He would advertise it all over the place." Quinn then offered to *double* his own contribution if Pound would agree to exclude Horace; Pound refused. When he wrote to Quinn in July, Pound remarked about how slowly the money was coming in:

> The sons of bitches of editors and publishers OUGHT to spot up but they *don't* and *won't* and even the by-you-so-scorned Liveright is the best of 'em. He is still young enough to think an author ought to be paid a living wage. NO elderly publisher even does think that.

Under a constant bombardment of invective from New York, Eliot's initial enthusiasm for Horace in Paris withered away, so that he eventually began to parrot Quinn's view of things. The creator of Leopold Bloom, however, had at no time any interest in anti-Semitism and simply ignored Quinn. So, too, did Pound, who had not yet been infected by the virus. It was not until he had begun living in sunny Italy's Rapallo in 1925 that he became anti-Semitic. Horace remained, indeed, the "pearl" among publishers in New York.

Quinn reacted predictably to Eliot's call for help:

> YOU DON'T HAVE TO TIE UP WITH LIVERIGHT I COULD
> EASILY ARRANGE FOR YOUR NEXT BOOK WITH ANOTHER

PUBLISHER THAN LIVERIGHT, IF HIS TERMS ARE NOT
IN EVERY WAY SATISFACTORY.

But Eliot was too much a man of his word to back out of his contract with Horace. A new and far more favorable one for Eliot was
quickly hammered out by Quinn; Horace signed it in late July.
Now every issue seemed resolved except the vital one of where *and
how* the poem would appear prior to the book's publication at the
end of the year.

After Eliot had accepted the terms of the *Dial* offer, he was
aware that Horace might well feel cheated by having to give way to
the magazine—it would result in his having to delay publication for
months. Eliot offered to forgo his $150 advance, but Horace had a
much more interesting idea how to redress matters. In a meeting at
Quinn's offices in New York, attended by Gilbert Seldes and
Horace, an agreement was reached that included Horace's selling
The Dial 350 copies of *The Waste Land* at standard discount rates—
the magazine would use them to solicit subscriptions. The agreement also stipulated that *The Dial* would publish Eliot's poem
without the notes that he had added. The purchase of the books thus
insured Horace against any loss in delaying publication of the little
book—he would wind up with both the cash and the glory.

It was the second part of this agreement that has left its indelible
mark on literary history. At the beginning of the year, while still in
London, Horace had written Pound a letter that contained the
plaintive line "I'm disappointed that Eliot's material is as short.
Can't he add anything?" (emphasis added). As Horace saw it, no matter how large the typeface, 450 lines of verse make a very tiny
book. After sorting through a number of possibilities with Pound,
Eliot prepared the famous (or infamous) twelve pages of supremely
erudite prose "notes" that followed the poem in Horace's edition—and have done so in all later editions. Since the agreement
denied the use of the notes to *The Dial* Horace would thus be able

to offer the public more than just the text of the poem. If you liked
The Waste Land, here was the key to it supplied by the author himself. These twelve pages of notes have furnished three generations
of students with the material for term papers and dissertations
about the meaning of Eliot's poem. The notes may have added as
much confusion as clarity. Eliot was always somewhat evasive
about them, but it is clear that Horace's concern about the length
of the little book he was about to publish was decisive in their
preparation.

The Waste Land was an immediate sensation when it appeared in
the November 1922 issue of *The Dial;* the success was augmented
in December when Horace rushed his edition to the bookstores
before the end of the month. Among those who talked about modern poetry, *The Waste Land* was the main topic that year and the
next. The first printing of 1,000 copies was quickly exhausted, and
another 1,000 were printed—an unprecedented event for a book
of "difficult" verse. On February 5, 1923, Horace wrote Pound
upon receiving a number of the new *Cantos:*

> God bless you. . . . If we can get as much publicity from them as
> The Waste Land has received, you will be a millionaire. The Waste
> Land has sold 1000 copies to date and who knows, it may go up to
> 2000 or 3000 [more than 5000 copies were in fact sold]. Just think,
> Eliot may make almost $500 on the book rights to this poem. And
> Gene Stratton Porter makes $40,000.00 to $60,000 a year out of
> her books. Well, it's all in a life time, so who cares.

As early as March 1923 Eliot had turned against Liveright
because he felt that the American publisher was cheating him. He
wrote Quinn:

> I am interested to hear that Liveright has sold 1250 copies of my
> book. . . . I am all the more surprised that I have so far had not a

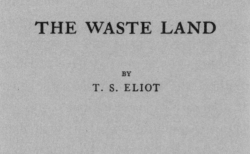

THE WASTE LAND

BY
T. S. ELIOT

"NAM Sibyllam quidem Cumis ego ipse oculis meis
vidi in ampulla pendere, et cum illi pueri dicerent:
Σίβυλλα τί θέλεις; respondebat illa: ἀποθανεῖν θέλω."

NEW YORK
BONI AND LIVERIGHT

Title page for *The Waste Land*.

Author's collection

penny from him. . . . I am very annoyed about this, although it is the sort of behavior which I have been led to expect from Liveright. I am sick of doing business with Jew publishers who will not carry out their part of the contract unless they are forced to. . . . I wish I could find a decent Christian publisher in New York who could be trusted not to slip and slide at every opportunity.

As will be seen, money was always in short supply at B&L. This factor, combined with carelessness concerning payment dates, had prevented Eliot from receiving his royalties on time. We know that he did receive them eventually, but it is clear from his letter that he regarded the lateness as just a part of Horace's Jewish practices. *The Waste Land* was the first and last book of T. S. Eliot's to be published by B&L.

(2)

My book will never come out now.
    —James Joyce, 1920

No contract for *Ulysses* had been signed when Joyce had agreed in principle to accept Horace's Paris offer. In the jittery climate of literary censorship created by the New York Society for the Suppression of Vice in the person of its director, John S. Sumner, Horace proceeded cautiously—perhaps too cautiously, in view of the outcome. He turned to Joyce's agent in New York, John Quinn, for help in determining if *Ulysses* would be prosecuted for obscenity if he dared publish the book in its entirely. Quinn may have been the wrong man to ask advice on the issue: he had already been burned once by the book. In 1920 he had gallantly defended Margaret Anderson and Jane Heap, the editors and publishers of *The Little Review,* in the courts of New York against charges of publishing obscene material by their serial presentation of Joyce's novel. It was John S. Sumner who launched the charges; he became Horace's chief enemy in the attempt by the Society to suppress anything remotely erotic. Sumner was aided by the U.S. Postal Service, which had burned several of the issues containing the *Ulysses* material. Quinn made a major tactical error by apologizing to the jury for the presence of the erotic material, describing it as "disgusting," while admitting that he himself did not understand *Ulysses*: "I think Joyce has carried his method too far." The jury agreed with Quinn and found the defendants guilty; they were fined $100 and led off to be fingerprinted. The case was a major defeat for free expression and frightened many publishers from undertaking books with any erotic content.

Quinn made another tactical blunder—he refused to appeal the decision to the Supreme Court—thus creating an intellectual climate in which literary material deemed obscene by the Society was without protection in the courts. Under these circumstances, Horace was obviously looking for some sort of encouragement, but Quinn did not take kindly to Horace's inquiries. He wrote Joyce on May 11, 1922, telling him:

> [Liveright] ought to know better than to ask for a legal opinion about contracts without submitting to me copies of them. He *does* know better and his letter is a piece of Jewish impertinence.

Whatever Quinn told Horace at that time is unknown, but it successfully deterred him from proceeding any further with immediate plans for publishing *Ulysses* in 1922; he did, however, make another strong effort in 1927.

In his letter to Joyce, Quinn had been offering his Irish client some other advice about dealing with Horace, who had made an offer to include *A Portrait of the Artist as a Young Man* in the Modern Library. Joyce was willing, but feared hurting the feelings of his book's original publisher, Ben Huebsch. Quinn's stance in the matter was directed not only against Horace but also against the guiding idea behind the Modern Library—that is, good books in cheaper editions for larger audiences. He wrote Joyce a diatribe against the Modern Library for its merely *existing:* "The inclusion in the Modern Library is a decadence, a declension into the sunset proclaiming the dark night of literary extinction." Out of sheer ignorance about the realities of publishing, Quinn attacked Horace for not having included Conrad and Kipling in the series. He was wrong about Kipling—*Soldiers Three* was among the first dozen Modern Library titles. As for Conrad, Horace would gladly have contracted for all the Conrad titles that Doubleday was willing to part with—which was none.

Nearly everything Joyce wrote would eventually appear in the

Modern Library, but those publications were to occur under radically changed circumstances.

(3)

> Do you suppose I like to go on losing money on you
> miserable highbrows? But no matter what you write, you
> know I always want to publish your poetry and I know that I
> do and will do more for it than anyone else.
>   —Liveright to Ezra Pound, April 5, 1923

As for Pound, the maker of the *Cantos* remained loyal to Horace,
recommending him to all his literary friends as the one American
publisher to be trusted. He remained on the B&L payroll for years
as a scout but never produced very many books that Horace actually bought. The major occasion on which Horace took Ezra's
advice concerned the inane phenomenon of positive thinking
known as "Couéism" that swept the United States at the beginning
of the twenties: All one had to do to be successful and happy was to
tell oneself, "I am getting better and better every day in every
way." Horace had been offered a book on the subject, but turned it
down on Ezra's say-so:

> Liveright has mistrusted my judgment ever since I told him Coué
> was bunk, thus costing him millions, as he took my word for it, and
> failed to think of the bunk-profits.

When Wyndham Lewis began making overtures to Horace in
1925, he cautiously asked Pound if it was true what he'd heard
from T. S. Eliot about Liveright. Pound replied with a list of the
American publishers who might take on Lewis:

HOWEVER, Liveright is my publisher, and the only one I have any dealings with.

Huebsch I believe to be dishonest, perhaps only when really bankrupt which he really is.

Knopf broke his word to me, so I nacherly am shy of him. The American McMillan is known to be a bandit. . . .

At ANY rate Liveright is the only man in America with enough pride to WANT to bring out a book.

The rest are worms, humble worms, with no self-respect to appeal to.

If it be wondered how the man who wrote these words became the virulent anti-Semite of the 1930s and 1940s, it must be recalled that Pound's feelings about Jews never applied to the individuals he knew, such as Louis Zukovsky, Jacob Epstein, and Horace.

While Pound and Horace had their quarrels, they held each other in high regard—so much so that they could frequently adopt a bantering tone in their letters to each other. In 1927, when Ezra complained that *Personae* was not receiving its fair share of advertising, and that maybe Horace had not really *read* his poems, Horace replied in a suitably outrageous manner:

What do you mean, you darn fool, telling me that I should take a day off to read the book myself? I've read it twice and it's a swell little piece of literachoor. However, I'll think the whole thing over and maybe I'll spend some more money advertising it. Goodbye dear love.

It was Horace's idea to bring out *Personae* in 1926: "I reiterate that what I think will go and sell year after year is a fine big juicy book of your collected poems." When Pound complained that the sales for the book were too low to support him—750 copies in the first year—Horace responded with a suggestion:

Why in the devil don't you write a novel, a shortish one, of about 50,000 or 60,000 words? If it's nice and naughty (I don't mean with any unprintable short four letter words) and understandable, I think we ought to be able to sell 2000 copies in a limited edition, signed by your noble self, for $5.00 a copy. And then if by some chance it really caught on, we could publish a trade edition at $2.50. My idea is based on your most amusing letters to me. Your novel, I imagine, would be some sort of buffoonery of modern life. I don't know whether you are acquainted with Carl Van Vechten's Peter Whiffle, and God Forbid that I should ask you to follow this, but what I have in mind is a super Peter Whiffle.

Pound's response to this idea and constant reminders about it was uncharacteristically restrained: "NOVEL, indeed."

(4)

I am a genius in a nice, small way.
—HBL to Lucille Liveright, January 13, 1922

Liveright has been here, advantage over other publishers is that he was in wall street first, not an office boy in a boîte d'édition . . . he seems to take more chances than the others.
—Ezra Pound to Ford Madox Ford, January 13, 1922

AFTER six days in Paris with Pound in January 1922, Horace left for a three-week stay in London, a place he found to be a busy hive of writers and their agents—all of them bent on selling something to the brash young man who had made such a stir in U.S. publishing. In this, his first London visit, Horace became acquainted with virtually all of the more important agents and through them acquired a number of writers whom he continued to publish throughout the

twenties. The impact of Horace's personality was felt by many in
the British publishing world, especially among the literary agents
who listened carefully to what Horace was telling them about what
would happen if some of their more popular authors would abandon their current publishers in the United States: By switching to
Liveright, they would enjoy a vast increase in both sales promotion
and advances. But convincing these people was hard work.

European buying trips have not changed much since Horace
began making his: The U.S. editor or publisher is under a constant
bombardment of manuscripts, galleys, outlines and proposals from
every agent in London who is aware that a prospective buyer has
arrived. The visitors from the United States spend their days speed-
ing around town to see people in their offices or by inviting them
to their hotels. The number of contacts that can be made in a single
day varies, but there are those who might see up to five or six,
starting with an early breakfast. Many of the sellers offer the U.S.
editor an "inside chance" to buy something that will sweep the
country, if not the world, but it is understood that the editor *must*
make a decision by the following morning. Every time the editor
returns to his or her hotel lobby a half dozen messages have
arrived—all urgent—which damage the working schedule.

If the editor/publisher is at all well known, invitations to parties
and dinners are also in order, and the American visitor may be out
till the small hours; as these hours advance, the feeling of guilt and
dread about all those manuscripts lying back there in the hotel
room unread grows sharper. The reading of the day's offerings
supposedly takes place at night, but the visitor frequently falls
asleep before much progress can be made. Events begin to get jum-
bled up in the visitor's mind; this schedule requires some sort of
diary or note-taking scheme so that matters can be properly dealt
with when the trip has been concluded. The pace is killing;
Horace, predictably, loved every moment and would have gone to
Europe every year if he could have made the time available.

The trips are expensive—the American cannot make do by staying at second- or third-rate hotels—only the very best will do. The preferred London hotels have not changed notably since Horace's day: Brown's Hotel and the Savoy were Horace's choice in 1922 and 1923 and have remained favorites among U.S. editors. They are costly, and in time many editors begin to feel that they are trapped in a fast-moving taxi whose meter never stops ticking. The big question in all this frantic endeavor is: Will all this time and effort pay off? After two weeks some editors begin to doubt their own sensibilities. Buying nothing on a trip may be taken as an admission of defeat. If they have found little or nothing, they may feel compelled to buy things at the last moment, *anything* to justify this enormous expense.

In a letter written to Ezra Pound a year before his first London visit, Horace had set forth his views on how American literary taste was swayed by small influential groups; the situation has not changed since 1920. He also told Pound what he hoped to find in London:

> The American public, as you know, is almost hopeless: the so-called intelligentsia could be gathered together in the smallest theatre. If for some reason or other an author of real worth reaches an audience of from three to ten thousand people over here, it is because the would-be intellectuals have been practically beaten into the frame of mind where they are ashamed not to read him. For this reason, what I am looking for most of all is really good novels which at the same time have some popular appeal. Conrad, Swinnerton, Maugham, Rebecca West . . . are selling very well over here now, and of course Wells, Bennett, May Sinclair and that group are most profitable properties. I . . . feel horribly vexed that through some fluke I missed out on getting D. H. Lawrence's next two novels. Another publisher [Toby Seltzer] has them, much to my disgust. . . . I tell you these things because you have been so very kind in answering my first appeal for advice.

Pound, of course, was the wrong man to be asking about contemporary fiction; his only help to Horace in this area was his espousal of Hemingway.

In his steady stream of letters to Lucille back home, Horace kept coming back to how difficult it was to keep up the frantic pace, the constant round of lunches, dinners, parties, and visits that filled his days and nights:

> Here I am again, rushed for time! At one o'clock sharp I must keep my engagement with Mrs. Belloc Lowndes, who takes me to lunch at the Ivy Club. At 3 Curtis Brown (damn him!) . . . at 5:30 I call at 10 Adelphi Terrace on G. B. Shaw & at 7.30 I give a small dinner here at my service flat to John Cournos . . . Aldous Huxley & Julie [Lasden] who has agreed to act as hostess.

He expressed continual delight over the kindnesses the English literary establishment bestowed on him.

His remark about being a genius in a small way was prompted by his success with Rose Macaulay, the English novelist who has recently won much posthumous fame for her later books: *The Towers of Trebizond, Letters to a Friend,* and *The Pleasures of Ruins.* At that time in London probably only Virginia Woolf rivaled Rose Macaulay in her knowledge of literature—like Woolf, she conducted a salon of sorts and was widely known for her charm and wit. She first appeared on Horace's list in 1920, when the New York branch of Curtis Brown in London had sold him her comic novel *Potterism,* a book that quickly sold 35,000 copies. The U.S. branch had been willing to try out Horace with an obscure book or two (Macaulay had never had a wide sale), but after the extraordinary success of *Potterism* in America, they planned to move her to an older, better-established house—a Christian house, if Horace's suspicions were correct.

The only way to avert the loss of Macaulay to Harper or Henry

Holt was to make her aware of how much her American publisher cared about her work—as well as how captivating he could be. Rose, like nearly everyone else in London that month, found Horace irresistible—irresistible enough to promise him her next three or four novels in direct contradiction to the wishes of Curtis Brown. In dealing with Rose Macaulay, Horace was not bound by the dictum that forbids "praise to the face," for he was capable of referring to her, in the presence of one of her closest friends, as a writer who was not just the popular novelist she purported to be— she was actually in a class apart. Besides holding on to her as a writer, Horace very much wanted her to write a novel that would contain a strong love story—*Potterism* had not. But Macaulay could not see herself in this role.

During a lunch at Rose's home in the country, her close friend Dorothy Brook told Horace that Rose "looked down" on love stories: "Anyone can write that—we look to Rose for something else, which no one else can do." But Horace was not shaken, telling Brook firmly that "Rose Macaulay, Mrs. Brook, is a *great writer.* Now all great writers must deal with the greatest subject in the world at one time or another." Rose immediately replied that she had no ambitions to be a great writer and that her touch was for "trivial topicalities." Horace did not give up on the idea, and a few years later she wrote books like *Told by an Idiot,* which, despite taking up the "greatest subject," managed to sell three or four thousand copies *less* than *Potterism.* Unperturbed, Horace continued to publish her annual novel with both profit and pleasure.

He showed his trust in Rose's business judgment when he asked her at the end of 1928, just after his partner Donald Friede had left the firm, a question that had vexed him for years:

Would you think it good or bad business to change the name of the firm to Horace Liveright Inc.? I've pretty much run the whole show for $9\frac{1}{2}$ years of our 11 and everyone over here knows it.

Please don't think that I mean that people like T. R. Smith and Julian Messner haven't been tremendously important. I simply mean that I've been carrying most of the burden. I'd value your opinion.

She may or may not have approved the change, but in the next few weeks Horace had to face the fact of Rose's finally leaving him for Harper—again under pressure from Curtis Brown. The situation looked hopeless, but Horace cabled her anyway:

WOULD FEEL ALMOST LIKE GIVING UP PUBLISHING BUSINESS IF THE
AUTHOR OF POTTERISM WHICH WAS ONE OF MY FIRST BIG SUCCESSES
WOULD LEAVE ME. . . . SINCE CHANGE OF FIRM'S NAME HAVE
ZEALOUSLY TRIED TO BUILD UP BIGGEST PUBLISHING FIRM IN AMERICA
AND WILL BE HEARTBROKEN IF YOU DO NOT HELP ME IN THIS POLICY.
. . . WILL BE IN LONDON FEBRUARY [1929] AND URGE YOU TO HOLD
UP ANY CHANGE OF PUBLISHERS UNTIL THEN.

It worked; Rose could not resist Horace's appeal, and he obtained her new novel. But trying to retain Macaulay was a losing battle; in the last sad days of Horace's loss of control of his firm in 1930 he found that she was leaving him for Harper after all. Unlike many publishers in similar situations, Horace responded by taking Rose out to a festive lunch to meet his daughter, Lucy (Rose was touring the United States at the time) and buying his former author an enormous bouquet of flowers for her departure from the United States the following day. On the *America* Rose wrote Horace a note begging his forgiveness for not having told him the sad news herself and, instead, leaving it up to her agent, Curtis Brown:

As you know, my personal relations towards you have always been those of friendship and liking, which made it difficult to move & to write & say I was leaving you. However, I do hope these relations will continue all the same; your magnanimity yesterday makes me think they will.

Back in early 1922 in literary London, the word about Horace's wit and charm began to spread—he was the man of the hour. Accordingly, numerous parties, dinners, and receptions were given in his honor, where he talked with G. K. Chesterton, Aldous Huxley, Hugh Walpole, Arnold Bennett, Walter de la Mare, H. G. Wells, and Rebecca West. He wrote capsule descriptions to Lucille about some of his new acquaintances: West, he said, "is Wells' mistress & is, I think, a Jewess. Tremendously brisk air." As for Wells himself, "He was most cordial . . . he is only 56 & looks about 48—a very prosperous grocer, with a high voice & a *slight* cockney accent—and of course, Macmillans don't do any advertising."

The line about Macmillan indicates that Horace felt that no writer was beyond his reach; he set about to lure Wells away from Macmillan and George Bernard Shaw from Brentano. He made no secret about his ambitions, as Sinclair Lewis noted in a London letter to his American publisher, Alfred Harcourt: "Seen Liveright several times; he's hustling like the devil & hints that he will bring home some big authors of older firms." He failed to get Wells and Shaw, but remained buoyed up by his enthusiastic reception. Although he understood that some of it was just hype, he wrote Lucille,

> Please don't think that I'm not sound enough to realize how little it all means in terms of *immediate* returns, but I'd almost stake my life that when changes in contracts are made that a lot of interesting, or rather important authors will remember me and my visit.

While often telling Lucille how much he missed her, Horace revealed an ambivalence about her absence:

I've wanted you with me and yet at the same time realized (now
this may hurt you, but it's a real honest baring of my soul) that for
my *first* trip here it possibly has been good that I've been alone.
People invite an attractive man (and they all tell me that the others
call me that) where they might think a second time about asking a
man & his wife. . . . You would have been alone a lot of the time
. . . [you] would have shrieked with horror at my . . . drinking
scotch, all sorts of wines & liquors morning, *noon* particularly &
night, at my reading till dawn.

He assured her, however, that there had been no flirtations and
that he had "never lost my balance for a minute, but I'm a bit
weary of my role as the intelligent, progressive American publisher."

It would be difficult to believe that Lucille could avoid detect-
ing the curious contradictions in Horace's letters from London—
essentially that "I miss you terribly but maybe it's a good thing
you're not here." He constantly reminded her about the temptations in his path: "Julie Lasden [a family friend] has kept me from
either suicide or adultery or both. (I've had so many "gay" parties
offered me, particularly by Noël Coward & his theatrical
crowd.)"* Although Lucille's letters to Horace have disappeared,
his replies to hers make it evident that she became increasingly
suspicious about his activities on these long trips away from
home—suspicious enough to often place him in a defensive
stance. At the same time, however, he persisted in drawing attention to what she plainly knew for herself—that he was extremely
attractive to other women and was fully aware of it: "And I'd give
a thousand millions, if I had it, to be sleeping in the bed next to
yours. (I've had many invitations but not one has even faintly
interested me.)"

Equally obsessive were Horace's attempts to reassure Lucille

---

*Horace published Coward's little book of satires, *Terribly Intimate Portraits,* in 1922.

that he had his drinking under control, a subject that caused ever-growing concern on her part. Although she was worried about alcohol and other women, she certainly could not deny his ferocious energy in pursuing writers for the B&L list. Just prior to his departure from London, Horace cabled Lucille that one of his traveling companions was of special interest to him: SAILING AQUITANIA TWENTY EIGHTH WITH JOSEPH CONRAD MAY GET HIM.

In the first few years of Horace's new life as a publisher, Lucille usually spent the summers up on Cape Cod or in Atlantic City with young Herman and Lucy. This arrangement was not always the case, for Horace occasionally took care of the children while Lucille took time away from her family to join her parents in their travels. In her absence, Horace wrote her dozens of letters, many of them concerned with their marital problems.

Horace constantly refers to Lucille's "nerves" as the chief cause of their difficulties. "There is one thing clearly sure & evident, my dear. The children are quiet, less nervous when you are away so you *must* make up your mind to fuss less about trifles—bother them less & *talk very low*. Even Herman is shouting less." An undated letter from this period indicates that Lucille had only herself to blame for those nerves: "Ada [Horace's sister] writes that you are taking poor or no care of yourself—drinking a lot of coffee & that you were *terribly nervous* on Saturday—if you think that's playing fair, I don't—but my dear girl, I can't get very sore. . . . I hope you've turned over a new leaf and are getting your nerves in really good order."

He had some startling notions about how to cure Lucille of her nervous problems: "I hope, dear girl, that you're more 'settled' and having a good time with [illegible] or someone else. Have a *real* fling & your nerves will right themselves—I'm a good doctor." This theme of Lucille's taking a lover to alleviate her problems continues through 1919, as when he tells her,

You could come to me from Ruskin's arms *if you felt the urge,* and I would enfold you with the same emotion that my heart appeared to hold at the time, as though Ruskin had never lived.——But a fool I can't abide, which has nothing to do with sex——and I wouldn't be very sympathetic about mistakes you made in any affairs.——As for myself, I've had none in nine years——but I've had very little temptations, though your conduct very, very often has given me much provocation.——If I were strongly tempted, I might fall, but oh, how careful I'd be & how calculating. Because I know that, in the real sense, my fine sweet words with you from April to May 20th 1910 was my last *love* affair and I feel that too was yours. Anything else that happens is adventure & we'll truly come back to each other——who knows, maybe *more* truly——with all inhibitions (if there are any) released.

Horace concluded by advising her to lead her own life and not be an appendage, "a mother and a wife." He noted that he had his work "to help me to express myself" and that "if what you've been having isn't enough, find out what you can & what will add to the sum total of your life. Life's mighty short——*live it.*"

Today many would substitute "depression" for Lucille's "nerve" problems. While it is easy to indict Horace for advancing self-serving ideas on the order of, "If Lucille can have an affair, then it's all right for me to have one," it is also possible to view the Liverights' dilemma in a modern perspective which grants Lucille the freedom to make her own choices. In a striking way, Horace's very modern approach to these problems appears in the pages of a well-known book he commissioned only a few years later, Bertrand Russell's *Marriage and Morals.* The existing evidence indicates that Lucille was reluctant to make such a choice, but Horace didn't give up easily. As late as September 1919 he returned to the idea of his wife's having an "adventure." She had met a "Mr. Hath [illegible]" and Horace was pleased that he had arrived at wherever it was she was staying. "Did he come back & did he try to kiss you—I'll be terribly disappointed if he didn't. I'm rather mixed up in my feelings about what you should have done—You really might benefit generally from a little emotional or sexual experience of that sort."

Despite the constant bickering about nerves and affairs—alleged or real—Horace and Lucille's marriage was kept viable by their intense devotion to each other and the two children, Herman and Lucy. It can be conjectured that the marital difficulties would have disappeared or at least been minimized if Lucille had been willing to work with Horace at B&L. He had encouraged her to do so, but she had rejected the idea. He was aware that she had the superior literary judgment and taste to become an excellent editor, but her own low self-esteem—as askew as Horace's—made it impossible for her to emulate Blanche Knopf, who became the most valued member of that firm outside of the founder. When Walter Lippmann had thrown her the challenge before her marriage to Horace, she had rejected it on the grounds that she was unworthy. Now, when the stakes were far more meaningful, she repeated her refusal. She just as surely disliked her role of mother and housekeeper for a man who often failed to return home at night. The reasons for his absences were plausible, but they did little to appease her concern.

Horace often displayed an intense need for Lucille's approval. He tells her in another letter of September 1919 that her recent letter had

made me very happy.—For the first time in a long while it showed that you really felt for me in my *hunger* for mental ease. I'll get it some day—I must—I must make you & Herman & Lucy & myself really happy—as I know how to be happy, or at least as I think I do. It may not come through the publishing business . . . but come it will someday—somehow.

He concludes on a note close to desperation: "But you *must, must* love me—a loser or a winner . . . why don't I succeed—like anyone you can name?—am I lazier, stupider—what?"

These last lines indicate some of Horace's deep-seated fears— and perhaps his low self-esteem. Even when things appeared to be going very well, he anticipated failure and disaster. In a flash, however, his mood might turn around completely and then he faced only a series of triumphs. Significantly, when things were, objectively, good, they had to be portrayed as even better than they were. For, as Louis Kronenberger commented, Horace did not write his mother that Dreiser and O'Neill were waiting for him in the reception room; instead, he reported that Conrad and Galsworthy were sitting there.

First Success

> What are you doing for Dreiser? I've got Dreiser and
> O'Neill, the two greatest American authors, and what have
> [you] editors done for me? Nothing!
> —HBL, 1924

(1)

HORACE was teasing the literary editors of the day when he complained that they were not paying enough attention to the B&L list. The truth was very much the opposite; Horace studiously courted all the major literary editors of the daily newspapers in New York. In the twenties there were eleven significant ones. At regularly scheduled lunches and dinners, he would go over his spring or fall list. He dared to tell these editors which books of his were worthy of front page coverage, even suggesting the names of possible reviewers. No U.S. publisher had ever had the gall to deal with the press in quite this way, but Horace's unfailing charm and enthusiasm were hard to resist. In addition, the books he was publishing *were* worth all the attention he demanded. In the early years of the decade Horace published a series of landmark books that are

as widely read today as they were at the time of their original publication.

One such book was Freud's *General Introduction to Psychoanalysis,*
which Horace published in 1920 in part because of his relationship
with a man he'd commissioned to promote the B&L list. In 1919 he
retained young Edward Bernays, the founding father of public relations in America, to take some new B&L titles and attempt to create some sort of publicity for them which might generate feature
stories in the newspapers. He had become aware of Bernays and his
work through his recent acquisition of Leon Fleischman as a vice
president. Horace employed this tactic—hiring wealthy young
men as vice presidents—to raise cash whenever things became
tight. The aspiring vice president was required to put up a substantial sum of money for the privilege of learning about publishing at
the most exciting house in town. Fleischman was only the first of
such vice presidents, whose tenure was usually brief. Among them
were several men who went on to create their own firms, including Bennett Cerf and Donald Friede.

Fleischman's sister Doris was married to Bernays, and it was this
connection that brought Bernays's pioneering work in public relations to Horace's attention. Born in Vienna, Bernays had come to
America as a small child. His father was Ely Bernays; his mother was
Freud's sister Anna. The family relationship was intensified because
two Freud siblings married two Bernays siblings: Ely Bernays's
younger sister married Sigmund Freud. Considering it a familial
responsibility, Bernays undertook the difficult task of obtaining a
U.S. publisher for his uncle's *General Introduction* for an American
public that had been exposed to a series of cheap popularizations of
Freudian theory. The name of Sigmund Freud was not unknown in
America, but his work had been appearing piecemeal under various
imprints—some of them medical-book houses—and no single volume summed up the basic principles of the new "talking cure." But
there was also a more pressing issue, the dire financial straits of the

Freud family in postwar Vienna. The Austrian crown had become nearly as worthless as the German mark. Freud's life savings had been wiped out, as had his life insurance policy. Dollars were urgently required, and Bernays asked his uncle to appoint him as his agent in America, to set the record straight about the nature of psychoanalysis as well as to refill the family coffers.

In discussing his uncle's work with Horace, Bernays had only his inscribed copy of the Viennese edition of the "Introductory Lectures" that Freud had given there from 1915 through 1917. As part of his work in Paris with the Peace Conference of 1919, Bernays had received the book as a gift from Freud, who learned of his nephew's presence there by the gift of a box of cigars from the U.S. mission. Armed only with the German text, Bernays set out to convince Liveright that the publication of Freud's basic work would attract not only an elite audience but also a general one. Horace's decision to publish was based on his intuitive feelings about Bernays, much the same way as he trusted Ezra Pound's estimate of *The Waste Land*. Horace's staff—Smith, Komroff, and Messner—were appalled at the notion of publishing what appeared to be a densely written German text about medical matters and predicted disaster for the undertaking. But Horace could not ignore what he called his "hunches" and drew up a contract, with Bernays acting as his uncle's agent.

Horace was fully aware of the special problems posed by such a book. Because of its erotic content, it would have to be priced at three dollars—a stiff price at this time—and be presented to the public with considerable dignity. Bernays had no doubt that B&L was the right house to publish such a radical volume with any chance of success and accepted Horace's contract, which guaranteed Freud an advance of $3,000. Bernays then arranged for a speedy translation as well as commissioning an introduction from G. Stanley Hall, the eminent American psychologist who had invited Freud to Clark University in 1909. But, without warning,

complications arose when Freud cabled Bernays's father: TELL
EDWARD STOP TRANSLATION. EXPECT LETTER.

When Bernays received Freud's letter, he was dismayed to discover that his uncle had granted his English champion, Ernest
Jones, the English-language rights to *General Introduction* as part of
the publication plans for the newly created International
Psychoanalytic Press in Vienna. With the book just about to go on
press, all seemed lost, but Bernays was able to convince Freud that
Horace's contract was for U.S. rights only and that the B&L edition
would not damage Jones's efforts to publish in the United
Kingdom. Bernays's tactful handling of the impasse worked, and
Freud withdrew his objections.

The publication of *General Introduction* had a material effect on
Freud's reputation in America. The book's circulation among educated readers transformed Freud from a Viennese physician with
curious ideas about sexual behavior into a seminal figure in modern
thought—it gained him a degree of respect he had heretofore only
obtained from professionals in the field. The success of the volume
was slow but steady, surpassing the expectations of Horace, Freud
and Bernays; by the end of the decade *General Introduction* had sold
more than 20,000 copies. It has never been out of print.*

There was a curious aftermath to Horace's first publication of
Freud. As will be seen, Horace had some idiosyncratic ideas about
business debts. When cash was plentiful, all went well and B&L
paid its bills as promptly as any other publisher. But it often happened that Horace had spent a great deal (or all) of the monies
normally retained as reserves against current royalties. The
money was spent on an extraordinarily wide range of editorial
projects—it became a legend in publishing that Horace would
offer a two-hundred-dollar advance to any writer who appeared
with what he thought had the making of a good book. This method

*As his royalties continued to appear in the 1920s, Freud commented, "It is the only book that
pays."

of editorial acquisition worked after a fashion or, more properly, worked *some* of the time—a lot of those advances were never recovered.

On two occasions, Bernays had to employ the services of an attorney to collect his uncle's earnings. Paradoxically or, more correctly, right in character, Horace fully approved of Bernays's course of action, finding it both "natural and desirable." This skittish behavior on royalties was dangerous—it furnished T. S. Eliot with still another reason to look for an "honest," Christian publisher. As for Bernays, he knew very well that Horace had no thought of robbing anyone—everyone *would* be paid eventually. He regarded Horace as a saint among publishers, but one who lacked good business judgment.

(2)

> Books were handled in the same way they had been published—for a select audience and not for a larger public. Book publishing was static in the content of its books and in its promotion . . . but Liveright changed all that.
> —Edward L. Bernays, 1965

STILL extraordinarily active for a man in his hundredth year, in 1992 Edward Bernays told me of his exciting year of work with Horace and the early days of B&L. Before encountering Bernays, Horace had broken new ground by building up an extensive network of relations with the most prominent tastemakers and journalists of the day, people like Floyd Dell, Ernest Boyd, and Burton Rascoe. By keeping these people informed about B&L's authors and their doings, Horace enjoyed the results of a steady stream of major reviews that influenced sales. Now, with the aid of Bernays, he wanted to push the process further.

Bernays found Horace difficult to "size up" on their first meeting. He was immediately aware of Horace's exuberance, his dedication to radical publishing and his willingness to gamble. But in some way Horace remained puzzling to Bernays, who blamed that fact on the publisher's "overpowering ego," a sample of which he encountered on that first day:

> When Leon [Fleischman] and I entered Liveright's office he was standing before the window facing the street, his John Barrymore profile outlined against the light—purposefully, it seemed to me. I did not realize then that he was only 31 years old . . . he seemed at first glance so much older, poised, sophisticated and authoritative.

Bernays was neither the first nor the last to note this theatrical quality—it was as integral to Horace's personality as his taste for the grandiose or his passion for the outrageous.

Horace believed that Bernays's ability to generate publicity might be used to advantage in the book business. At that time Bernays considered himself as an image maker who attempted to crystallize public opinion about a product or a person by supplying the press with a steady stream of information in the way of feature stories about his clients. (Among his many clients were Nijinsky and the Russian Ballet, Henry Ford and Henry Luce.) The two men agreed that books might be marketed *in the same way as any other product:* by aggressive promotion in the press and a thorough backup operation of constant advertising. They were also convinced that publishing a book was as much an *event* as the opening of a play or an opera. If the press could be convinced of this, an enormous amount of free advertising could be obtained.

Working on a retainer basis, Bernays offered to publicize five of Horace's new titles, among them Hutchins Hapgood's *The Story of a Lover,* a novel which contained—for the time—a strong erotic element, so erotic that Hapgood chose to publish it anonymously.

Bernays's solution to this problem was to contact the press agent of four young women who were thought to have expertise in these matters; the women included Mary Pickford, the two Gish sisters, and a forgotten fourth queen of the silent screen, Alice Joyce. The agents were glad to cooperate. Lillian Gish was quoted as saying, "In the crucible of love there could not exist the waste of the carnal; there could only be the pure gold of loving affection." Her sister, Dorothy, rivaled her by stating, "On the loom of life was the warp and woof of all worth having—that it was one of the few good things that money could neither buy nor ravage." Alice Joyce was less fancy: "Love is life, laughter and lightning, but most of all, love, is love."

When newspapers received Bernays's feature stories containing these utterances which appeared to have some mysterious connection with the Hutchins book, they found it hard to believe there would be no charge for their use; assured there would be none, they gave them front-page treatment.

As things worked out, neither Horace nor Bernays needed the young ladies to publicize the book: the New York Society for the Suppression of Vice went after it in the courts (unsuccessfully), and this suit was probably responsible for the bulk of the 11,000 copies sold before the book was removed from the stores.

Then Bernays attempted the impossible, to make the writings of Waldo Frank accessible to the American public. A dense and difficult writer, but widely regarded as an original thinker and close student of the national psyche, Frank never sold widely, with the exception of *Virgin Spain,* but Bernays thought he could turn things around with his latest book, *Our America*. With the aid of his wife, Doris, Bernays wrote up a series of feature stories that, in effect, "psychoanalyzed" cities like Chicago and New York. He managed to get the papers to run the stories, but they had little effect on sales—in this case amounting to about 4,000 copies. Some of Bernays's experiments failed, but his techniques left their mark on

American book promotion, and most of the basic concepts developed by working with Horace have become industry practice. As for Waldo Frank, Horace doggedly continued to publish Frank's experimental novels, despite his personal dislike for them and their disappointing sales, some less than 1,500 copies. Horace felt it was his *duty* to publish writers like Frank.

During Bernays's time with Horace, the B&L ads began to take on the appearance that distinguished them sharply from those of other publishers. They were starkly assertive, using bold-face type surrounded by lots of white space. Whenever possible, the newsworthy aspects of the books were emphasized. So, too, was the B&L logo which Horace began using in 1922, a cowled monk sitting at a desk with quill in hand. Many publishers use these logos on all their title pages in addition to their house ads—Knopf's Borzoi dog and the Scribner's burning lamp are among the more familiar. Horace's enemies liked to point out the absurdity of a monk in a logo for a firm that was gaining a reputation for publishing the most daringly outspoken books, the kind that often wound up in the courts on obscenity charges.

After his one-year tenure with B&L, Bernays and Horace remained friends and saw much of each other in the years that followed. Looking back, Bernays has some theories about his old friend—theories that seek to explain some of Horace's later behavior as "ego problems." He believes that Liveright was deeply ashamed of his lack of formal education and that he feared that this lack "would not support his social and intellectual aspirations." In short, Horace felt inferior to the bright people who surrounded him. Although Bernays's impressions come long after the events, and there is a certain hindsight at work here, his views contain some measure of truth.

A year or so before Horace's first London trip, the Liverights abandoned apartment living and moved to New Rochelle, just north of

New York City on Long Island Sound. They were renters for a time on Seafield Street but soon purchased the house across the street. Their new home was sufficiently large for Horace to entertain several overnight guests in addition to maintaining a small staff of servants. The commute to Manhattan was under an hour, but Horace often found it necessary to remain in town long after the departure of the last train from Grand Central. Many writers are profoundly lonely, and Horace's willingness to discuss their projects with them until the small hours was gratifying. New York had further attractions: Horace had lost none of his passion for the theater and was a first-nighter for every major opening in town at a time (1921) when there were seventy-six legitimate theaters.

While it can be argued that the late hours and the nights in town were the chief threats to Lucille and Horace's marriage, it is also true that, once B&L had become successful, Lucille found her place in Horace's life ambiguous at best. Her father's money was still invested in the firm, although Horace began to regret this situation more and more. He could never lay his hands on enough cash to repay Mr. Elsas what he'd invested and thus had to be the recipient of Elsas's objections as to how his money was being spent. Lucille's life in New Rochelle was a life apart from Horace, and as time passed the gap between them widened. Other women may have played a part in this as well, but there is no doubt that the marriage underwent ever-increasing strains in the early 1920s.

(3)

ONE of the most important publishing contacts Horace made in London was Jonathan Cape, who had started his own business only the previous year. The two novice publishers got along very well at the outset, but it is likely that Horace later came to share William

Faulkner's opinion of Cape as something of a stuffed shirt, "A Limey . . . snapping his false teeth in the girl's garters." In time Cape began to refer openly to B&L as a "rag-time outfit," meaning that he didn't approve of the way business was conducted on West Forty-eighth Street. This was to be the identical judgment he would make of his American partner, Harrison Smith, who followed Horace's example by locating a relaxed, fun-loving publishing house in a New York brownstone. Cape's anger at Smith was perhaps compounded by Smith's placing Faulkner's *The Sound and the Fury* on his first list. Probably Cape believed that only ragtime outfits would publish writers like Faulkner.

In the next few years Cape took on a number of B&L authors for the British market, among them Eugene O'Neill, Waldo Frank, and Sherwood Anderson. But in the beginning, in 1922, Cape offered Horace the very first book he published, Charles Doughty's massive two-volume work, *Travels in Arabia Deserta,* originally published by Cambridge University Press back in 1888. Cambridge had printed only 500 copies, and sales had been so poor that the hefty volumes had quickly been remaindered. T. E. Lawrence, or Lawrence of Arabia as he has become more widely known, had a passion for Doughty's book and regretted that it had been allowed to go out of print. He indicated in an interview that he would be willing to write a preface or introduction to the book if a publisher brave enough to undertake the endeavor would step forth.

The Doughty project did indeed require bravery. The two huge volumes ran to more than 1,400 pages of a dense text filled with scores of line-cuts accompanied by more than a dozen fold-out maps and charts, some of them in full color. When Cape and his partner in the enterprise, Lee Warner of the Medici Society, contemplated the costs, they may well have hesitated, for this was long before the days of cheap offset printing. *Travels in Arabia Deserta* would have to be reset to bring it before the public again. Typesetting alone would cost at least £1,500. Since it was clearly a prestige book, Cape decided to price it accordingly at nine guineas, or about $45 in 1920s money. With an introduction by Lawrence, *Travels* made back its costs and gave Cape what he wanted most at the beginning of his great career as a publisher: recognition. He was unable, however, to interest any American publisher in acquiring the U.S. rights until Horace arrived in London. If Cape believed that publishing Doughty helped his firm get off the ground, why wouldn't it work for B&L? Horace made him an offer which he instantly accepted.

When he returned to New York, Horace bore with him the two volumes that were to be an unprecedented marketing challenge to his staff. *Travels in Arabia Deserta* is an immense work that some have declared to be close to unreadable or, at best, only of interest to serious students of the Arabian desert. Horace used a far more aggressive version of Cape's snob-appeal approach, one that might be summed up as "How can you consider yourself an educated person if you have not yet encountered the world of the Arabian desert through the writing of Charles Doughty, a living master of English prose?" Also following Cape's example, Horace hedged his bets on *Travels* by pricing it at $17.50, an enormous sum for a book in 1923—seven times the price of an ordinary book then. His strategy worked; B&L sold 4,600, copies, which produced a net profit for the firm of more than $10,000, but, again, as had been the case with Cape, an additional advantage was obtained in reaffirming B&L's sense of risk and daring.

Shortly after his marketing experiments with Bernays, Horace became the publisher of some extraordinarily popular books—so popular that their profits enabled him to move to far more expensive quarters by the beginning of 1923. The first such book—the first B&L best-seller—has a curious history, made even more so by the disparities in the accounts of how the firm came to publish the wildly successful *The Story of Mankind*. Its affable, Dutch-born author was Hendrik Willem Van Loon, a writer with a Ph.D. from

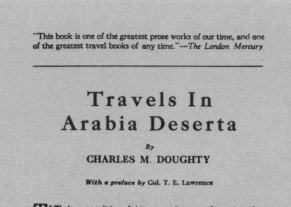

"This book is one of the greatest prose works of our time, and one
of the greatest travel books of any time."—*The London Mercury*

Travels In Arabia Deserta

By
CHARLES M. DOUGHTY

With a preface by Col. T. E. Lawrence

THE cheapest edition of this extraordinary work was issued in
1921 at Fifty Dollars. The first edition (1888) which consisted only of a few hundred copies has been long out of
print and brings over One Hundred Dollars when offered for sale,
which is seldom. Messrs Boni & Liveright in co-operation with
Jonathan Cape and the Medici Society (London), consider it a very
great privilege to be able to offer to libraries and the Public for the
first time this very handsome and *absolutely* complete edition of this
famous work for the price of $17.50.

1300 pages. Maps and Illustrations.   2 volumes.   Boxed.
Buckram gilt binding. Large 8vo.

$17.50 Net

BONI and LIVERIGHT
61 West 48th Street   *Publishers*   **New York City**

B&L brochure for first American edition of *Travels in Arabia
Deserta*, 1923.
Liveright Publishing Corp., W. W. Norton Co.

Munich who was working as an Associated Press correspondent
while also teaching history at Cornell. His teaching career came to
an abrupt end when the citizens of Ithaca, New York, discovered
that Van Loon's views on the European war were not theirs—he
was promptly fired for being pro-German. Albert Boni had known
Van Loon for years and had noted with great interest how the erudite ex-professor liked to illustrate his conversations at lunch with
little sketches made with burned-out matches on paper napkins.

Boni felt certain that the sketches would appeal to children and that Van Loon should write a brief, simple text to accompany them. As for a subject, how about *Ancient Man*? This was the title that B&L published in 1920; it was to be Boni's last editorial contribution to the firm, if, indeed, his account is correct.

An alternate version was given by Horace's long-term production chief, Manuel Komroff, who became a popular novelist in the thirties and forties. In his account, it was not Boni but rather Tommy Smith, who discovered Van Loon's talents while Smith was still working at the Century Company. Van Loon had himself conceived of a series of small books for children which would constitute a history of the world. But Century was not interested, and it was only after Smith began to work for Horace in 1919 that he contracted for the first volume, *Ancient Man*, as well as the rest of the volumes that Van Loon had completed. Since *Ancient Man* had been submitted to sixteen houses before reaching B&L, Van Loon had by this time completed the other volumes in the series. The sale of *Ancient Man* was a modest 4,000 copies, but Horace noticed that the little book was being bought by parents for their children as well as by adults, who found the pictures irresistible, thus justifying Van Loon's statement that he "wrote for people aged 12 to 72."

Horace was aware of the worldwide popularity of H. G. Wells's *Outline of History,* a fat compendium of historical fact addressed to a world hungry for information about a civilization that had just concluded a bloody four-year struggle. Wells's book gave its huge audience a grasp on history that was made painless by its author's easy-to-read style. Thinking about all this, Horace reflected that Van Loon's style was even easier to read than Wells's, so why shouldn't a book made up of the individual parts of Van Loon's series—all of them, in fact—appeal to that same mass audience? Van Loon had arranged his sections chronologically (The Classical World, The Middle Ages, etc.), and it required only a few hours' work to produce *The Story of Mankind.*

Left to right: Burton Rascoe, Hendrik Willem Van Loon, and HBL, 1922.
UPI/Bettman

When Horace told his staff about his plans for Van Loon, he's said to have used the language of the gambling trade: "Let's shoot the works." He had to repeat himself before they got the drift, but Van Loon's permission to proceed in this startlingly new way was obtained within the hour. *The Story of Mankind* became the No. 2 national best-seller for 1922 and was No. 9 in the following year. Van Loon's hundreds of drawings were expensive to reproduce, thus raising the retail price of the book to five dollars—a huge sum at the time, equivalent to forty to fifty dollars today. Nevertheless, the book sold 113,000 copies, producing a net profit for the firm of $136,000, figures that showed the publishing world that a new and significant presence had entered the scene. As if determined to prove that *The Story of Mankind* was not a onetime fluke, B&L published Gertrude Atherton's novel about sexual rejuvenation, *Black Oxen,* in the following year. It became the No. 1 best-seller in fiction for 1923, the year when Horace moved the firm to a more fashionable part of town.

(4)

My dream . . . is of some cottage on the coast of the Mediterranean, where amid sunny rocks I shall sit surrounded by devout women and disciples, aestheticising the days away, my feet in the bluest and beautifullest of seas. For the accomplishment of this lovely destiny you will not mind dipping your hand a little deeper into your till than you do for strangers?
—George Moore to HBL, 1928

MOORE, a half-forgotten figure today, was famous for the outrageous demands he made of his various publishers. Unlike most writers, Moore granted these publishers the rights to print and sell his books for very short periods of time—usually for only a year— and would then take the rights back in order to sell them again to another publisher. He usually demanded—and got—a 20 percent royalty on the retail price of his books. His novels and stories usually appeared in limited, signed editions and were eagerly snapped up by rare-book collectors who believed they were buying the work of one of the best living English novelists. Moore has gone out of fashion, although his work has great importance in the history of Irish literature and influenced James Joyce. His naturalistic novels, for example, *Esther Waters,* now seem to be softened, English versions of Zola while lacking the horrific power of the author of *L'Assommoir.*

After he had published a limited signed edition of Moore's *A*

Story-Teller's Holiday in early 1919, Horace wrote Moore for permission to issue a trade edition of the book; his letter indicates his conviction about Moore's importance to his list:

> I live in the hope . . . that you will soon give us the opportunity to publish one of your books in a regular trade edition. The greatest living English author should give the wider public an opportunity to read his books.

But Moore would not consent to this trade edition for nearly another decade. He wisely knew that little support could be expected from the ordinary book-buying public in England or the United States. His wares were, he believed, for the chosen few who might appreciate them in beautifully printed, expensive editions. In addition, several of Moore's novels had attracted the attention of censorship groups on both sides of the Atlantic, thereby creating another good reason for issuing his books in small editions that would not disturb the authorities. In England many of these limited editions appeared with title pages that indicated the publisher's name in Gaelic, still another ruse to discourage censorship. So many limited editions of Moore's were printed that, sixty years after the death of the novelist, bookstores can still offer them for sale at modest prices. A rare-book dealer in New England once told me that unsigned Moore titles should be priced higher than signed ones since they were so rare.

It may be that Horace had a low opinion of rare-book collectors, for he had no compunction in deceiving them about what they would be buying when he published Moore's complete works in twenty-two volumes in the Carra edition. As the publication date approached, Moore began complaining that Horace's deadlines were tiring him out. Horace's reply indicates the nature of the editorial work required of Moore:

George Moore in the
twenties.
*Warder Collection, W. W.
Norton Co.*

I suggested that you (not anyone else in the world) make certain
textual changes in each one of the volumes, even though these
changes amount to only two or three words, so that it will be possible for us to advise collectors of your books that it will be necessary for them to possess the new collected edition if they wish to
have the most up to date texts of all your books.

Priced at the extraordinary sum of eight and a half dollars per volume, or $176 for the complete set, the Carra edition was ulti-
mately successful, although it took nearly a decade to happen; the
last of the books were remaindered in the thirties. Despite this,
B&L made a profit of $30,000 on the venture.

   After 1921 Moore refused to conduct any business with Tommy
Smith, either as his agent or as his editor at B&L. Moore discovered

that Smith had sold many of his letters, manuscripts and galley proofs to rare-book dealers in New York and London. From then on Horace dealt directly with Moore—the beginning of what amounted to a ten-year war between author and publisher over such matters as deadlines, production errors, merchandising schemes, and, most important, advances against royalties. To make sure that his troubles with Tommy Smith would not recur, Moore laid down a firm set of rules about the way his manuscripts must be treated if he was to remain with B&L:

> This is not the first time Mr. Smith has sold my letters, and it was on account of these sales that I ceased to do business with him [as agent]. . . . I am determined not to have my corrected books and manuscripts going hither from one sale to another.

Moore stipulated that he was to be given back his material the moment the printers had finished with it. Then, figuring that he had Horace on the defensive, he brought up an earlier proposition about publishing two of his plays, an option that Horace had refused. Moore's approach this time was sly:

> If you would like to publish these two plays at once you can make me an offer. If not, I have no choice but to look round for another publisher. Perhaps you would like me to publish with another publisher in view of the fact that you are publishing the collected works? A telegram will settle the matter.

Horace wisely refused to be intimidated.

Horace put up with Moore's unorthodox behavior because publishing his books gave the firm in its early days the prestige it needed; Moore liked Horace because of his ability to sell his books without fear of the consequences.

The House on
Forty-eighth Street

A job with any publishing house was a plum, but a job with
Horace Liveright was a bag of plums.
             —Lillian Hellman, 1969

Boni & Liveright . . . stood for America in the process of
exposing and defining itself; stood for the Zeitgeist, itself all
too fluid and mercurial, stood for something brooding and
lonely in American life as well as unruly and defiant.
             —Louis Kronenberger, 1965

(1)

WHEN Horace could finally afford greatly expanded quarters
for the firm, he acted with his usual disregard for tradition. Most (if
not all) publishers are located in office buildings scattered around
midtown New York, just the way B&L was until 1923. That was
the year Horace bought the five-story brownstone house at 61
West Forty-eighth Street, between Fifth and Sixth avenues. His
choice of a brownstone may have been influenced by memories of
the smaller British houses he'd visited on his first London trips.
Jonathan Cape, for instance, occupied a small town house at 30
Bedford Square for decades; so, too, did Faber & Faber on Russell
Square. When Horace renovated No. 61, he transformed a nonde-

script residence into what some have regarded as the source of nearly everything of value in modern American writing.

It was here at No. 61—"the house on Forty-eighth Street"—that the many legends about Horace were spun out in an atmosphere of laughter and good spirits that has been likened to a three-ring circus. Determined to make his new quarters appear as noncommercial as possible, Horace was successful in maintaining a convivial, home-style, partylike feeling at B&L that was hard to reconcile with the astonishing torrent of important books that kept appearing there as if by magic. If one single publishing house epitomized the era, it was surely B&L, the house that pulsed and glowed in the great heyday of the mid- and late twenties side by side with the boundless hopes of Americans who saw no limit to their expanding horizons.

The ceilings of Manhattan brownstones were high by today's standards: fourteen to sixteen feet for the lower floors was not uncommon. The floors were connected by narrow staircases that were unusually steep; it required healthy lungs to get to the top with any speed. Once B&L became a beehive of activity, these stairways became conversational way stations for those coming and going in the building. Louis Kronenberger, who worked for B&L for seven years, had his initial sightings of Dorothy Parker and Sherwood Anderson on the stairs: Parker was coming up and Anderson going down.

The street floor of No. 61 was devoted to storage and the shipping department, while the first floor proper was the domain of the accounting division. Here in front were the telephone switchboard and the young women who ran it. Horace always hired attractive young Irish girls for this task, convinced that they would "take no taffy and can talk back to anybody, high or low." To gain access to the upper reaches of the building, you had to pass the scrutiny of those girls who guarded the stairway against the constant tide of supplicants who begged entry. By all reports, many of the visitors were bootleggers eager to sell their wares in a richly hospitable environment.

Horace's office occupied the front of the building on the second floor. Here, with a grand piano and a huge, ornamental fireplace, Horace received his many visitors. Photos of the main B&L authors adorned the walls. On one side of the room a series of painted panels depicting plants and seaweed disguised the doorway that led to Horace's private bathroom. The bathroom had a zinc-lined shower—a novelty at the time, as was the telephone there. The office had its own bar, and few visitors left Horace's sanctum without at least a taste of something just off the boat. To dispose of his wastepaper, Horace purchased a gigantic Chinese vase, into which he rained a constant stream of printed material.

A good part of the entire second floor was taken up with the reception room, which Horace had decorated with furniture in the Italian Renaissance style, Oriental rugs, another grand piano and many oversized plants. A large wood-burning fireplace helped to give the huge room the appearance of a living room admirably suited for parties, which is what Horace had in mind. The stucco walls often displayed drawings and paintings fresh from the studios of young artists who had persuaded Horace into giving them a little show, where their work could be seen by some of the most noted tastemakers of the day. Three triple French doors at the back of the reception area opened onto a terrace built out over the yard below. Large parties spilled out onto this canopy-covered area, especially in the summer, when small groups of instrumentalists were hired to play the latest jazz from Harlem.

After 1924 and Horace's entry into theatrical production, one wall of the reception area was demolished, to be replaced by a new one with a floor-to-ceiling bookcase in its middle. The bookcase concealed the door leading to Horace's new premises in the adjoining building. Visitors to B&L were sometimes startled to observe this door being opened onto the appearance of a vision of loveliness who had just finished auditioning for Horace and his associates. The bookcase itself attracted some talk, for among the titles was a slim volume entitled *The Complete Works of Walter Scott*. Other titles were of the order of *With Gun and Tackle Through the Ovarian Canal*.

At the front of the floor above was Julian Messner's sales department. Messner was assisted by a series of bright young men, several of whom would found their own publishing houses. They included Richard Simon, cofounder of Simon and Schuster, and Bennett Cerf, who left B&L to found Random House with Donald Klopfer. A third assistant, Edward Weeks, left the sales area of publishing to become, for several decades, the editor of the *Atlantic Monthly*. Although he worked at B&L for less than a year, Weeks later recalled Horace's fostering a strong feeling of participation among all his employees regarding the current state of the firm. Horace called it "socialism in action," and it definitely meant an openness about matters that were usually cloaked in mystery at other houses. Weeks remembered that each day's reorders—the lifeblood of any publishing firm—were "placed on a round table in what had been the house's dining room; everyone from office boy to Smith and Messner read them avidly."

The rear of the third floor was occupied by both the editorial and production departments. At first sight, plump Tommy Smith seemed out of place as editor in chief at B&L. His pince-nez and exceptionally erudite knowledge of books seemed to indicate an academic background, but his working habits would rapidly cancel this impression. Besides erotica, Smith collected gossipy stories, and people from all over the building dropped in to hear the latest, or perhaps to share their own tidbits. He was also a "Mr. Memory," who could recall to the last dollar every advance George Moore had ever received, as well as thousands of other pieces of information, some of which were quite valuable. Few visitors left his office without sampling something from his vast store of potables. Book publishing with Horace Liveright, a place where you could try anything at least once, was exhilarating in a way the old Century Company had never been. Smith was tirelessly ebullient over his luck in having made the switch.

Down the hall from Smith was the B&L production department, managed by Manuel Komroff, a genial young Yale graduate with long, drooping mustaches who had worked as a journalist in Moscow with John Reed during the October Revolution. In late 1919 Komroff had been writing film criticism for *Film Daily* in New York. Just after lunch one day that year, he encountered Reed on West Fortieth Street in the company of Horace. One of Reed's first remarks during the conversation that followed was "You two ought to know each other." Nothing might have come of this, but in just a week or two Komroff received a call from Horace, informing him that Horace's dentist had recommended him strongly as a possible editor for the Modern Library, a job that had been created in part by the departure of Albert Boni. Komroff's strong literary background coupled with his knowledge of printing techniques made him an ideal person to hire. In practice, Komroff spent most of his time producing the firm's books—he had very little time for the Modern Library. Komroff stayed with B&L until 1926, when he, too, answered the call of Paris and began a long career of successful novel writing that stretched into the 1960s.

All the way up at the top of the building—actually the attic— was a series of small, low-ceilinged rooms that housed the rest of the editorial staff—the readers. Again, Horace had chosen some remarkable people for a job that has been compared to pearl diving in the North Baltic Sea at night. Many of the readers went on to achieve literary careers of distinction. In the early years of B&L, the readers included the wife of the playwright George S. Kaufman, Beatrice Kaufman, who was regarded by some as one of the wittiest women in New York. Working with her was Edith Stern, who began her own novel-writing career while working at B&L. So, too, did Louis Kronenberger—one of the few male readers—who started in 1926 and remained with B&L through 1933. Horace also published Kronenberger's first novel, a common practice at B&L. Budding authors saw their hopes gratified by a publisher who knew that most writers are more interested in fame than money. Horace lost money on nearly all the "house authors" that he published, but it was worth it to cement the bonds of loyalty. Kronenberger later worked for Knopf before becoming, for many years, the dramatic critic of *Time* magazine and the author of many works about the eighteenth century. Like his immediate boss, Tommy Smith, Kronenberger possessed a vast knowledge of literature accompanied by a graceful style that made his reports a joy to read.

But it was Lillian Hellman who became the most famous of all the B&L readers, although she had not been hired as one when she joined the firm shortly after the move to Forty-eighth Street. She had met Julian Messner at a party, and he'd been impressed by her intelligence; he hired her that same evening to begin work at a variety of tasks including copy editing and odd jobs in the advertising department. She loved the work at B&L, summing up her feelings in her memorable line, "a job with Horace Liveright was a bag of plums." She later commented on the strange clublike atmosphere that prevailed at No. 61, as well as the startling lack of job definition that characterized B&L: "Even the stenographers and shipping clerks often wandered around reading manuscripts, offering opinions about how to advertise or sell a book, and there was seldom a day without excitement." Some of the excitement was caused by Hellman's habit of losing manuscripts—a trait that did not endear her to Smith and placed her plums in danger.

The house was frequently awash with visitors, so many that they threatened the work output: "Some days no corner could be found for work because too many writers were in town." Hellman also describes the intense feeling of "belonging" that permeated many of the workers at B&L:

Sometimes one of the editors had been in mysterious trouble the night before and everybody went around to his house or hospital to call upon him; on no day could you ever be sure what you would see through a half-open office door, or how long lunch would be for Horace and the editors, or who was taking a long nap afterwards.

She retained vivid memories of the B&L staircases, where she built up her running skills: "All the men in the office made routine passes at the girls who worked there—one would have to be hunchbacked to be an exception—and one of the more pleasant memories of my life is the fast sprinting I would do up and down the long staircases to keep from being idly pinched or thrown by a clutching hand on a leg."

By all reports, the house on Forty-eighth Street was rarely a quiet place to work. As Louis Kronenberger put it, the place was "a living bulletin board":

There was a constant sense of people clattering up and down stairs, and emerging from conspicuously placed toilets; and even with the office door shut, you could hear telephone conversations through the walls. Having been summoned, say, to Liveright's office two flights down, I might be fifteen minutes getting back to what, with various encounters as I climbed the stairs, resembled a gossipy Alpine village—hearing who was in the building, who now was with the boss, noticing whose doors were closed, wondering which doors were locked.

The tradition of everyone knowing all about everyone's business could be exasperating, as Hellman discovered when she had an abortion—then illegal—performed by a doctor recommended by Donald Friede, one of Horace's bright young vice presidents. Although Friede swore to keep the event to himself, the next day

nearly everyone she knew well in the firm came round to her office
to offer her money or make inquiries about the child's father. The
abortion took place without anesthetic at Coney Island, with the
doctor's mother functioning as his assistant. Although feeling rotten the following day, Hellman went off to work, to be invited into
Horace's office for "a glass of midmorning champagne." Julian
Messner took her out to lunch that day; the two were greeted by
Tommy Smith on their return to the office. He told Julian: "Tell
that ninny to go home to bed. She shouldn't have come to work
today. Tell her to get out of here."

Hellman believed that Smith's agitation was caused by his wishing to fire her for her carelessness about manuscripts, plus other
assorted gaucheries that had plagued her working performance at
B&L. But this was not his intention. Instead, he invited her to take
a nap on his couch, which she promptly did. When she awoke,
Smith engaged her in a conversation aimed at defining the pattern
of her recent actions—her refusing to name the child's father or
to make any trouble for him. These refusals, plus her indication
that she would probably marry the father in the future, puzzled
Smith, for Lillian was a nice, "respectable" girl in his view. Smith
concluded the new-generation talk by saying, "So now we realize
that you're younger, different than the women we know. There *is*
a new generation and nobody here likes to think like that. But
we'd better catch up on it if we want to publish it. I don't think
we're going to like it, but maybe you'd better start telling us
about it."

Smith told Hellman that she might hold on to her job—if only
temporarily—if she would agree to come round to Horace's apartment the following Saturday night with two of her friends to discuss "the modern girl's attitude toward sex" with Samuel Hopkins
Adams, who, under the pseudonym of Warner Fabian, had written
the best-selling *Flaming Youth*. The idea behind the meeting was to
give Adams an up-to-date view on the situation, so that he could

write a proposed sequel to *Flaming Youth* with some accuracy. Strangely enough, considering Hellman's feisty temperament, she agreed to the proposal—perhaps the fact that she did so makes it clear how much the job meant to her. Smith's plan misfired badly, resulting in a drunken fiasco with all of them getting their feelings hurt. Adams was not at all interested in what Hellman and her young friends thought about sex in 1924—he had long ago made up his own mind about the subject and wasn't going to adjust it to any kind of pressure being put on him by B&L editors.

The weekly editorial meetings at B&L were decidedly on the informal side. Held in Horace's office, they usually began about 11:30. Horace might be having his shoes shined as his staff drifted into the room, some of them long after the meeting had started. It took some time to get things going, for there was almost always considerable gossipy small talk about what they had all done the night before. Phone calls were not screened; the members of the group

Self-portrait of
e. e. cummings in the
early twenties.
Warder Collection, W. W. Norton Co.

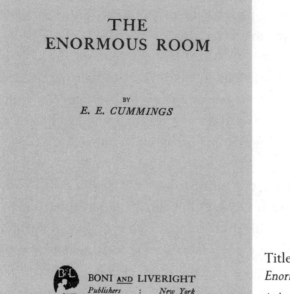

THE
ENORMOUS ROOM

BY
E. E. CUMMINGS

BONI **AND** LIVERIGHT
Publishers   :   New York

Title page for *The
Enormous Room*, 1922.
Author's collection

might listen with half an ear to what their colleagues had been up
to. These oddities aside, the B&L meetings were similar to those in
most other houses—there was a rough agenda of items to be considered. Projects were accepted or rejected; terms were proposed
for offers to be made. Horace ran the whole process as the showman he was, making witty comments at the expense of writers and
agents he despised and praising those he liked. At about one
o'clock or so, the meeting more or less fell apart, as people rushed
off for their agent/author lunches.

Besides the regulars like Tommy Smith, Manuel Komroff, Julian
Messner, and Bennett Cerf (to be succeeded by Donald Friede and
Fred Hummel), others including Beatrice Kaufman, Louis
Kronenberger, Leane Zugsmith, and Edith Stern might also be
invited. It was all very casual, but the results of these meetings con-

tinue to astonish one with the high quality of the books Horace's staff chose for publication. An examination of any 1920s B&L catalogue testifies to the astuteness of these editors, with Horace always having the last word.

As indicated earlier, the advertising for the B&L list was bold from the start. The selling copy was unusually flamboyant. There was often an urgency in the ads which seemed to scream HOW CAN YOU AFFORD *NOT* TO BUY THIS BOOK? These ads were produced in the rear of the same attic that housed the readers. Here reigned another of Horace's choices—the kind of man other publishers would avoid hiring. This was Isador Schneider, a Marxist poet and experimental novelist who, like so many of Horace's discoveries, later went on to Paris to pursue his literary career. One of his chief assistants was Leane Zugsmith from Kentucky, who admired the novels the firm published by a fellow Southerner, William Faulkner. He dated her on a number of occasions when he visited New York in 1928. As did other B&L employees—Kronenberger, Komroff, Stern, and Schneider, Zugsmith began a long literary career by having her first novel published by the firm; in the thirties she published several proletarian novels.

(2)

It was the damnedest thing. They spent more money for liquor in that place, I think, than they did for books. I mean, it was incredible.
　　　　　　　　　—Donald Klopfer, 1967

Most people I knew in the twenties worked very hard, as I did, and if we seemed to play a great deal also, it was because we had the energy to do so.
　　　　　　　　　—Burton Rascoe, 1947

> Although the doings at our office parties could involve public
> endearment, stained and ripped garments, periodical passing
> out in public, disappearing couples, maudlin recitals,
> unmanageable guests, almost as much spilled liquor as
> swilled, and almost as many gate-crashers as guests, what
> alone might have set Liveright entertainments apart was the
> prominence of the guest list.
> —Louis Kronenberger, 1965

ASIDE from the continual round of parties, people were forever
paying visits to the premises as if B&L were their own private club.
For some, B&L was a bank where they could replenish dwindling
funds. For others, B&L was akin to a favorite bar where they could
meet their friends, new and old. Young women were always very
much in evidence, as Louis Kronenberger remembered:

> Many other ladies came to the office, sometimes to call for some-
> one they were lunching with, or they came back after lunch, or
> appeared in mid-afternoon or towards sunset; and sometimes
> doors stood wide open upon impromptu drink-in-hand get-
> togethers, and sometimes doors were locked.

Horace's parties became legendary. Much has been made of
them, especially the amount of alcohol consumed and the extraordinary guest lists that Horace assembled for these occasions. The
plentiful supply of beautiful young women was drawn from the
theatrical world, particularly so after 1924, when Horace began
producing plays. The young ladies accepted his invitations gladly—
you never knew whom you might meet at one of these events.
Besides the women, Horace's endless supply of good liquor was
vital when it was hard to come by. After January 17, 1920, obtaining liquor became a daily problem—the passage of the Volstead
Act made the manufacture and sale of alcohol illegal in the United
States. Life in New York in the twenties and early thirties was the

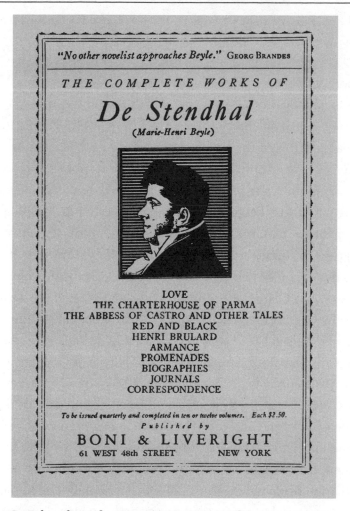

"No other novelist approaches Beyle." GEORG BRANDES

THE COMPLETE WORKS OF

De Stendhal

(*Marie-Henri Beyle*)

LOVE
THE CHARTERHOUSE OF PARMA
THE ABBESS OF CASTRO AND OTHER TALES
RED AND BLACK
HENRI BRULARD
ARMANCE
PROMENADES
BIOGRAPHIES
JOURNALS
CORRESPONDENCE

To be issued quarterly and completed in ten or twelve volumes. Each $2.50.
Published by

BONI & LIVERIGHT
61 WEST 48th STREET   NEW YORK

B&L brochure for *The Complete Works of Stendhal,* 1924.
Liveright Publishing Corp., W. W. Norton Co.

world of the "speakeasy," and B&L was right in the center of it.
Kronenberger thought that:

> Boni & Liveright was an actual *part* of the speakeasy world. Not
> only were there perhaps six speakeasies to one publishing house on
> our block; they were virtually all B&L branch offices. Long before
> Madison Avenue gave business a social facade, Forty-Eighth Street

did. . . . Horace's scarlet-walled, black-ceilinged bathroom—a bit
of a showplace—had its barroom aspects too.

There were two kinds of parties given at the B&L offices. There
was a formal or official gathering which today would be comparable to a "launching" party for a major new book or for an author
who had just joined the house. Then there was the far more informal "Let's have a party!" function, which was more rambunctious,
sexier, and often just plain drunken. According to Hellman, these
parties might just keep going until the guests ran out of energy.
Burton Rascoe, a chronicler of the period, recalled that many of
the parties at Horace's were "impromptu; they started in the afternoon, usually on Friday, and lasted until one in the morning."

Rascoe, now largely forgotten, was one of the major tastemak-
ers of the twenties, a critic with a far wider appeal than his friend
Edmund Wilson at *Vanity Fair*. Rascoe's daily column, "A
Bookman's Day Book," appeared in the New York *Tribune* and was
syndicated nationally. A Southerner, Rascoe read in several languages, was largely self-taught, and was extraordinarily kind to
Horace's books and authors. They shared a common dislike for the
Algonquin group of writers, many of whom returned the feeling.*
Horace repaid Rascoe for his kind reviews by publishing in 1929 a
compilation of some of his best columns, a book bound to please its
author but one also guaranteed not to sell—which, however, was
not Horace's purpose. In his memoir, *We Were Interrupted,* Rascoe
recalled just how easy it was to get a B&L party going. After a long
welcoming lunch for Bertrand Russell at the Algonquin, to mark
the publication of his first book for Horace, *Education and the Good
Life,* Horace, accompanied by his guests including the philosopher
Horace Kallen and the Rascoes, returned to Forty-eighth Street in
fine spirits. Horace immediately called up a number of important

*Nevertheless, Horace published Dorothy Parker and George S. Kaufman.

people to invite them over to meet Russell. Tommy Smith called the caterers; the liquor was already on the premises. And, as Rascoe recalled, "a four piece orchestra appeared out of nowhere . . . within half an hour Mayor Jimmy Walker had arrived."

Rascoe reported no mishaps with the Russell party that afternoon, but this was not always the case, for sometimes these gatherings continued without a letup. Russell wrote his wife an account about that evening and his later adventures uptown:

[Liveright] insisted on taking me to Harlem where the rich niggers live—we went to a place called the Ebony Club—seven of us, Liveright & his lady [Dorothy Peterson], Sherwood Anderson, Dreiser, Genevieve Taggard . . . another lady whose name I forget, & I. I wanted to enjoy myself, but when we got there they invited black ladies to our table & one was expected to dance & flirt with them. To my surprise, the mere idea was unspeakably revolting to me, & I left the place and went home. I couldn't bear the jazz music or the futurist walls or the negro ladies got up like Americans or anything about the place. I just felt jungle poison invading all our souls. I believe you would have enjoyed it. I am too old.

Russell also informed his wife that Horace had attempted to obtain bed partners for his stay in New York, but that he had rejected the offer: "In spite of his efforts, I took up with no ladies." It would appear that Horace often tried to fix up visiting B&L male authors with girls with whom they might spend their nights in New York. From all reports, many such young women were in regular attendance at Horace's parties and were ready and willing to oblige. After Horace entered theatrical production, many young hopefuls began to attend the festivities at B&L—they too offered hospitality. The pairing off of couples at the parties was assisted by the stunning cocktails that Tommy Smith mixed not only for the social events but for any and all occasions in his office. The best

HBL sitting at the Algonquin Round Table, 1923. Back of table, left to right: Heywood Broun, Dorothy Parker, George S. Kaufman, Alexander Woollcott, and HBL. Behind them: Robert E. Sherwood and Frank Case. In foreground, center: John Weaver and Marc Connelly.

The Algonquin Hotel

thing you could say about the drinks served at Horace's is that they were far safer than the kind served in the numerous speakeasies that surrounded No. 61.

Drinking could be dangerous in the twenties, because no one could be sure what he or she was consuming. Many of the beverages served in speakeasies were actually chemical "experiments" of a kind designed to produce a palatable intoxicant. Occasionally, errors crept into the manufacture of the booze, resulting in excruciating hangovers for the victims at one end of the scale and paralysis or death at the other. The presence of wood alcohol in the brew caused most of the havoc. In the month of October 1928, forty-two New Yorkers died of wood alcohol poisoning. It was, indeed, the time of bad liquor. Every time you took a drink in the age of Prohibition you were gambling, but since the odds were pretty much in the drinker's favor, Americans took to serious drinking with a passion unmatched since then. It even became fashionable to boast how you had "tied one on last night."

Bennett Cerf loved to recall the party to which Ford Madox Ford had been invited and at which the portly novelist had sat down rather too quickly on one of Horace's recently purchased couches. Ford's weight immediately reduced the fragile seating to matchsticks. Forty years after the event, Cerf could still hear the hideous crash and enjoy the sight of the walruslike writer lying on the floor: "I'll never forget that moment. It was a great day."

Horace gave so many parties that some of his guests looked forward to them as the place where they met their friends on a regular basis. Festive feelings usually prevailed, but Louis Kronenberger's most vivid memory of the B&L parties was "of Hart Crane violently plastered and very pugnacious. And sometimes I saw Horace drunk, I suspect on not very much liquor." As was the case with his new young friend Scott Fitzgerald, it seems likely that Horace was extremely vulnerable to alcohol—it took comparatively little to make him drunk very quickly with unpredictable results.

Fifth Avenue and
42nd Street, 1927.
HBL's ad for
Napoleon at top of
picture.
Liveright Publishing Corp.,
W. W. Norton Co.

One regular guest was Herbert Bayard Swope, the young editor of
the New York *World*. Swope was a great host in his own right, as
well as an authority on just about everything. Swope's parties near
Great Neck were so sensationally lavish that Scott Fitzgerald used
them as the model for Gatsby's. Bennett Cerf recalled his legendary hospitality: "Anybody you'd see on the front page who
arrived from Europe that day was at his house that night, from the
Prince of Wales up and down." Through his friendship with
Swope, Horace made many contacts with writers he might not
have encountered on his trips to London and Paris. One of the
"anybodies" in 1924 was the very young Noël Coward, who began

to come to Horace's parties as well after he'd agreed to publish Coward's little book of satires.

Another regular at Horace's was James John Walker, Mayor Jimmy Walker, whose reputation as the most colorful, uninhibited mayor of New York City has gone unchallenged. Like Swope, Walker was also a greeter to all the famous visitors to the city; he adored celebrities from the theatrical and literary worlds. His feelings concerning the Volstead Act were well known, placing him in the awkward position of being the chief enforcer of an act that he personally despised. After their work together in defeating the Clean Books League bill in Albany in 1923, Horace and Walker maintained their friendship.

From the world of high finance came the princely Otto Kahn,

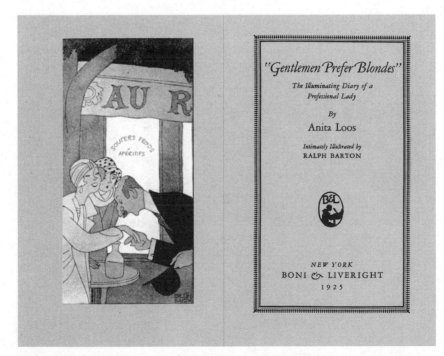

Title page for *Gentlemen Prefer Blondes.*
Author's collection

who was Horace's ear on Wall Street whenever he needed money—a situation that never ceased. Kahn also became Hart Crane's patron at the time he was completing *The Bridge;* Kahn was better at patronage than as a stock market tipster.

George Gershwin also came to Horace's to play the piano for the kind of people he liked playing for, especially the beautiful girls present at all Horace's affairs. When Horace began to produce plays in 1924, he starred the young actor and singer Paul Robeson in the play *Black Boy,* which flopped; Robeson didn't, however, and was a regular guest. These parties understandably absorbed a good part of B&L's overhead, but Horace had no doubt that they were worth every cent spent on them—they opened doors that might have remained shut—doors open to the future.

Firebrand at Work

No woman was ever ruined by a book.
—Mayor Jimmy Walker, 1923

(1)

THROUGH most of the twenties Horace's arch-enemy was the greatly feared John S. Sumner, secretary of the New York Society for the Suppression of Vice. The name of this organization today has faintly comic overtones and seems to have nothing to do with the world of book publishing. But from the time of the First World War until the late 1930s, the Society possessed extraordinary power and authority over writers, publishers, and librarians. The avowed aim of the Society was to encourage the publishing and reading of "good" books by the suppression of "bad" ones. Perhaps the single most amazing fact about the Society was that many self-styled liberals endorsed its aims. Who, after all, likes to come out in favor of dirty books?

From the end of the Civil War until the turn of the century, numerous antivice societies sprang up in many major U.S. cities—

the one in Boston was called the Watch and Ward Society. All the societies were designed to protect the young from being exposed to the evils of prostitution and narcotics. They were also to be protected against the potent effect of "vulgar and degrading" crime books, as well as such hoary erotic classics as *Fanny Hill, Only a Boy,* and *The Lustful Turk.* The vice societies made no effort to harass the trade publishing industry, for this industry was completely self-censored. No publishing house in New York, Boston, or Philadelphia would dream of publishing anything that would disturb the sensibilities of Victorian readers. When the Boston publisher James Osgood discovered that the Watch and Ward Society disliked Walt Whitman's *Leaves of Grass,* he simply canceled the contract. Purity, if such it can be called, prevailed in American letters to a degree that many would now find perplexing. There was virtually no eroticism in books published in the United States—in fact, there was little literary sign at all that the sexes were physically attracted to each other. If any writer dared to demonstrate that this might be the case, the editorial blue pencil was poised to eliminate the source of possible complaint. The depiction of everyday life in most contexts was considered to be unsuited to literature. One prominent American, Julia Ward Howe, author of "The Battle Hymn of the Republic," once published a definition of the tasks assigned to literature:

> [It] . . . must bring pure and beautiful ideals to . . . the human mind. The brutal, the violent, the excessive, do not need to be increased and multiplied in the pages of a book. . . . It becomes the guardians of society to keep a watchful eye on the press.

Many agreed with her, and the vice societies prevailed with the approval and support of the church, the police, and most educated Americans. What was to change Howe's definition was the entirely different world about to be found in the novels and plays of

Theodore Dreiser, Eugene O'Neill, and Sherwood Anderson—all three on Horace's list.

In the years between the turn of the century and the beginning of the First World War, a number of public-spirited individuals—the people who financed and staffed the vice societies—regarded prostitution and venereal disease as moral rather than social problems. It took little time to establish a connection between the reading of "bad books" and sexual promiscuity. The formula was simple: If we can just rid ourselves of these bad books, we will be eliminating the twin social blights of prostitution and venereal disease. The leaders of the vice societies were able to persuade political reform Progressives to join them in their campaign against bad books. The suppression of such books became, in their eyes, an act of social hygiene.

It was Anthony Comstock, a crude and bumbling man, who founded the New York Society for the Suppression of Vice in 1873, thereby creating the word that has characterized literary prudery ever since. There is a tradition that the word was uttered in anger by George Bernard Shaw when, having been accused of writing filth, he shouted at his accusers, "Comstockery!" Comstock ruled the Society until his death in 1915, when his successor, John S. Sumner, was appointed secretary. Like Horace, Sumner had also been a stockbroker before taking up his life's work of searching out and destroying what he considered noxious. As Mencken defined him, Sumner was the new "snouter" for the Society. Unlike Comstock, Sumner had at least a semblance of rationality in his fear and loathing of what he called "smut." He was capable of telling writers and their publishers just exactly where they had gone wrong and strayed from the path of purity. But he could be accommodating, as in the famous *"Genius"* case, when Sumner agreed to sit down with H. L. Mencken and together remove the objectionable passages from Dreiser's novel. When they had nearly finished their work, both men were shocked to discover that Horace had announced (with Dreiser's permission) a complete and unabridged edition of the novel that Sumner had forced its original publisher to remove from sale in 1916. Strangely enough, he took no action against the complete text of the book he had spent weeks bowdlerizing with Dreiser's closest literary friend.

At the beginning of the twenties, Sumner had two publishers targeted for prosecution over the "filthy" items they were offering the public: Horace Liveright and Toby Seltzer. Seltzer's crimes included publishing (under his own imprint) the limited edition of D. H. Lawrence's *Women in Love,* Arthur Schnitzler's *Casanova's Homecoming,* and the anonymous *Diary of a Young Girl.* Until Seltzer's time, most publishers caved in immediately when the Society attacked a book—this was the case with a Polish novel by Stanisław Przybyskewski, *Homo Sapiens,* published by Alfred Knopf in his first year of business. Upon being summoned to court to defend his book, Knopf capitulated and agreed to destroy all the existing stock and melt down the plates. As a relatively poor young publisher, Knopf could see no way to challenge Sumner's authority. But Seltzer thought times were changing and decided to fight the case. After obtaining expert testimony about the literary quality of the three books in question, he won his case and all three were cleared. It was the first serious setback for Sumner and his Society—they *could* be defeated if the case were brought into court and fought vigorously.

It was Horace, however, who proved to be Sumner's nemesis in the courts. The two men struggled over the legal right to publish half a dozen books, with Horace winning most of the battles. He encountered Sumner's wrath on so many occasions that he placed the law firm that employed Arthur Garfield Hays, the famous trial lawyer, on a retainer basis. Hays took a special delight in defending clients whose freedom was being curtailed in any way whatever. After a series of court cases, Horace eventually commissioned Hays to write an account of them—the result was *Let Freedom Ring*

(1928), a book that is still cited for its revelations about how con-
stitutional freedoms can be successfully defended; it is still in print.

When Sergei Eisenstein began working with Horace in
Hollywood in 1930, he was initially put off by Horace's reputation
in Europe as a publisher of "off-color" books, books that would be
considered innocuous today but in the twenties excited the wrath of
the professional smut hunters, who saw no difference between writers like Dreiser and Petronius on the one hand and run-of-the-mill
pornography on the other. Horace's reputation as a publisher of
erotica began with B&L's publication in 1920 of James Huneker's
first and only novel, *Istar, Daughter of Sin*. Huneker, an important
music and art critic of the day, had expected that his regular publisher, Scribner's, would take the book, but when they read the
manuscript they demanded cuts in the story about the literary and
artistic world of New York and Paris. The book recounts the activities of a Wagnerian soprano called "Istar" who deliberately
debauches a theological student. Other characters included a young
prostitute and Moana Milton, identified as a "maternal nymphoma-
niac." Huneker had embedded his tale in a thick crust of talk about
Henry James, Petronius, Ibsen, Rémy de Gourmont, and Stendhal.
It made little difference: Huneker's book was unpublishable as submitted to Scribner's or any other trade publisher in New York.

Huneker included Tommy Smith among his close friends, and it
was he who now decided that B&L was the logical house for the
book. He suggested issuing it with the words "privately printed" on
the title page and the entire edition to be sold at ten dollars a copy
on a subscription basis. Every copy of the book they now called
Painted Veils was sold prior to publication. Smith had stumbled onto
this manner of publishing books whenever they were in danger of
suppression through his long association with the Irish novelist
George Moore. In England, Moore's publisher, William Heine-
mann, had introduced the practice of issuing nearly all of the later
Moore titles on a subscription basis. The idea was to convince

would-be censors that this method of publishing kept the book out of the reach of the general public—it was to be a collector's item for those who could afford it.

Two years later, Horace and Smith took the same approach with a work from antiquity—W. C. Firebaugh's unexpurgated translation of Petronius's *Satyricon*—in two volumes and priced this time at an extraordinary thirty dollars, perhaps three or four hundred dollars in 1990 dollars. Sumner became aware of the book's publication and employed a novel approach in dealing with publishers who used the "privately printed" scheme. Manuel Komroff recalled that Sumner's efforts were aided unwittingly by the greed of one of B&L's clerical employees, one Harry Salzman, who made a practice of buying at top discount several copies of books he thought would increase in value. One day a Sumner agent appeared at B&L to purchase a copy of the *Satyricon* and was told that it was now out of print but that perhaps Harry might be able to help. He did just that by selling the visitor a set of the books for a price in excess of the published one. Harry was then presented with a summons for selling obscene material directly to the general public. It demanded the presence of Tommy Smith and Horace in Magistrate Charles Oberwager's court. Arthur Garfield Hays attempted to have the case dismissed on the grounds that such an expensive book could in no way interfere with the morals of the general public. But the magistrate insisted that the case must be heard.

The *Satyricon* of Petronius is a Roman work dating from the middle of the first century A.D., composed of fragments of prose and poetry. Only a small part of the work has survived, but these fragments give us a vivid re-creation of life in the days of Nero. The best-known section is that of a fantastic dinner given by the ostentatious *nouveau riche* Trimalchio.* There is a considerable amount of talk about sex in the surviving fragments, much of it

---

*At one point in 1925, F. Scott Fitzerald thought of calling *The Great Gatsby Trimalchio in West Egg.*

unabashedly homosexual, and until Horace's edition, no one had dared to publish an unexpurgated text. Sumner was convinced that Petronius was a danger to the mental health of Americans in 1922.

When Tommy Smith was asked by Magistrate Oberwager just what the *Satyricon* was all *about,* he was able to tell him something about its importance as a work of literature. The judge's reply was short: "I suppose I have to take your word for all this?" Smith replied, "Give me two weeks. . . . I'll prove it to you."

> In two weeks we were back. . . . I had gone to various libraries and to friends and we came into Magistrate Oberwager's court with over 80 [critical works]. Books in Latin, French, English, Dutch, Swedish. . . . Liveright and . . . Hays helped me take them out of the cartons and pile them on Magistrate Oberwager's desk.

The sheer bulk of so many testimonials to the literary value of the *Satyricon* convinced the magistrate: all charges against the book were dismissed, and the magistrate's opinion was soon published by Horace in pamphlet form. In his brief, Oberwager had some important things to say about literary censorship:

> the mere existence of isolated passages is not of itself sufficient to condemn a literary work as falling within the prohibitive pale, for, if such were the rule, an attack could be launched at almost every classic on the shelves of our libraries. . . . If one is to condemn simply because of the existence of isolated passages of obscenity, we are to condemn to a fate of obliteration Shakespeare, Chaucer, Voltaire, Rousseau, Boccaccio, Balzac, Flaubert, Zola, and even the Bible.

He implicitly attacked the standards of judgment exercised by Sumner:

> Judge Charles A. Ober-
> wager's decision rendered
> in the Magistrate's Court
> of the City of New York in
> dismissing the complaint
> of Mr. Sumner, Secretary
> of the New York Society
> for the Suppression of
> Vice, against Boni & Live-
> right, who were charged
> with violation of Section
> 1141 of the penal law of the
> State of New York for
> publishing "The Saty-
> ricon of Patronius
> Arbiter."

Judge Oberwager's
Satyricon decision, 1922.
Liveright Publishing Corp., W. W.
Norton Co.

The works of art and literature of an ancient age cannot be judged by modern standards. The good of possessing those literary and cultural records of the past that constitute the very spiritual continuity of civilization cannot be outweighed by any imaginary evil that is alleged against the Satyricon.

Oberwager concluded his decision with a plea for freedom of expression:

To suppress the Satyricon is to suppress one of the two extant* Latin novels of the post-classical age . . . and thereby depriving stu-

*The other is probably Apuleius's *Golden Ass*.

dents of any knowledge of the actual life of the Roman people. AS LITERATURE IS AN INTERPRETATIVE DESCRIPTION OF HUMAN LIFE, IT CANNOT LIMIT ITSELF TO THE INTERPRETATION OF ONE SIDE OF HUMAN NATURE ONLY, FOR OTHERWISE IT WOULD DEFEAT ITS OWN AIM OF TRUTH AND POWER. Upon the facts and the law, the summons are dismissed and the defendants are discharged.

Sumner refused to accept the decision, and took his complaint to the district attorney of Manhattan, who handed the matter to the city's chief magistrate, William McAdoo, hoping that he would appeal Oberwager's acquittal. Unexpectedly, McAdoo refused to push the case, telling reporters that any further attempts by the vice society to suppress the *Satyricon* would only serve to encourage people to purchase the book. Undaunted, the district attorney then convened a grand jury as a preliminary step on the road to a trial of Liveright and Smith. Horace then demonstrated what his enemies decried as his "Barnumism," by announcing that he would supply all twenty-three members of the grand jury with personal copies of his expensive book so that they could read it at their leisure. By the time the jurors had been selected, however, someone recalled that no further copies of the *Satyricon* were now available. It was then agreed that the jury would have to spend two hours a day in court listening to the entire work read aloud—a task guaranteed to take at least a week. At this point, the district attorney gave up trying to suppress Petronius; Horace had won.

(2)

[The Clean Books League law will be] horse-high, pig-tight and bull-strong.

—John Ford, 1923

SUMNER realized that a radically new way must be found to combat the filthy publishing practices of men like Horace Liveright and Toby Seltzer. In the early twenties, conservatives became more and more incensed about the seemingly ever-increasing flow of literary material being published that dealt openly with sex. If Sumner's Society managed to drag a book into the courts, the charges against it were frequently dismissed by the adroit legal maneuvering of lawyers like Arthur Garfield Hays. To cope with this situation, a Clean Books League bill was presented to the New York State legislature in 1923, a bill which would have effectively created an ironclad instrument for censorship in the world of book and magazine publishing. The principal force opposed to this all-out threat to intellectual freedom was Horace Liveright, exercising his "firebrand" qualities to the utmost. He was in a particularly advantageous position to do so. In the spring of 1923 there were no B&L titles currently under attack by the Society. This fact was of great importance for his credibility as a disinterested individual.

The impetus for a Clean Books League bill began with the deep anguish felt by John Ford, a sixty-year-old Roman Catholic justice of the New York Supreme Court. Early in 1923 he had become aware of something that stirred his wrath to warlike proportions. His sixteen-year-old daughter had borrowed a copy of D. H. Lawrence's *Women in Love* from a lending library and found parts of the book puzzling. She turned for answers to her mother, who preferred to pass the book on to her husband. Ford later commented on his initial reaction to the book: "If that book dealer had been in reach of my hands at that moment, I should have done him bodily harm." Turning to the police for assistance, Ford discovered that they could do nothing to help him. It was not long, however, before he encountered Sumner and members of his Society, who realized at once that they had made contact with a valuable asset in their campaign.

War plans were quickly drawn up when the Society held a conclave of interested parties at a New York hotel. Among those attending were emissaries from the Roman Catholic Archdiocese, the Boy Scouts, the Girl Scouts, the Knights of Columbus, the Salvation Army, the Colonial Dames of America, and a half dozen other organizations. The outcome of the meeting was the declared intention of creating a Clean Books League, which would attempt to create legislation to wipe out the poison emanating from New York publishers. Within a month or so, the Jesse-Cotillo bill had been drawn up and rushed through the Assembly without challenge; the Senate gave the bill two readings, and it was shortly to be put to the vote.

The Clean Books League bill, actually an amendment to the existing obscenity law of New York, was unlike previously formulated ones in regard to obscenity cases in that an indictment against a book could be undertaken on the basis of any *part* of the book without regard to the rest of the book. In addition, jury trials would become mandatory under the provisions of the bill. To make absolutely sure that cases might not be lost, the bill rejected any notion of expert testimony as to the merits of the work—the opinion of the vice society would suffice to establish the fact of obscenity. Lastly, the bill stipulated that a "filthy or disgusting" book could be suppressed even if it were not sexually stimulating. It meant, in fact, that almost anything could be suppressed at the will of the New York Society for the Suppression of Vice—that free speech and expression were about to be banned in New York State.

It now seems bizarre that no other publishing house worked with Horace to organize opposition to the passage of the bill, which was a dead certainty. For the better part of two months, Horace spent huge amounts of his time and money fighting for a cause that the people in his own industry failed to support. Horace had outlined in detail what exactly was in the bill to John Hiltman of Appleton, the president of the principal book publishers' organization at the time, the National Association of Book Publishers. The Appleton Company refused to send any delegates to Albany to show its opposition; its decision was supported by four other prominent New York houses. The prevailing wisdom in the trade was that it was foolish to go against what appeared to be a national groundswell of popular opinion that supported some kind of censorship; it was politically incorrect to be against this threat to freedom. The bottom line appeared to be, "If you are against this bill, you must be *in favor of* dirty books, yes?" Only two houses in New York opposed what was happening: Harcourt, Brace and Putnam's, with George Palmer Putnam actually expressing support for Horace.

Although *The New York Times* came out unequivocally against the bill, most New York book publishers remained aloof and noncommittal. Was there perhaps another reason for Horace's almost complete lack of support in an endeavor that concerned every publisher in New York? There is evidence to indicate that literary anti-Semitism played some role in the book trade's reluctance to attack something so threatening to their survival. The publishers most frequently indicted on obscenity charges were Liveright, Toby Seltzer, and Ben Huebsch. Manuel Komroff, the production manager for B&L, reports that one of their salesmen encountered support for the bill among the old-guard salesmen who resented the new, radical houses:

> Some of the book salesmen who sell Brentanos are as mad as hell. They say it's those cheap little publishers, who have been springing up from nowhere, that cause all of the trouble in the book business. The old publishers have been established a hundred years and now these new boys are poaching on their preserve . . . the old publishers would be happy to have a bill that would prevent the circulation of the kind of books these fellows are printing. They're all goddam Jews!

The salesman told Komroff that he had heard the same complaint from a variety of sources.

Horace had tried the Authors' League of America and came up against the same resistance. In fact, there were some prominent individual writers who openly supported the bill, Booth Tarkington and Hamlin Garland among them. A widely read magazine article by Mary Austin, famous for her books about the American Southwest, may shed some light on their behavior. Austin deplored the disappearance in literature of the "love tradition of the Anglo-American strain . . . [which] touches more and higher planes of consciousness, than the love life of any other socially coordinated group." The tradition was "asphyxiated in the fumes of half-assimilated and fermenting racial contributions." She attributed this to "Semitic" writers: It was the "peasant" sexuality of these Baltic and Slavic writers that made their eroticism so unhealthy.

In May at the annual meeting of the American Booksellers' Association in Detroit, the issue of the pending bill was raised; an older member spoke in favor of it. Only one younger (and courageous) local bookseller declared that it was not the job of booksellers to dictate the taste of their customers. His remarks about the evils of censorship were stricken from the official record of the convention. At the annual convention of the American Library Association, a young librarian stood up to declare that it was not the duty of members of her profession to exclude books "on the grounds of their possible moral effect on mature readers." But, again, there were few in agreement with her.

The only support Horace could muster came from two of the most prominent magazine publishers: William Randolph Hearst and Bernarr Macfadden, both of whom were aware that John S. Sumner was just as much against *True Confessions* as he was against D. H. Lawrence. At this point, Horace may have recalled some of the lessons he had learned from the original opinion molder,

Edward Bernays. The opinions to be swayed now, in 1923, were those of men who had been elected to public office in the State of New York—how could they be reached effectively? The method was clear—through the influence of the most politically knowledgeable man in the state, Democratic minority leader James ("Jimmy") Walker or, as his biographer Gene Fowler called him, Beau James. Horace and Walker had much in common. Both men had yearned for theatrical success; both had written lyrics for shows. They were both songwriters—Walker is best known for his "Will You Love Me in December As You Do in May?" Horace and Walker were impeccable dressers, even thought of as dandies by some. Like Horace, Walker carried a walking stick on most occasions. Both men can fairly be said to have epitomized the American twenties. The biggest talent they shared was their mastery of the art of publicity.

Walker happened to be a member of the same law firm as Arthur Garfield Hays. Horace now had two superbly skilled legal talents working with him to overturn what had become a tidal wave of support for the bill. Horace had already taken a public stand in an article he published in a widely read magazine, *The Independent:*

> The absurdity of censorship lies mainly in its application. *Only* the highest quality of intellect and understanding is capable of acting as a censor, and it is obvious that no man nor woman of fine intelligence will act in any way as a censor of the arts; therefore such activity is left in the power of those individuals who have little, if any, sense of value in literature, drama.

He concluded with words that few would challenge today:

> A censorship over literature . . . is stupid, ignorant, and impudent, and is against the fundamental social principles of all intelligent

Americans. There is no place for such crudity in our present civilization, and even the most conservative press and individual opinion have expressed themselves against it most emphatically. Who is
really in favor of it?

Jimmy Walker would recall these last words in the remarkable
performance he gave before the State Assembly in Albany.

Walker apparently preferred to keep his plan of attack on the
bill to himself, allowing Horace to go his own way. Horace was
convinced that he might attract some degree of attention with the
personal appearance in Albany of some of his more celebrated and
articulate writers. He asked Gertrude Atherton—his best-selling
author and the *grande dame* of American letters—to talk to John
Ford and the committee that had written the bill. Mrs. Atherton
said that she had read Boccaccio's *Decameron* at the age of sixteen
and had not understood all of it but that even if she had, "What
harm does the book do that hasn't already been done?" John Ford
was shocked and enraged.

Horace then booked an entire parlor car on the New York Central railway to transport a group of writers. This time the cast
included Theodore Dreiser, Waldo Frank, Edgar Lee Masters, a
reporter from the Hearst papers, and the invaluable Mrs.
Atherton. When Jimmy Walker saw this motley group at the State
Capitol, he is reported to have asked its leader, "For God's sake,
Horace, what did you bring these nuts for?" Walker made it clear
that there was no chance for any of the visitors to address the
assemblymen; they could present their views to the members of a
committee created at that very moment by the ever resourceful
Walker.

Walker exploited Horace's fondness for gambling for the cause.
So he arranged for Horace to play at the Ten Eyck Hotel with those
congressmen who would be pivotal in the coming vote on the bill.
He thought that Horace's losses in a series of rigged card games

might gain a necessary vote or two. Horace consented and agreed to lose steadily to the politicians, who enjoyed taking a presumably rich New York publisher "to the cleaners." His cash kept running out, and he was forced to call his chief accountant in New York for additional funds which were dispatched daily by messenger.

Even so, Walker was not at all optimistic about defeating the bill. The night before the votes were to be cast (May 22), he gave Horace a visitor's pass to the gallery above the main floor. The next morning,

> Promptly at ten o'clock the clerk began reading the roll and one by one the members replied. . . . Jimmy Walker's name was called but there was no response. Liveright was worried. He thought perhaps Walker had had a long night of drinking and therefore could not appear. When the clerk finished reading the roll call he went back to the few members who had not replied . . . but when Walker's name was called there was again no reply.
>
> It was then announced that the first order of business would be the voting on the Clean Books Bill. As soon as these words were spoken the folding doors at the back of the hall flung open and Jimmy Walker moved swiftly down the aisle. . . . "What's going on here!" he called in a loud voice. "Voting on the Clean Books Bill," some [one] replied. "Point of order," called Walker in a loud voice. "Mr. Chairman . . . no one has yet said a word against this measure. And as a special privilege I now ask for 60 seconds to tell the assembly how I feel about this bill."

He launched into a spirited, witty attack on those who would prevent the public from reading what they chose to read. He began by appealing to the men's feelings about their mothers:

> There is not one among us who cannot tell the story of my dad's sweetheart who afterward became Dad's wife, and who lived in days when there were as many salacious books as there are today

and who for all that grew into a life of saintliness and went down to her last resting place just as clean and pure in mind and heart as the day she was born. That is all there is to this talk about books of the kind against which this bill is directed ruining our young girls. They haven't got to read them if proper influences dominate their homes.

Although short, his speech contained a magical sentence that has lingered on for most of this century as a succinct summing up of what's foolish about censorship. His next paragraph began with the bombshell *"No woman was ever ruined by a book."* [Emphasis added.] The assembly burst into tumultuous laughter.

It is one of those strong men who are worrying about salacious books in the hands of little girls who are ruining them. This debate makes me think of the Volstead Act and in connection with that of how many vote one way and drink another. Some of the best tellers of shabby stories in this Senate have been worrying their hearts out during the debate today about somebody reading something which may not be good for him or her.

From that moment, there was little doubt about which way things would go: The bill was defeated by a coalition of New York City Democrats and conservative upper New York State Republicans—the vote was fifteen votes for the measure and thirty-one against. Although this was a solid victory for the anticensorship forces, Sumner and Ford introduced new versions of the bill in 1924 and yet again in 1925, but each time it was defeated by a larger margin.

Horace was given a testimonial dinner attended by most of New York literary society, although some believed that Horace organized it himself. Even H. L. Mencken attended the affair at the Brevoort Hotel on Fifth Avenue on the night of June 14, 1923. For a brief moment Horace was the hero of the hour—the man who had said "no" and won. The Dinner Committee included Eugene O'Neill, Burton Rascoe, Heywood Broun, Elmer Davis, Fannie Hurst, and Lawrence Langner. The 150 guests were just as notable: Zoë Akins, Carl Van Vechten, and Ernest Boyd among them. Horace chose this occasion to announce B&L's resignation from the National Association of Book Publishers, which had denied him assistance. The chief speaker of the evening was Jimmy Walker, who graciously paid full tribute to Horace as the main force behind the bill's defeat. Edward Bernays enjoyed himself so much that he didn't want the evening to end:

> After the speeches, libations and general rejoicing at the bill's defeat, I commandeered the party and all of us, including the musicians, walked half a block to our home at 44 Washington Mews, where we carried on merriment through the night. At one point a policeman knocked at the door and warned us to quiet down. I beckoned to the leader of the senate majority, James J. Walker,   ·
> known later as the Party or Night Mayor of New York. He walked to the door with me, grinned, and the policeman saluted the senator and moved on.

(3)

Certainly we cannot go as far as Liveright is willing to.
—Maxwell Perkins to F. Scott Fitzgerald, May 10, 1927

BY 1926, Horace's reputation as the bravest, most unpredictable publisher in America was publicly proclaimed in Waldo Frank's profile of him in the pages of the recently established *New Yorker*. Frank created an imaginary argument with a supposedly irate reader:

"What! *this man?* . . . During the war he brought out the best revolutionary and pacifistic books that he could muster. He has sponsored half the advanced novelists who pollute our homes, half the radical thinkers who defile our customs, half the free verse poets who corrupt our English.

"He has defiantly come out for minorities in a land where the Majority is sacred. He has fought such noble democratic measures as Censorship, as Clean Book Bills—and with his own money! money doubtless ill-begot through the sale of works by renegades like Debs and Dreiser. He stands, first and last, for the Revolt of our misled youth against every proper tradition of the land. . . . He has popularized Petronius, Nietzsche, Moore! He has been indicted by the State of New York for a subversive publication. And you entitle a sketch of him *100 per cent American!* . . . Sir, how dare you?"

Frank concluded that one had to accept Horace's methods of publishing even if they seemed out of keeping with what he published: "HBL can sponsor a book like a lover of the truth and sell it like a patent medicine hawker. He has done more to put 'life' into the literary market than any of his fellows."

Horace occasionally defended some of his books that he didn't particularly like, Maxwell Bodenheim's being prime examples. Bodenheim is virtually unknown today, although his murder in Greenwich Village at the hands of a half-deranged vagrant made national headlines in 1954. He had by then reached the end of a long period of decline into alcoholism and poverty and was reduced to eking out a living selling his poems to passersby in the streets for a dollar a poem. Horace had known him well in better days when both Pound and Eliot thought that Bodenheim had a genuine poetic gift.

In the early twenties, as part of his bookselling rounds in Chicago, Horace became acquainted with Bodenheim as well as

Maxwell Bodenheim in the twenties.
Warder Collection, W. W. Norton Co.

Ben Hecht. The two dominated the so-called Chicago Renaissance with their fiery personalities, and both became B&L authors. Hecht's lush but now virtually unreadable fiction published by Horace included novels such as *Count Bruga,** *Gargoyles, Humpty Dumpty,* and *The Florentine Dagger.* Hecht's sales were respectable,

*Hecht and Bodenheim later quarreled bitterly, and they wrote novels about each other: *Count Bruga* concerns Bodenheim, who then wrote *Duke Herring* in retaliation.

but eventually he quarreled with Horace. His departure from B&L was close to the end of his novel-writing career; in 1926 he left for Hollywood, where he became the highest-paid screenwriter of the 1930s. A year after Horace's death, Hecht wrote, produced, and directed a venomous film about him: *The Scoundrel*.

Bodenheim was as fiery as Hecht but with a difference. Unlike the strictly commercial Hecht, Bodenheim regarded himself first and last as a poet and only wrote his sexy novels to support himself. These novels are now as unreadable as Hecht's, but in their day they were considered naughty enough to incur the wrath of John S. Sumner, who decided to take action against Bodenheim's 1926 *Replenishing Jessica*. With Arthur Garfield Hays as his attorney, Horace had to defend himself on obscenity charges for having published what was actually a dull, rather innocuous book.

The *Jessica* case might never have come to trial had not Horace made a series of determined efforts to restage a suppressed French play, *The Captive*, by Édouard Bourdet. This highly praised drama about a woman's discovery that she is a lesbian was shut down by the New York City Police Department after a successful run of several months. *The Captive*, a serious work, was accorded exactly the same treatment as Mae West's travesty *Sex*—both plays were "raided" by the police, who brought the entire casts down to the station house for questioning about their appearances in the allegedly obscene works. Disturbed that a work of this quality could be closed down so easily, Horace set out to restore *The Captive* to the New York stage. He obtained the production rights to restage it and he also attempted to get an injunction against the police department that would effectively prevent a second closing. After months of angry negotiations with the authorities, Horace realized that he would never persuade them to grant the injunction; *The Captive* never reopened. But Horace's efforts to restage the work had annoyed the then acting mayor of New York, Joseph McKee, who decided that he could retaliate against Horace by reopening a two-year-old indictment of *Replenishing Jessica* which had been dropped by the city in the wake of Sumner's various defeats in the courts. Horace, Tommy Smith, and Bodenheim were named as defendants.

Both Tommy Smith and Bodenheim were quickly set aside as parties in the case. Horace stood trial alone as the "offender against common decency." In later years Arthur Garfield Hays became internationally famous for his brilliant courtroom strategies, and the *Jessica* case demonstrated one of them. Since the jury was to consider whether or not the novel was obscene, why not have them hear every word of it from the lips of the prosecution? Surprisingly, Judge Charles C. Nott agreed, and the reading by the prosecution's team of the 272-page novel began. The case had by this time attracted the attention of the New York daily papers, whose reporters flocked to Judge Nott's courtroom. Headlines proclaimed the novelty of having an entire novel read aloud to a jury. What the jury heard was not perhaps what it expected in the way of lubricious entertainment: *Replenishing Jessica* was just a dull, plodding account of a woman's quest for fulfillment. The novel was so vapid that Judge Nott was hard pressed to keep his jurors awake. *The New York Evening Telegram* noted that one juror was caught napping; another sat there listening but holding his head in his hands. When Horace begged to be excused from the afternoon's reading session, the jurors demanded that they, too, be excused. When the last page had been turned, Horace took the stand in his own defense. He explained that many editorial changes had been made in Bodenheim's manuscript, mostly deletions, in order to make the book suitable for publication. He mentioned that Tommy Smith had done much of the editing. The assistant district attorney asked Horace if Smith was the same man who had compiled the *Poetica Erotica* that he had published. His question provoked Judge Nott, who abruptly declared: "I'm not going to have another book read at this trial!" He then allowed the jury to retire;

their verdict of "not guilty" required only fifteen minutes of delib-
eration. *Jessica* was soon back in the stores and eventually sold
about 30,000 copies.

Despite the hilarious aspects of the *Jessica* case, and the considerable amounts of money involved in legal fees and the time spent in
court, Horace considered all such defense efforts well worth it: he
was changing the temper of the times. Prosecutors would now
think twice about bringing novels into court.

The Voice of Love:
Sherwood Anderson

Yet there were a few moments when [Anderson] spoke, as
almost no one else among American writers, with the voice
of love.

— Irving Howe, 1951

(1)

As if the fates wished to recompense him for the ceaseless
warfare he experienced in dealing with Dreiser, Horace was
rewarded in his relationship with Sherwood Anderson. With
Anderson there was none of the distrust, suspicion, and outright
hatred that characterized the ups and downs of Horace's thirteen
years of struggle with B&L's moody star author. Oddly enough,
however, there were eerie resemblances between the careers of
the two writers that became apparent only during Horace's last
years with the firm. But Horace and Anderson liked and respected
each other from the start. Anderson always remained aware that it
was Horace who had made him, if only briefly, a best-selling
writer.

Unlike the pensive, sour Dreiser, Anderson possessed an ineffa-
ble openness and sweetness that made him attractive to nearly

everyone—even to Dreiser, who had little good to say about most writers. He struck many as a nonliterary type; Faulkner thought he resembled a riverboat gambler, while others saw in him a man who might know more about horses than about editors and publishers. Perhaps it was because of this fact that Bertrand Russell found him so fascinating: an American novelist who conveyed the impression that he might be in touch with feelings beyond words.

Because of the stark simplicity of his style, Anderson was considered to be a writer's writer. His work usually appeared in the pages of the tiny-circulation, avant-garde literary magazines of the day: *The Seven Arts* and *The Dial*. He was able to write novels only after he walked out of his job in advertising; he published his first novel, *Windy McPherson's Son,* in 1916, when he was forty. He followed that with a second the following year: *Marching Men*. The appearance in 1919 of *Winesburg, Ohio,* under the B. W. Huebsch imprint, established Anderson as a major figure in modern American writing, although essentially he was read only by other authors. Huebsch then published *Poor White, The Triumph of the Egg,* and *Horses and Men,* thereby consolidating Anderson's reputation in America. Despite the radical books he published, Ben Huebsch was actually far more backward in merchandising than many of his more conservative competitors. His methods were especially ineffective when attempting to launch a talent not likely to please a mass audience. Anderson found it impossible to support himself through his book earnings. Although he admired Ben Huebsch and was grateful to him for continuing to bring out his books despite their poor sales, by 1924 he began to think he might have to take his books elsewhere.

In his *Memoirs* Anderson spoke of Huebsch's methods of doing business. He sarcastically claimed that his publisher had taken two-inch advertisements in both *The New Republic* and *The Nation* to announce *Winesburg,* advising their readers to get the book from their local public library! Despite Huebsch's willingness to publish daring writers like James Joyce, he failed to promote them. According to Anderson, his sales force consisted of a single traveler, a "cockney Englishman . . . [who] would open the door of a book store, stick his head in and say, 'You don't want any tosh books, do you?' Evidently they nearly all said they didn't." In addition, Huebsch had qualms about touting his wares, preferring merely to announce their existence. When he did advertise one of Anderson's later titles, *A Story Teller's Story,* Huebsch avoided using any of the superb reviews the book had received, thus incurring the wrath of Horace's brother Otto, who became the novelist's literary agent in the early twenties: "It is beyond my understanding. He may think there is some violation of the proprieties in selling the book in this way but I am pretty careful myself and I can tell you that quotations from these wonderful criticisms would be used by every decent publisher."

Anderson was a familiar name at B&L: Horace had included *Winesburg* in the Modern Library as early as 1922, only three years after its original publication. In 1923 Tommy Smith had commissioned Anderson to write a preface to the ML edition of Dreiser's *Free and Other Stories.* By late 1924 it was clear that Huebsch's pitiful campaign to sell *A Story Teller's Story* had failed and that the book would wind up by selling as badly as had all the others. Aware that Anderson had a novel under way, Horace wrote him a seductive letter:

What I would like to do is this, Sherwood. Read the manuscript of the [new] novel . . . come down to New Orleans and talk the whole situation over with you. I think I can convince you that I'm your man. I don't pretend to either legerdemain or necromancy but I have in a short time built up the best book organization in the country. . . . I don't want to take the long New Orleans trip unless I have an even chance. . . . I know all about your relations with Huebsch and I, too, am fond of him and don't think anyone can accuse me of ever having played the game anything but fairly. After all, though, business is business. It is your business to write books and it is your publisher's business to sell lots of them.

Horace's attempt to sway Anderson failed, for the writer's loyalty to Huebsch was strong:

The truth is I would just find it too hard and uncomfortable for me to make a change. When I started to do it last year I felt like a dog. I wanted to do it and at the same time didn't want to. . . . There is no question of your not doing the right thing by Ben [Huebsch]. It was me who opened the ball with you but, really, I guess in doing so I wasn't quite myself.

But Anderson left the door open by concluding his refusal with an invitation: "I hate not to make it seem necessary for you to run down to New Orleans. It's a great town really and you would like it. Why don't you come anyway."

Horace graciously refused the ambivalent invitation:

I am heart-broken not to have a valid excuse to get to New Orleans at this time. But I have a funny conscience that will amuse you when you get to know it better. I simply couldn't come down now realizing what the situation is.

But Anderson remained a prize that Horace was determined to win for the B&L list. Apparently abandoning his conscience problem of the previous autumn, he arrived in New Orleans in March 1925, accompanied by Lucille. The Liverights were visiting New Orleans as part of their vacation trip—a trip motivated by what appears to have been a final attempt to save their failing marriage.

Horace's heavy drinking and his hard-to-conceal affairs were the two main factors that plagued the Liveright marriage. Horace's letters written to Lucille at this time reveal a steadily worsening atmosphere between them. Hoping to repair the damage, the Liverights decided on a whirlwind vacation trip through the Deep South, with New Orleans as the last stop before returning to New York. Perhaps some time spent together without the children might help them. Their initial meeting with Anderson on Bourbon Street in the French Quarter—a chance one, according to Anderson—did not serve to dispel the marital tensions:

> So one day I was walking in one of the streets of New Orleans and there was Horace Liveright. He had come down there. He was striding along with a beautiful woman on his arm. Horace was famous for his women, that I knew. I had already, on many occasions seen him with many women and they were always beautiful. He stopped and introduced me to the woman he had brought with him to New Orleans.
>   "Meet Mrs. Liveright," he said and I laughed.
>   "But why does he do this to me?" I thought.
>   "I'll not let him get away with it," I thought.
>   "Mrs. Liveright, oh yeah?" I said.
>   Well, it was Mrs. Liveright and I was sunk and so was Horace. There was an uncomfortable moment.
>   "It may have been an uncomfortable moment for you but it was more than that for me," Horace later told me.

Later that afternoon Horace talked with Anderson in a café in the Quarter and made an offer that "took [his] breath away." It was a simple one: in order for Anderson to devote himself entirely to the writing of fiction and stop wasting his energies writing low-paying articles, B&L would agree to pay him $100 a week for a period of five years. These weekly payments would accrue against all the Anderson books that the firm published—whatever their nature. It was an extraordinary offer—in modern terms a quarter-of-a-million-dollar contract that gave him the freedom to write what he pleased. Horace was principally interested in his fiction but was willing to go all the way with Anderson in order to get his future novels. In short, Sherwood Anderson was to be subsidized by Horace.

Horace's pitch was irresistible: Anderson returned his signed contract to New York a week or so later, telling his new publisher that he had informed Ben Huebsch that he was leaving his firm—a decision that left Huebsch feeling betrayed. Anderson also told Horace, "I feel you are taking a gamble on me. I am going to give you the best I have in shop. . . . Now that I've come with you I want to build up in you a feeling of confidence in me."

Horace's astonishing offer was something that Anderson always regarded as a miracle. After the consistent failure of more than half a dozen books, he had been faced with his recurrent nightmare of having to return to the world of advertising to make a living, after having walked away from it in disgust a decade earlier. He had told Horace about his fears in New Orleans: "I'll have to go back there, begin again to write of tooth paste, of kidney pills, of how to keep your hair from falling out." Horace had listened carefully and it was at this point in their talk that he had made his proposition.

Under his contract with B&L, Anderson would also be earning a straight royalty of 15 percent, a more than respectable figure that was surpassed among the firm's writers only by Dreiser's 20 percent. Within a week or two of signing the agreement, Horace and Anderson began discussing the publication of his new novel, *Dark Laughter,* which Horace hoped would establish him as a best-selling American novelist. Anderson felt that the book must live up to Horace's expectations:

Since you were here I have been working on it every minute of every day, in fact have kept at it so hard and long that each day when I got through I was so exhausted I could hardly get up from my desk. All this is not because I have had any sense of hurry about

it. In the first place I believe it is largely because a certain weight
has been lifted off my shoulders for the time being, of which you
know . . . I am convinced that it is going to be a ripping novel. It
walks and sings . . . bet on this novel, Horace, it is going to be
there with a bang. . . . Keep your thumb on your ear and when you
go to bed at night say a little prayer that it is going to be as good as
I think it is going to be.

When the completed manuscript of *Dark Laughter* arrived in
New York, Horace told Anderson that, despite a few reservations
about minor matters,

Sherwood, you've written a great book. . . . After telling you that
Dark Laughter is a great book, there is nothing left for me to say
about it. Nor am I going to reiterate how hard we are going to
work to make it a big success . . . it's going to be great fun to show
the public what can be done with a Sherwood Anderson novel.

After warning him that the economy was not all that it might be
and that the great American public might just find the book a bit
over their heads, he assured Anderson that such fears left him
unmoved. Horace also prepared his new friend for revelations that
might startle him.

But please believe, my friend, that I have no failure complexes. I
haven't had any for some long time and I think I'm the gayest sin-
ner you know. When we see each other again and have a real talk,
I will expound a philosophy of life to you that may shock you a bit,
but which I'm sure you'll understand.

As the time grew nearer to the publication of *Dark Laughter,*
Horace began to imagine how Anderson was feeling down in New
Orleans: "I'll keep you posted pretty carefully on what happens on

the book, Sherwood, because you're pretty far away and must be almost as excited as I am. Business is fun sometimes, isn't it?"

Published in the early fall of 1925, just three months prior to *An American Tragedy, Dark Laughter* received mixed reviews, but with the benefit of Horace's huge advertising campaign began to sell briskly. For the first and only time in his life, Sherwood Anderson received the attention of the American public, which now began to take him seriously as a major novelist. *Dark Laughter* sold nearly 30,000 copies in its trade edition and proved again that Horace could market a literary book as well as those of his professional best-selling writers like Gertrude Atherton and "Warner Fabian" (Samuel Hopkins Adams).

Although Horace had succeeded in accomplishing what he'd set out to do—making Anderson a best-selling author—it was a sad fact that *Dark Laughter* was a relatively poor book, possessing all the faults of its predecessor, *Many Marriages.* Both books exhibit the erosion of Anderson's talent. A certain woozy sentimentality had begun to appear in his work after 1923—a quality that even affected his autobiographical book of 1924, *A Story Teller's Story.* Paradoxically, Anderson sought to express this vagueness of feeling in a language that aimed at exactitude, a futile task at best. This new softness in his writing provoked the distain of his two most distinguished pupils, Hemingway and Faulkner, who satirized it— Hemingway in a short novel, *The Torrents of Spring,* and Faulkner in an introduction that he wrote for a collection of caricatures of artists living in the French Quarter of New Orleans.

Some critics have blamed Anderson's decline on his fascination with the work of D. H. Lawrence, while others have believed he became corrupted by associating with literary people in big cities, thus losing his early natural simplicity. Certainly Anderson did become obsessed with style. Whatever the cause, Horace was faced in the next few years with the increasingly familiar problem of subsidizing a writer for whom he had the highest regard but who had—at fifty—entered a period of irreversible decline.

(2)

To Horace Liveright
Who isn't afraid to play, doesn't take life as a funeral procession, keeps going, is loyal and generous with his friends, is no moralist and gets there because he isn't afraid. . . .
—Anderson's inscription in HBL's copy of Dark Laughter

Something happened and everyone knew it.
—Raymond Carver, 1987

WITH the money he'd earned from *Dark Laughter* over and above Horace's weekly checks, Anderson bought a farm in Virginia as well as two country newspapers, one Republican and one Democratic, in nearby Marion. Here Anderson settled down to write a series of novels that would maintain his now established fame among the critics and that would sell enough copies to earn out his subsidy. But, as Carver puts it, "something happened" that prevented the realization of the dream. Anderson continued to write until the year of his death in 1941, but never again with the power and grace of *Winesburg* and the half-dozen stories that guarantee his permanent place in American writing.

The Anderson books that Horace published after *Dark Laughter* were *Sherwood Anderson's Notebook,* another autobiographical work, *Tar: A Midwest Childhood,* and a collection of poems, *A New Testament.* Only *Tar* had any appreciable sale (6,000 copies) and by the end of 1927 Anderson's debit balance with B&L had reached $1,200. Unlike Dreiser, Anderson possessed a conscience and decided he had to take action after discovering that he could not

Sherwood Anderson in the early thirties.
Liveright Publishing Corp., W. W. Norton Co.

produce books that were tied to money paid in advance. He recalled that

> I had to give it up. I took a train to New York. "Please, Horace, quit it."
>
> "Quit what," he asked.
>
> "Quit sending me that money." I tried to explain how it affected me.
>
> "But," he said, "I have made enough on the one book. I am in the clear. Why should you worry?"
>
> I had a hard time convincing him. He even became suspicious.
>
> "Are you not satisfied with me as your publisher? Is that it?"
>
> It seemed . . . impossible to him that a writer should refuse money.
>
> And so I was released.

Once his "money shackles" had been removed, Anderson felt free of the onerous burden he had borne for three years; his friendship with Horace continued to flourish. Occasionally Horace regarded Anderson as someone to whom he might confess what he believed were his failings—his worries about the number of women in his life. Anderson tried to reassure him:

> You are what you are, Horace. You like women—when they are nice, drinks, good living. So do I. I hope you have the grace not to be much concerned with sin. When it's nice. You will always have my vote. Shut up.

Anderson was of an age to regard the B&L offices as a sort of "mad house" in which excitement was the order of the day:

> When you went to see him . . . often enough the whole outer office was filled with chorus girls.

Horace . . . was putting on a musical comedy and there they were. It wouldn't have surprised me . . . to have had one of the women jump up and taking a practice swing kick my hat off. . . . Men and women were rushing in and out, phones were ringing. Horace was talking on the phone to casting agencies in regard to some show he was producing, he was buying or selling shows . . . authors were coming and going. It was a bedlam, a mad house, and yet a man felt something very gratifying in it all.

What was perhaps most gratifying was Horace's complete trust in Anderson's recommendations concerning the new writers that he brought to B&L: "And there was his check book, always at hand, often with a bottle of whiskey on the desk beside it." In later years Anderson asserted that hc had introduced the first work of both Faulkner and Hemingway to Horace, but his account may only have been correct about Faulkner.

Although disconcerted by Anderson's refusal to continue accepting his weekly subsidy, Horace was pleased to remain his publisher despite steadily decreasing sales on his new books. As Horace saw it, it was his *duty* to publish Sherwood Anderson; one day, with luck, he would produce another best-seller. Only one event disturbed their mutual satisfaction. Horace heard a rumor that Anderson had complained bitterly to the critic V. F. Calverton that B&L was not pushing his work as well as it might. The occasion was the publication in 1929 of a little book of sketches that Anderson called *Hello Towns*. The advance orders for the book totaled 1,526 copies, a new low for his work. In addition, Horace decided not to continue the established practice of issuing a limited, signed edition of his books. When Horace heard Calverton, he fired off an angry letter to Anderson in which he defended B&L's abilities to sell books. Anderson was quick to respond:

Have you gone crazy? I just got your letter about my knocking
Horace Liveright Inc. What kind of a man do you think I am. I have
never been so well used by anyone in the publishing world as by
you and everyone connected with the firm. In addition to that I
have thought of myself as your friend. . . . Who ever told you that
I have ever said anything against you or your firm. . . . What does
it matter to me whether you sell "Hello Towns" or not? Why damn
it man, don't be silly. I am your friend. For Heaven's sake write
and tell me where you got this story.

Horace had flared into explosive anger—Dreiser excepted, he
demanded complete loyalty from his authors and was deeply hurt if
he felt he was getting less than that. Apologetic, he quickly told
Anderson that the whole incident had resulted from a misunderstanding: "I quite agree with you that this shouldn't have upset me
so much because so little said in publishing circles is anything but
gossip." Playfully, Anderson responded by telling his contrite
friend,

If I were somewhat younger I would attempt to Jack Dempsey you
when I next saw you for upsetting me in this way. . . . I do not like
my friends to feel me capable of such disloyalty and you may be
sure that when I have any such feeling you shall be the first to hear
it, and direct from me.

Anderson first encountered William Faulkner in New Orleans in
1924. Meeting almost daily for several months, their friendship
blossomed as they traded tall tales. Anderson thought that Faulkner
should abandon writing newspaper sketches and turn his hand to fiction; Faulkner agreed and began a novel. Anderson had promised
Horace that he would send him the work of young writers of talent.
In hindsight, Horace's supreme gift from Anderson was the chance

to publish Faulkner's first novel, a book he called *May Day*. After its acceptance, based in part on Anderson's recommendation, someone at B&L—probably Louis Kronenberger—retitled it *Soldiers' Pay*. Published in April 1926, the book was well received and sold 2,500 copies—a sale common then for first novels.

When Anderson recommended that Horace publish Faulkner's manuscript, he carefully neglected to tell him that he had not read it himself. For by this time his friendship with the young Mississippian had cooled considerably.

Faulkner's and Anderson's friendship had come to a sudden end in 1925 and was not to be resumed until they met again in New York in 1931. What caused the strain between the two has always remained a mystery. The commonly offered explanations are clearly inadequate. The one most frequently cited is the satirical introduction Faulkner wrote for his friend William Spratling's little book of caricatures of artists living in the French Quarter, *Sherwood Anderson and Other Famous Creoles,* but this was published nearly a year after the cooling. Also too late to qualify was the mocking portrait of Anderson in Faulkner's second novel, *Mosquitoes,* published by Horace in 1927. A more likely cause of the quarrel—if it can be called that—lay in Faulkner's doubts about the older man's abilities as a writer. As far back as April 1925, while still outwardly friendly with Anderson, he had written a study of his works for a Dallas newspaper in which he accused his teacher of having an "elephantine kind of humor about himself," adding that Anderson did not have "enough active ego to write successfully about himself." Harsh words from a pupil who had published only a few sketches in one of the local papers.

Perhaps the real reason for their quarrel is Anderson's discovery that Faulkner had lied to him about the war wounds he had supposedly suffered in a plane crash on the Western Front in 1918. Anderson, believing every word of Faulkner's tale, had published a story about his meeting with the maimed aviator—the truth made him look like a fool.

But Faulkner never lost his personal regard for Anderson, and he dedicated his 1929 novel, *Sartoris,* to him with the words "TO SHER- WOOD ANDERSON through whose kindness I was first published, with the belief that this book will give him no reason to regret that fact." More important, Faulkner published in 1953 a brief study of his work in which he explained perhaps better than anyone else just what had happened to his old teacher. Faulkner pointed out that Anderson's creative drying up back in the twenties had been due to his passion for exactitude:

> The exact word and phrase within the limited scope of a vocabulary controlled and even repressed by what was in him almost a fetish of simplicity. . . . He worked so hard at this that it finally became just style: an end instead of a means: so that he presently came to believe that, provided he kept the style pure and intact and unchanged and inviolate, what the style contained would have to be first rate: it couldn't help but be first rate, and therefore himself too.

The purity of language that Anderson strove for in his later fiction is used to evoke characters who never come alive. They become mouthpieces for Anderson's notions about life; they fail absolutely as human beings.

(3)

> I am pretty sure that writing may be a way of life in itself. . . . I think the whole glory of writing lies in the fact that it forces us out of ourselves and into the lives of others. In the end the real writer becomes a lover.
> —Sherwood Anderson, 1940

IN April 1929 Anderson responded to one of Horace's querying letters by writing that he'd begun work on a new novel and that he'd probably move to a new location in order to finish it without interruption. In the initial phase of writing the book he felt that he had now lost the block that had prevented him from undertaking a long work of fiction, telling Horace, "I am feeling like a young bull, in fresh green pastures. I will tell you everything about the story when I see you." A few months later he requested Horace to begin advancing him money to complete the book, to be paid in monthly installments. He then made a curious request: "When you go to bed at night give a little pull on your left nut. This that the Gods will be good and that I will keep on writing." In reply, Horace reassured Anderson about the advance and concluded by noting, "Your bedtime suggestion for me comes just too late to be pleasurable— take that out of your eye, my boy!"

By the end of the year it appeared that Anderson had succeeded in getting close to finishing the new novel—a book he decided to call *Beyond Desire*. It had been over four years since B&L had published a new Anderson novel, and Horace became excited about the prospect; by 1929 Horace badly needed a best-seller. Just before Christmas, however, Anderson wrote Horace a rueful account of the way things were with his book:

I may have been spoofing myself and you . . . in saying that I had it about done. I did have all the scenes of the book, the people, events etc., but it did not have any real movement. . . . I think you know Horace that I have to have this book right, not only on account of its chances of success but also because of myself. I want to whip out of me this sense of deficit I have had. . . .

I wish I could say definitely that, in a week, two weeks, a month, I will be through this job but I can't. I have to take it as it flows. All I can say is that I will do nothing else, think of nothing else.

Only two days later Anderson telegraphed more bad news for
Horace:

> AM SORRY BUT WILL HAVE TO WITHDRAW PROMISE OF
> THE NOVEL FOR THIS SPRING STOP HAPPENINGS IN
> MY OWN LIFE HAVE UPSET ME AND WILL HAVE TO
> GATHER MYSELF TOGETHER STOP ANYWAY IT IS NOT
> A GOOD PIECE OF WORK STOP FORGIVE MY BEING
> OVERSURE

Horace's reply was of the kind that endeared him to Anderson:

> DEAR SHERWOOD IT'S TOO BAD ABOUT NOVEL BUT OF
> COURSE I UNDERSTAND AN AUTHOR CAN'T WRITE
> WHEN HE CAN'T STOP MAY THIS COMING YEAR BE
> THE HAPPIEST YOU HAVE HAD IN YOUR LIFE
> AFFECTIONATE GREETINGS

The truth was far worse than just having to withdraw an unfinished novel from Horace's spring list. The book that he had virtually completed was left unfinished; it has never been published.
Anderson's "happenings in my own life" probably refers to the
depression he appears to have been encountering. He drove his car
off a road in North Carolina just after telling his new, young wife,
Eleanor Copenhaver, "I wish it was all over." Although the car left
the road, it did not flip over; the Andersons were safe. Shortly after
this he wrote an old friend: "Lots of times I said to myself—why
don't I die?"

Faulkner surmised that Anderson had faced the unbearable truth
when "he found himself to be a one or two book man . . . after *Dark
Laughter,* when he had reached the point where he should have
stopped writing." But Anderson didn't stop: in the decade or so left
him, he published several collections of sketches about life in the

depression years. When things were going badly for Horace in 1930 he expressed sadness over his friend's inability to continue with his novel: "It's an awful shock to hear that you're off novels." He concluded by telling Anderson that his plans to reissue his earlier books had run aground: "The omnibus volume has been postponed for the time being, as have many other things."

The only thing that survived from the aborted novel was its title, *Beyond Desire,* used for his 1932 novel about Southern textile-mill workers. This was far below the quality of his previous books. In the early thirties Anderson confided to friends that he now wrote mainly to please his new wife, but these friends knew that the truth was deeper—Anderson went on writing in order to define himself as a human being; he *had* to write to live.

By 1933, when Horace had sold or given away nearly all his possessions, including many of the books in his once extensive library, he managed to hold on to a few that had special significance for him. One of them was the first numbered copy of the limited edition he'd published of *Dark Laughter,* which Anderson had inscribed for him, praising his courage. Anderson, too, deserves our praise for his refusal to surrender to the terrible truth about the loss of his talent. Faulkner again said it best: "I knew that I had seen, was looking at, a giant in the earth populated to a great—too great—extent by pygmies, even if he did make but the two or perhaps three gestures commensurate with gianthood."

A Cup of Coffee

If I can't sell twenty thousand copies of your next novel, I'm
willing to quit the publishing business.
—HBL to Dreiser, June 15, 1921

(1)

Horace's ongoing problems with Dreiser only worsened.
Dreiser's mistrust continued throughout their relationship, but
Horace never doubted that Dreiser was his flagship author, the one
writer who epitomized what B&L stood for in American book publishing. Come what may, no matter what he did, Dreiser *had* to
remain on the list. Horace was also aware that with little or no
provocation Dreiser was capable of ditching him in a moment for
another publisher. His perpetual hope was that Dreiser would one
day deliver his long-awaited major novel that would make all the
tribulations worth enduring. As has been indicated, Dreiser was
aware of Horace's need for him and proceeded to use it as a
weapon by flirting with the other New York firms who courted
him. Every three years or so Dreiser would renegotiate his basic
contract with Horace, each time raising the ante.

Similar to the Anderson situation, Horace gave Dreiser a four-year contract at the beginning of 1923 that guaranteed him $4,000 a year. The money was a monthly drawing account against the royalties to be earned on all his books, including future ones. This was generous support for an author whose books had yet to sell significantly, but the contract also provided more than $2,000 to permit Dreiser to buy from their original publishers the plates and rights to all his earlier works. The royalty rate for all his books was to be 20 percent, again high for any writer and particularly one who was not a best-seller. Dreiser, for his part, agreed to supply Horace with at least two full-length novels.

Dreiser reacted to the new contract by telling Horace that he was prepared to work with him only upon the condition "that I get a square deal." He stated this in a letter in which he expressed his anger over the poor sales figures on *A Book About Myself*, which sold less than 3,000 copies. Despite the fact that Horace had spent disproportionate sums advertising it, Dreiser's reaction was predictable: Horace hadn't spent *enough* on promotion, and he was also lying about the sales figures, which must surely be higher than the ones reported. Horace's rejoinder indicates how carefully he had to deal with his star author:

> I cross my heart and swear to our Lord that your note of yesterday absolutely mystifies me . . . Your letter leaves no interpretation open other than that you question whether you have always gotten a square deal from me. Thank God our books are open to all of our authors or to anyone else who has any direct or indirect right to be interested in them . . . The only thing in this business that I have the slightest regret about is that when I first came in and knew nothing about publishing ethics, Albert Boni put several titles in the Modern Library which legally were non-copyright, but all of which we should have paid for. And as soon as I learned of these things, I paid back every cent that was ethically due, although it hurt pretty badly when I did it.

Let me reiterate what I have frequently said to you: That I am heart and soul for your work; that we have now a very big investment in it, and that from now on you will see a very much greater concerted campaign for the sale of all your work. . . .

In spite of your letter, which it is possible I have misinterpreted, my admiration and affection for you remains the same.

To justify his monthly stipend, Dreiser kept submitting material of doubtful appeal to B&L. Since he fancied himself a poet, Dreiser thought Horace was just the man to publish his rough and ready lyrics. It is not to Horace's credit that he told Dreiser, "I have read your Poems and think that in many ways they are as masterly as those of the great Whitman." A more realistic note was sounded when he told his poet that the work could be expected to sell between 400 and 500 copies. He also advised Dreiser that he should cut out at least a third of the poems and suggested that his young friend Edwin Justus Mayer, the author of *The Firebrand* (a play Horace produced in 1924), would be glad to do the cutting for only fifty dollars. He concluded his buttery letter with a dig at Dreiser's distrust: "I am going to make you believe more and more that Liveright's word is as good as his bond." The poems, *Moods: Cadenced and Declaimed,* actually sold a little better than Horace had predicted: 900 copies in the trade edition and 500 in the limited.

But no matter what Horace did to please Dreiser, it never sufficed, and he kept on with his flirtations and overtures to other publishers. Nothing ever came of these approaches, for there was not a single other publisher in New York willing to come up with the terms demanded by Dreiser—not to speak of putting up with constant vilification.

Even under these rather strained circumstances, Dreiser became a regular at Horace's parties on West Forty-eighth Street—he liked the beautiful young women on display there as well as the excellent liquor always available. He even reciprocated the hospitality, once

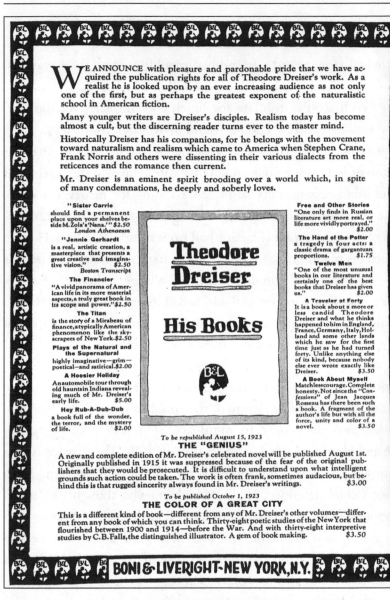
Boni & Liveright ad for Dreiser's works in *Publisher's Weekly*, 1923.

Van Pelt Library, University of Pennsylvania Library

inviting Horace for a celebratory luncheon at his new home in the country near Putnam, New York. The day turned out badly, however, when Horace and a friend had trouble finding their way and arrived very late. Their host greeted them in character with the words "Well, you're too late for lunch and too early for dinner!" Thus dismissed, Horace and his friend drove back to the city.

It was not until 1925 that Horace began to believe that his investment in Dreiser might finally pay off. This was the novel that the publishing community had been awaiting for nearly a decade. As the hundreds and hundreds of pages began to flow into the hands of Tommy Smith (Dreiser had now refused to allow Horace to touch his manuscripts) Horace began to worry about the book's title—wouldn't it be too depressing for a large audience? His suggestion was that Dreiser call his novel *Ewing* or *Warner* (Clyde Griffith's family names in earlier versions) and use the words *An American Tragedy* as a subtitle; Dreiser wisely refused.

Few novels in American literary history have been greeted with the burst of praise that welcomed the publication of *An American Tragedy*—two that come to mind are Steinbeck's *The Grapes of Wrath* and Hemingway's *For Whom the Bell Tolls*. There were only a few negative reviews, and the most significant of these came from Dreiser's chief defender, H. L. Mencken, who thought the novel was abominable, the worst written of all his books, and more than twice as long as it should be. But Mencken's was a voice alone: The critical stampede made the book an instant success. Published in December 1925 in two fat volumes in tiny type and retailing at five dollars, by January 1931 *An American Tragedy* had sold a total of 76,000 copies in the trade edition. The net profit on the book for the firm was more than $60,000, but it is likely that Horace's deepest satisfaction lay in the fact that he had finally published a Dreiser work that *sold,* after all the dubious items he'd had to bring out in the previous five years.

Horace immediately saw its theatrical possibilities and commissioned Patrick Kearney to turn the novel into a play, which he produced in October 1926. Again the contract with Dreiser gave him
a larger percentage of the royalties than was usual. But Horace
demanded that B&L be given 30 percent of the film rights if they
were sold before a play was produced and the price exceeded
$35,000. Dreiser naturally balked. The publisher's normal share of
such rights is seldom more than 10 percent. The matter of the
movie rights was left up in the air, but it is important to keep in
mind that 30 percent was the figure that Horace thought he was
entitled to.

Was Horace's initial demand to take a 30 percent share in the
film rights excessive? Horace calculated that he was entitled to a lot
more than usual. Besides his having supplied Dreiser with the idea
of basing his novel on the famous Gillette case, he had labored for
weeks with Kearny on the dramatic rendering of Dreiser's work,
very much in the same way he later worked on the adaptation of
Bram Stoker's *Dracula*. This was effort far beyond that of a literary
agent earning the usual 10 percent. In addition, only through
Horace's efforts had the movie people begun to take an interest in
the property—most of the interest traceable to his upcoming play
production.

Hollywood production companies had shown little interest in
the novel—it was a best-seller, but what kind of movie can you
make about a hero who dies in the electric chair? Horace, however,
was aware that a Broadway production, especially a successful one,
would alter the situation greatly. He turned to his old friend Jesse
Lasky of Famous Players–Paramount. A lunch was arranged at the
Ritz-Carlton Hotel to discuss a film sale. The producer Walter
Wanger was also invited. So, too, was Dreiser, whose presence,
Horace thought, would be helpful in the negotiations.

What actually happened at the lunch table on March 19, 1926,
was described by both Dreiser and Liveright in their letters to each

other about the event. In addition, Lasky published a cursory, non-committal account of the lunch in a ghostwritten autobiography not noted for its candor. The account of Bennett Cerf in his memoirs has no firsthand information, for Cerf was not present at the event and had left B&L a year before it happened. The truth of what did occur is of interest, because it demonstrates as does no other single quarrel just how far Horace was prepared to go to keep Dreiser with his firm. The incident may well be a classic case of misunderstanding on both sides, but it created a situation in which Dreiser came closer to leaving Horace than he ever did again.

In the few days preceding the lunch, Horace had supposed that $35,000 was the top figure they could obtain from Lasky, while Dreiser said he thought they could get $100,000. Now, with a signed contract in hand for the play, Horace began to think that maybe $60,000 might be possible. On the way over to the hotel he asked Dreiser to "take care of me," a phrase which meant that Dreiser was to give him the 30 percent of the purchase price. Horace later claimed that Dreiser acquiesced to his request; as Dreiser recalled it, he had merely smiled at Horace's audacity.

When the two men entered the Ritz-Carlton, Horace believed he had Dreiser's assurance that he would receive 30 percent if the sum was over $60,000; Dreiser was just as sure that he was never going to give his publisher such a cut. At a critical point in the negotiations, when the price was nearing $100,000, Horace excused himself briefly. Why he departed the scene at such a time has always remained a mystery—it was certainly a mistake. When he returned it was to discover that the three men had agreed on a price of $90,000, and that only $10,000 of it would be his. When Horace protested loudly that Dreiser hadn't "taken care of him" as promised, Dreiser asserted that he had not made an explicit promise. At this point, Horace shouted, "You're a liar!" to Dreiser, who then asked Horace to stand up. When he refused, Dreiser threw a cup of lukewarm coffee in Horace's face and stomped out of the restaurant.

Dreiser left the building convinced that Horace had arranged the lunch with his friends in order to rob him of his property—that the lunch was strictly a "set-up" situation. He wrote Horace an angry three-page letter setting forth his views about what had happened before and after the meeting. He demanded an apology from Horace for calling him a liar; not a single word was devoted to the coffee-throwing incident. But he also told Horace that after he'd left the table he attempted to persuade Lasky and Wanger to come through with either $15,000 or $20,000 as Horace's share of the sale, but that they would not pay more than $90,000 and therefore Horace's share would remain $10,000.

Horace's reply required two letters, for the novelist was not satisfied with the apology contained in the first one. In it he had emphatically denied there had been any "set-up," and also indicated why both men had lost their tempers:

> I may have had too much to drink—you may have had too much to drink. I don't know, only a great diagnostician could decide upon this, but at any rate my memory is that . . . When I asked $100,000, $70,000 for you and $30,000 for me, I thought you were pleased; at least you made no comments to the contrary. . . . I left the table thinking that you would have gotten the $100,000 which would have let me in for $30,000. I left the table so that you could speak unconstrainedly.

Horace proceeded to tell Dreiser that he was certain that he could convince him that his services on the deal were surely worth at least $20,000 and that he would like to discuss the matter, not in a letter but in a "five minute talk." But Dreiser demanded an out-and-out apology for being called a liar, as he made clear in a talk with Horace's new partner, Donald Friede.

In a second letter, Horace offered Dreiser what he wanted:

You are proud and I am proud but as Friede has told me again how
deeply hurt you feel at what I said at the table at The Ritz that day,
my appreciation of your feeling overcomes my pride, and I want
you to know how sorry I am that no matter what might have provoked my display of temper, I should not have said what I did. One
gentleman should not talk this way to another, particularly in front
of comparative strangers. So I hope that you will accept my apologies. . . . Dreiser, the incident should be closed so that as we work
along together in the future, it doesn't prove a thorn in the flesh of
either of us.

Horace capitulated to all of Dreiser's demands. He simply felt
that he couldn't afford to lose him; it was obvious from Friede's
recital of the writer's woes that he was once again on the verge of
leaving B&L. Only a full apology and a modified contract filled
with new blandishments could avert the disaster that Horace
sensed was fast approaching.

Horace's decision to debase himself before his boorish author is
painful. Alcohol, of course, played a part in the restaurant fiasco,
and knowing that he had been out of control may have influenced
Horace in deciding to apologize. But there is obviously some other
factor in his willingness to be humiliated. It would seem that, once
Horace had decided that Dreiser was of crucial importance in
American cultural life, it followed that a list without Dreiser would
lower his prestige as a publisher. To prevent this happening,
Horace would go to any lengths, even to such servile behavior
toward a man who delighted in humiliating him. It can safely be
claimed that few publishers in New York would have put up with
such behavior.

Dreiser's anger over the nastiness at lunch was mollified by
obtaining even better terms in his B&L contract. Furthermore,

both Doubleday and Harper's had come through with elaborate schemes for his future; Horace hoped to better their offers. He began by guaranteeing that B&L would spend $10,000 that year in advertising *An American Tragedy*. If Dreiser delivered another novel during the run of the contract, another $10,000 would be spent on that book. Moreover, not only would Dreiser continue to receive a straight 20 percent royalty on all books sold, but now the monthly drawing account was increased from $333 to $500. The most startling item in the contract was that Dreiser was to become a member of the board of directors of B&L. He would now be in a unique position to judge just how well his publisher was treating him. This new contract was of a kind that has seldom if ever been drawn up by an American publisher. There would be no further talk of "doctoring the books," for Dreiser now had the right to inspect them at any time he wished. He would also be a participant in deciding the way his books were marketed; it was the ultimate writer's dream come true.

Even in strictly editorial matters Dreiser held the upper hand. Disliking Horace's radical cutting of his earlier books, Dreiser had requested and obtained the services of Tommy Smith as his personal editor. But Smith proved to be as adamant as Horace was about cutting and had lopped off 50,000 words from the *Tragedy*, producing the oft-quoted quip by Dreiser about the surgery: "Hell, what's fifty thousand words between friends?" Predictably, Dreiser later changed his mind about the wisdom behind the editing; he could only be pleased for short spans. In 1928, feeling that Horace had removed too many poems from his *Moods* collection, Dreiser demanded that the book be reissued in an expanded edition; Horace complied. Before the book could reach its public, however, the entire printing was destroyed because Dreiser insisted that the newer poems be interspersed with old ones (the B&L production department had, quite naturally, added the new poems at the end). He denied that he had approved their being at the back of the book—now he demanded the book be reset; it was and then sold 903 copies.

One might have thought that peace would then have prevailed between Horace and Dreiser, but not even a truce occurred. At the end of 1927, for example, only a year and a half after signing his new contract, Dreiser again became restless and appeared about to breach his contract by signing with another house. Horace hired a lawyer to prepare a report about B&L's legal position which was strong enough to make Dreiser desist from making any move, at least for the moment. In reading through the Dreiser–Liveright correspondence, it is impossible not to note the adversarial stance taken by the novelist on every possible occasion. For example, he concluded a scolding letter of early 1929 by telling his publisher:

> You have now the privilege of writing me a letter in which you will state what did happen from first to last. This begins with your telephone message to my studio and what happened at 130 West 57th Street. I am not willing to wait longer than Monday afternoon next for your reply.

(2)

> [Dreiser] was essentially a German peasant, oafish, dour and distrustful of all mankind, and he remained that way to the end of the chapter. It was always unsafe to assume that he would react to a given situation in the manner of what is called a gentleman. . . . His customary attitude to the world was that of any other Yahoo, say an Allegheny hill-billy or a low-caste Jew. He trusted nobody, and was always suspicious of good will.
> —H. L. Mencken, 1941

CASH was always in short supply at B&L, and at least one of Horace's attempts to obtain it seems to have been tinged with mad-ness. He now turned to his chronically unhappy author to have him supply the firm with some of the funds it had been paying out to him for over a decade. Dreiser had invested his huge royalties from *An American Tragedy*—book, play, and film—and had accumulated an impressive holding. Horace's attempts to have Dreiser invest in the firm led to the preparation of fact-finding documents that give us an accurate picture of how the company was run and why it resembled no other firm in New York, and how it was possible to keep selling over a million dollars' worth of books in a calendar year and still manage not to make money.

In late 1928 Horace approached Dreiser with a complicated proposal in which the writer would work in an editorial capacity and would guarantee to bring new and famous writers to B&L. In return, Dreiser was to receive 25,000 shares of the "new" B&L stock for his investment of $25,000. Cannily, Dreiser turned for information and guidance to an outside firm of auditors, who prepared for him a detailed account of B&L's finances. As a member of the board of directors, Dreiser was in a position to supply the accountants with the necessary information.

The confidential report began with a brutally frank assessment of how Horace had been running his business:

> The corporation has the benefit of astute management. It is being operated as the property of one man. In the course of such operation, such management may be desirable. The utmost advantage is taken of every situation, with the net result that the corporation is able to continue in business with practically no attractive net assets of any substantial amount. It is not too much to state that the corporation is being conducted on borrowed money.

The three-page report contained detailed information about B&L's "unusual" finances (i.e., declaring a dividend in a year the firm lost money). It drew special attention to the basic fact that the cash position of the firm was dangerously low. It also drew attention to the extremely low profits produced: $11,000 in 1925, $8,500 in 1926, and $1,203 in 1927. Profits as tiny as these might be considered "paper profits." The report concluded with some accurately prophetic judgments about the future of B&L unless the firm introduced some fiscal reforms:

> It would be desirable to see the corporation's affairs so reconstructed as to make its actual quick assets equivalent to at least twice the actual quick liabilities; with a reasonable cash reserve, so that the corporation may have a sound basis for . . . meeting conditions that must arise before long, when the wave of general prosperity on which a good many businesses have been riding with temporary success, subsides, and business in general has to meet conditions of depression.

These last words, written in February 1929, indicate that Dreiser's advisers knew their business. Unquestionably Horace's way of running his firm was decidedly unorthodox, even bizarre by some standards. His "peculiar" practices came about through a variety of causes. While producing the most distinguished list of literary titles in the United States for most of the decade, Horace was also deeply involved, as will be seen, in the production of plays on Broadway, thus tying up much of B&L's funds. In search of cash, Horace returned to his old love (or hate), the stock market, at a particularly trying time of boom-or-bust economics. But the plays and the stock market speculations don't completely explain why the firm's cash position was always so alarmingly low—they neglect Horace's exceptional generosity to his employees and to the authors he published.

In many ways B&L resembled most other New York firms. Where it differed from them was Horace's determination to hold on to noncommercial writers like Dreiser and Sherwood

Anderson, even to the point of subsidizing them; the same applied to other B&L authors as diverse as Djuna Barnes, Hemingway, Faulkner, and Hart Crane. Unfortunately, Horace's financing of Dreiser and Anderson came at a time when both writers had passed their prime. With the single exception of *An American Tragedy,* none of the later Dreiser or Anderson titles ever earned more than a fraction of what was advanced on them. In addition, Horace gained a reputation of being a soft touch: A writer with a plausible outline or a sample offering might often obtain a $200 advance, but few of these bets paid off. If Horace could have responded to the charge that it was "bad business" to play the long shots this way, he might have replied, "What about the incredible luck we had with Emil Ludwig's *Napoleon* and Anita Loos's *Gentlemen Prefer Blondes,* books that became the number one best-sellers for over a year? And what about Dreiser, for that matter? Who would have thought that a four-hundred-thousand-word novel in which the hero winds up in the death-house would sell seventy-five thousand copies?" All these books were indeed long shots, the wild success of which surprised their publisher as much as anyone.

How much of a gambler was Horace in his B&L years? The answer must be that he indeed was a gambler in a business that is a gamble to begin with. All book publishing, by its very nature, relies on chance to some extent; Horace simply took more chances than any of his rivals. The results of his policies remain astounding when considered within the framework of literary history. From a purely business point of view they were dangerous to the point where his firm was incapable of building up any reserve capital for the time when no *Napoleon* or *Blondes* magically appeared. Disaster was always just around the corner, and it may be that Horace liked it that way—that the element of danger appealed to him.

Reading the confidential report may have frightened Dreiser, for nothing came of Horace's scheme to make him invest in the firm.

He continued to deliver a series of books to fulfill his 1926 contract: *Chains* (short stories) in 1927 and the enlarged *Moods* in 1928, along with *Dreiser Looks at Russia* (travel sketches). He followed these with *A Gallery of Women,* a two-volume collection of stories, in 1929. Only the story collections had any sale to speak of— 13,000 copies or so, but scarcely enough to wipe out his debit balance with B&L. There were several years in which he earned little or nothing of his monthly stipend. Dreiser never published a full-length work of fiction with B&L in the twenty years left to him after the publication of *An American Tragedy.*

When B&L failed in 1933, Dreiser had great difficulties in replacing Horace's beneficence. After Simon and Schuster became his publishers in 1935, he made what was, for him, a singularly candid, even generous admission to its vice president Leon Shimkin: "Since Horace Liveright died I have never had a publisher."

Parade of the Vice Presidents

I pray to God to send me temptation and to give me not the strength to resist it.

—HBL, 1929

Liveright was head and shoulders above all of us, and particularly above me, as an inspired publisher. He knew this to be true and he didn't care who knew it. . . . He was a man born to be unhappy, born to be ridden by ambition and a will for power.

—Donald Friede, 1948

(1)

MANY of Horace's days and nights were spent devising ways to obtain new funding. It had been so from the very beginning in 1917, when Lucille's father had agreed to underwrite Horace's publishing venture with Albert Boni. He'd gone ahead, with the understanding that his young son-in-law would return his original investment with interest, which seemed likely, especially after Horace's stunning successes in the early twenties. As the years passed with the debt left unpaid, however, Mr. Elsas pressed the matter, but with no success. Horace continued to spend the firm's income as fast as it arrived. There were always exciting ways to spend it: advances to new writers, stock market transactions about which he now had the (sometimes) sage advice of the great financier Otto Kahn himself, or producing plays on Broadway. In addition, tensions between the two men increased with the marital difficulties of Horace and Lucille.

Perhaps inspired by the need to know precisely how his money was being spent, Elsas had persuaded Horace to hire in 1919 one of his own employees, a young accountant named Arthur Pell who had recently graduated from City College. Pell would eventually take control of Horace's company and would still be running what was left of it in the 1960s. His principal function at B&L in the early years was to be the watchdog over Mr. Elsas's money, attempting to make sense of the firm's tangled finances. Pell's task was pretty hopeless, for as indicated by the findings of Dreiser's auditors, Horace's unorthodox fiscal practices defied all current standards. Spending relatively large amounts of money on advertising and promotion in order to increase sales meant that the cash position of B&L was always precarious. This investment, coupled with the never-ending stream of generous advances for new books, swallowed up virtually all the cash generated by the firm. There was almost nothing left for contingencies. In 1926, a year after Donald Friede became co-owner, he and Pell devised a scheme to deceive Horace regularly about the firm's actual cash position. They secretly instructed B&L's bank to show a balance that was always five thousand dollars less than it actually was, thus assuring themselves that one of Horace's sudden whims would not wipe them out; there would always be at least five thousand that he couldn't spend.

Pell had other reasons to complain about Horace's profligate ways. There was the expense of lavish parties at 61 West Forty-eighth Street and the steady stream of cash paid to bootleggers. In addition, Horace still thought of himself as a socialist publisher and occasionally shared the corporate wealth with his employees. For instance, when he unexpectedly received $20,000 from a subsidiary rights sale on Emil Ludwig's *Napoleon,* Horace promptly divided the money up among those most directly connected with the book's publication. Pell never saw a penny. In his opinion, Horace just couldn't bear the notion of money sitting around idly in a bank—it had to be spent immediately.

When Horace finally paid his debt to Mr. Elsas, he could have rid himself of Pell without interference. Nevertheless, Horace chose to keep him on as treasurer. By that time, Pell knew all the little secrets that kept the firm afloat; he became the in-house financial wizard. Even Dreiser trusted him sufficiently to take his advice about the stocks in which to invest the considerable book and play royalties earned by *An American Tragedy*. When Horace's methods of raising money failed, Pell was called into action. Unfortunately, he sometimes had to obtain funds at prohibitive rates from private money lenders, thereby placing B&L in an even more vulnerable position than it already was.

Pell was to be a thorn in Horace's flesh for thirteen years. His chief task was to avert the financial disaster that always seemed to loom just ahead despite many of the wild and unexpected successes that the firm enjoyed. Whenever Horace would attempt to justify his unexpected expenditures in the face of the appalling fiscal condition of the firm, Pell would say, "Horace, you've got easy talking, easy talking." He had occasion to say it frequently. Pell had few admirers: Many have felt that he possessed an appalling vulgarity that Horace must have found difficult to bear. His publishing philosophy was simple: Reduce all costs as radically as possible, and you are bound to make money. He was unable to comprehend the success of the books Horace published. On his own for thirty years after Horace's death, Pell never achieved any distinction either in immediate sales or in the survival value of his list. In later life, Pell had much of the Victorian stage miser about him, even down to the Uriah Heep–like rubbing together of his hands. Donald Klopfer, Cerf's partner at the future Random House, once characterized Pell as "an unpleasant personality, to say the least." Cerf spoke more plainly when he said that Pell could not be trusted around the

corner, a fact that became clear to Cerf when he purchased the
Modern Library from Horace. In short, there was much that was
loathsome about Arthur Pell, but Horace discovered that he could
not run the company without him; he did not suspect that he was
paying the salary of a deadly enemy.

Horace had to use Pell in times of severe crisis, but he much preferred obtaining large sums of money from new partners who were
willing to invest in the firm. Their investment gave these partners
the title of vice president and supplied them with a hands-on working education in the art of selling books at the most advanced publishing firm in the country. The first of the new young partners was
Leon Fleischman, Edward Bernays's brother-in-law. A wealthy
man with strong literary interests, Fleischman became aware after
less than a year at B&L that many of the new and exciting writers
were working in Paris; it was the place to be then for young
Americans. Far more important, Leon's beautiful and wealthy
wife, Helen, desired to live there. Leon resigned his position as
editorial vice president of B&L in 1920, and the couple (with their
young son David) left for Paris, where Fleischman took on the job
of Horace's European scout. (After 1922 Pound also filled that
chair, but Fleischman was obviously expected to pick rather different books for the American market.) In his four or five years of
scouting, Leon became importantly involved in the acquisition of
Hemingway's first book to be published in the United States, *In Our
Time,* as will be seen.

   For a writer, one of the advantages of working at B&L was that
Horace might just publish your poems or novels even if there was
not the slightest chance of their making any money. He was perfectly aware that his literary hopefuls were thrilled by the mere fact
of publication; it also kept them happy in their work. When
Horace published Leon Fleischman's collection of poems,
Refractions, it sold 170 copies, a loss but a bearable one.

Starting with Fleischman, all three of Horace's major vice presidents shared a lively interest in the legal problems in America of James Joyce's *Ulysses,* first published by Sylvia Beach from her bookshop in Paris, Shakespeare and Company. In addition to Horace himself, both Bennett Cerf and Donald Friede, who followed Fleischmann in the v.p. succession, made determined efforts to get the novel published in the United States. However, Cerf's final success for Random House had much to do with the activities of Fleischman's wife, Helen, who was to regard that feat quite properly as a family affair.

It all began when the Fleischmans became friendly with both Nora Joyce and her husband soon after their arrival in Paris. The Joyces were delighted with the attractive and sophisticated young couple. Equally entranced, Leon became a charter subscriber to the Beach edition of Joyce's work. It is more than likely that most of what Horace knew about Joyce at the time of his first European trip in 1922 was obtained from Fleischman. But Helen Fleischman's fascination with Joyce and his family was not entirely literary.

Helen Fleischman was born Helen Kastor, the daughter of a wealthy New York Jewish family belonging to what Stephen Birmingham called "Our Crowd," Jews who believed strongly in assimilating themselves into American life. The Fleischmans pursued an open marriage and had many casual affairs with no crippling effects on their relationship until Helen met Giorgio Joyce, the novelist's only son. Although she was ten years older, Helen and George (as she called him) fell in love. Their affair resulted in Helen's leaving Leon, who returned to the United States alone. Young Joyce married Helen in 1928, after her divorce.

When she discovered that her new husband was, in fact, illegitimate and that this might well deny her the right to the family name, Helen insisted that Nora and her new father-in-law legitimize their union of a quarter of a century. Joyce unexpectedly capitulated to

Helen's demands—he wished deeply for the continuation of the
family name, and only Helen's giving him a grandchild would
accomplish this. (Stephen Joyce was born in 1931.) While the
pending marriage of the elder Joyces was being arranged in 1930,
so, too, were Helen's plans for a New York publisher for *Ulysses*.
Should a book as great as this be published by a stodgy little bookshop run by an expatriate? She began her campaign by urging Joyce
to cancel his contract with Sylvia Beach. Joyce might well have
made this decision on his own for a variety of reasons, many of
them resembling Helen's. Bennett Cerf, now the president of the
new firm Random House, had displayed to his close friend Robert
Kastor, Helen's brother, a strong interest in obtaining the U.S.
rights if he felt that he could win the court case that might follow
publication.

Once the famous trial lawyer Morris Ernst had agreed to defend
Ulysses in the courts when it came to trial, a contract was drawn up
in New York for Joyce's signature. It provided for a $250 advance
and a royalty of 10 percent. Since this was, indeed, family business,
Robert Kastor, who had been entrusted to take the contract to
Joyce in Paris, persuaded Cerf to quintuple the advance and to
increase the royalty to 15 percent. Before *Ulysses* could be cleared
in the courts, a copy of the contraband work had to be entered as
evidence in the case. This was accomplished by a friend of Cerf's,
who talked a reluctant customs inspector into confiscating a copy
that was in his luggage. Judge John M. Woolsey's famous decision
of December 1933 in the book's favor permitted Random House
to proceed with publication. *Ulysses* became Random House's first
general trade book and sold more than 40,000 copies in its first
year.

It is fair to say that the complicated history of the American pub-
lication of *Ulysses* might not have culminated with the Random
House edition of 1934 had not Horace originally taken on Leon
Fleischman as his vice president.

Fleischman's immediate successor at B&L was Bennett Cerf, who got more from his association with Horace than any of the other money-bearing vice presidents. Standing as tall as Horace, tirelessly ebullient, Cerf radiated an irresistible charm. His very slight lisp was no hindrance to telling countless funny stories. Everything he touched was enlivened by his wit and personal warmth. In 1920, only recently graduated from the Columbia School of Journalism, Cerf decided to try his hand at writing a financial column for the New York *Tribune*. Simultaneously, he held down a job at the Wall Street brokerage office of Sartorius, Smith and Loewi. After losing his job at the *Tribune* for writing an inaccurate story about a firm's fiscal condition, Cerf continued on at Sartorius, as unhappy in his job there as Horace had been as a broker in his day. The work on Wall Street seemed just too easy for a man of Cerf's overwhelming energy and enthusiasm, the same characteristics that made Horace wish to leave the relative security of the Street. It is more than likely that Cerf would have bought himself a seat on the Exchange had he not received a phone call in 1923 from Richard Simon, a Columbia College classmate who was then working for Horace as a salesman in New York. Simon came to the point immediately:

> You're always moaning about wanting to go into the publishing business. If you want to, I'm handing it to you on a silver platter. I've decided to go into business for myself with Max Schuster. When I told my boss, Horace Liveright, I was leaving, he said it was a terrible time to walk out on him, with the fall season coming up. He asked if I could suggest anybody to replace me.

Cerf, it appeared, was just the right man for the job at B&L, with his Phi Beta Kappa key and his journalistic experience, including having been the editor of the Columbia *Jester*. These qualities seem not to have much to do with book publishing, but both Simon and Liveright knew that he had money to invest and that he had expressed a desire to enter the business. A lunch was set up for the following day at the Algonquin, and Horace brought up the matter without subterfuge. He told the young aspirant, "You can go up quickly if you've got the stuff. I hear that you've got some money, and I need money very much. If you'd like to start with style, you could put a little money into the business."

How much? Cerf was informed that if he lent $25,000 to the corporation and purchased B&L stock, he would become an immediate vice president. It was the news that he'd been expecting to hear, but he demurred, asking Horace for a little time to think it over. Not a chance: Horace pressured his new catch by suggesting that, if he wanted to get on well with his new boss, he might just take Theodore Dreiser up to the ball game later that afternoon. Horace was bored by baseball, and spending an afternoon with the testy Dreiser was the last thing he wanted to do. Bennett Cerf did not return to his Wall Street job that afternoon or ever. It was the end of his career there and the beginning of a distinguished one in publishing. All did not end well that first day, however, for taking Dreiser to the game proved to be a fiasco. The novelist became bored after the fifth inning and wished to leave. Outraged but helpless, Cerf meekly followed his surly guest from the stadium.

Cerf remained with B&L for less than two years. He recalled the time he spent there as exciting beyond all his expectations. Although he deplored the almost nightly drinking parties and the prevailing sexual hijinks at the office, in general the colorful ambiance of Horace's little empire delighted him. Horace became, in certain areas, a role model for Cerf, who, after a few months, began to sport his own silver-tipped walking stick. In the area of conviviality, Horace had met his match in Bennett, whose enthusiasm and charm were striking. He shared with Horace many interests—a passionate devotion to the theater and everything about it, and a consuming interest in books and writing. They also shared an enthusiasm for the stock market, but with the big difference that Bennett knew when to stop.

Cerf became, in his own words, the "wide-eyed boy," who now found himself in the daily company of people such as George S. Kaufman, Ben Hecht, Dorothy Parker, and Marc Connelly, all of them displaying the wit that marked the conversation of so many visitors to B&L. It was an intoxicating experience, but it had to take second place to the new task at hand: mastering Dick Simon's job as Horace's chief salesman in the eastern part of the country. In his two years at B&L, Cerf struck up lasting friendships with the major book buyers in shops all over his territory, and acquired a knowledge of the business which was invaluable when he went off on his own as a publisher with Donald Klopfer.

Cerf might have been surprised that his new boss was in desperate need of cash, for 1923 was the year that B&L published Gertrude Atherton's novel about sexual rejuvenation, *Black Oxen,* which became the number one best-seller in fiction. The explanation was simple: The combination of Horace's remarkably heavy advance/advertising expenses and the outlay for buying the building on Forty-eighth Street had left the firm in a precarious position. (This may have been the reason why Eliot did not receive his *Waste Land* royalties on time.) What Arthur Pell and Julian Messner (or Cerf) probably did not know was that Horace was already planning to use at least some of the Cerf money to launch the first of his Broadway plays, *The Firebrand,* by Edwin Justus Mayer.

The contract that Cerf signed on October 17, 1923, reveals much about the control of the firm and offers clues as to why Horace was finally willing to sell the Modern Library to his young partner only two years later. The contract was countersigned by both Lucille and Horace—apparently Mr. Elsas was worried sufficiently about his equity in B&L to make his daughter the chief stockholder in the firm. Startlingly, Lucille owned $76,500 par

Bennett Cerf, 1925.

Manuel Komroff Collection

value of the preferred stock of B&L out of the total of $82,500 that had been issued to date. In the common stock area, Horace was identified as owning "at least 45" of the 360 shares issued. In short, this was the Elsases' company and not Liveright's. Cerf agreed to accept a weekly salary starting at $75 and climbing to $125 at the end of three years. His contract with B&L included an agreement to lend B&L $25,000 at 10 percent interest for a period of five months. It also contained an option clause by which Cerf could purchase $25,000 worth of the preferred stock if he chose, an option that he duly picked up. Cerf now had $50,000 of his money tied up with B&L.

Cerf's various accounts of his working life with Horace are characterized by a curious ambivalence about a man he admired. His praise for Horace is seriously undercut by his retelling of several damning stories which portray the publisher as either a hypocrite or a scoundrel. Most of these revelations contain details about Horace's sexual life. A few concern his drinking, but Cerf significantly fails to make any connection between the two. Even making allowances for the stricter moral codes prevalent at the time, Horace is portrayed as a man lacking character—which Cerf makes clear was certainly not the case. Cerf's account is puzzling. There is no doubt that his portrait of Horace is distorted, not out of any malice on his part but stemming from the enigmatic qualities of Horace B. Liveright himself.

Cerf delights in salacious details about Horace's unquenchable appetite for attractive young women, as when he tells us a "caught in the act!" story about encountering his new boss performing on what some called his "casting couch." Cerf had returned after hours with his date of the evening to show her the wonders of Horace's office. What they saw on the couch convinced Cerf that he would be fired the following morning. Instead, a strangely contrite Horace asked his young trainee: "What must you think of me, Bennett? I know you're a very moral young man. . . . This girl is a very promising young writer, and the only way I felt I could really get her was to have a little affair with her. . . . I'm ashamed of myself." Cerf concludes his tale by informing us that he told Horace he "understood fully."

In a similar vein, Cerf gleefully depicts an outraged Lucille bursting into a B&L editorial meeting just at the moment Horace was reading to his staff an amatory epistle from a young admirer. After Horace had quickly slammed his desk drawer shut on the incriminating communication, Lucille demanded to know what was in the letter he had just hidden. As Cerf tells it, Horace turned the tables by angrily demanding that Lucille open the drawer and read the letter aloud to his assembled staff. "She looked at him for a moment, wilted, and apologized. We were absolutely stunned. A performance by a master mountebank!"

Why did Cerf delight in telling these stories? Clearly the evidence was strongly against Horace, who seemed untroubled by having established the reputation of a man obsessed with sexually desirable young women—an appetite rivaling James Boswell's and John F. Kennedy's. It is clear that, despite his obvious admiration for much about him, Cerf was appalled by his style of life. But when Cerf and his later partner Donald Klopfer speak of Horace's "lack of integrity," it is apparent that they mean sexual integrity and not other areas of morals. Both men, for example, went out of their way to offer evidence that Horace's handshake on a deal was as binding a thing as there could be; there is not the slightest evidence to indicate that they ever regarded Horace as less than honest in his business dealings. Foolish, perhaps, but absolutely honest.

Horace's heavy drinking—after 1924 or so it was clearly alcoholic drinking—also fostered Cerf's doubts and mistrust. Little was known about alcoholism in the 1920s, and its victims were widely thought to possess serious moral flaws. Alcoholism today is widely regarded as a disease, but, to conservative Jews of the time, a *shikker* (or drunk) like Horace was especially despised for choosing to indulge in immoral behavior. Cerf, Manuel Komroff, and Donald Friede all asked the same questions: How could a man who tippled so much exercise such uncanny judgment? How could a man laboring under the effects of a blinding hangover turn out the volume of work that Horace performed day after day? Besides drink, they were bothered by his other distractions from publishing: How could a man who was producing several plays at once on Broadway function as a publisher? For that matter, what about Horace's continued fascination with the stock market? Cerf's explanation of how Horace was able to achieve his wonders while under the sway of his obsessions was brief and decidedly on the weak side: "by some kind of intuition he picked people who were going places—people for his office, as well as authors."

The testimony of a man's enemies may sometimes throw more light on him than that of his nominal friends. Ben Hecht hated Horace Liveright, but his portrayal of him as the publisher Joe Boshere in his 1930 novel *A Jew in Love* supplies us with evidence concerning Horace's amazing ability to produce a torrent of first-class work faster than anyone else in the business:

> It was his boast he could get more accomplished in an hour than his entire staff of ninety-eight employees could in a week. Accordingly . . . he fell to dictating letters, curtly rejecting manuscripts; to reading over readers' reports on other manuscripts. He accepted a half dozen of these, scribbled blurbs to be used on their jackets, cackling as he worked and reading each sentence aloud immediately it was completed. He examined the spring catalogue copy and screamed at its rotten language, its stupidity, lameness, ignorance; he ran through all the ad proofs, making changes in type and contents. The awe his willy nilly decisions inspired in the two men and Miss Stevens pleased him and kept him going despite his weariness.

Horace's ability to detect merit (or the lack of it) was particularly useful in coping with the tidal flow of new manuscripts submitted to B&L—more than a hundred a day in 1925. The news that Horace might not have time to read your manuscript became legendary. When Thomas Wolfe wished to describe the despair of his young novelist's alter ego, Monk Webber, he evoked his feelings in a rejection scene in the posthumously published *The Web and the Rock* when the firm of "Rawng & Wright," a thinly disguised B&L, is considering the immense bulk of his first novel—actually *Look Homeward, Angel*. In his caricature, Wolfe gives Mr. Rawng (Horace) a unique method for evaluating a manuscript:

He did not know about Mr. Rawng's feeling and smelling test. Had he known of the smelling test, he could only have hoped and prayed that all that he had written might smell sweet and wholesome to Mr. Rawng's voluptuous nostrils. But as for the feeling test—how could a manuscript ten inches thick and fourteen hundred pages long, *feel* anything but appalling to a publisher? . . . Its fate had been decided within an hour after its arrival. . . . Mr. Rawng had cried:

"My God! What's this?"

. . . He walked around it carefully, surveying it from every angle with suspicious, unbelieving eyes. He edged closer to it cautiously, reached out and poked it with a finger—and it never budged. Finally, he got his fat hand gripped upon it, tugged and heaved and lifted—felt its weight and groaned again—and then let it drop!

"Nah!" he cried. . . .

"Nah!" he said again, and took two steps forward, one step back, and paused.

"Nah!" he shouted with decision.

"Nah! Nah! Nah!" he shouted. "Take it away! The whole thing stinks! Pfui!"—and holding his nostrils with his fingers, he fled.

The truth about the rejection of *Look Homeward, Angel* was far more prosaic. Wolfe's lover, Aline Bernstein, submitted the man-

Left to right: "Carrie," Alfred, Hetty, HBL, Ada, and Otto Liveright in the mid-twenties.

Herman Liveright collection

uscript to her friend Horace, who passed it on to Tommy Smith. Smith's response was similar to that of most professionals: He wrote a rather stiff, uninterested letter, telling Wolfe why B&L would not publish his book: "[It] is so long—so terribly long." The letter infuriated Wolfe, who, years later, retaliated with his "Rawng & Wright" scenario.

(2)

> They all seem to have decided that Liveright is an awful crook . . . with this estimate I violently disagree. He has always played fair with me.
>
> —Bennett Cerf, 1925

> The Boni and Liveright office was the Jazz age in microcosm,
> with all its extremes of hysteria and of cynicism, of Carpe
> Diem, of decadent thriftlessness, and of creative vitality. To
> recapture its atmosphere one would not, like Proust, dip a
> madeleine into a cup of tea, but a canapé into bathtub gin.
> —Edith Stern, 1941

THE sale of the Modern Library for $200,000 to Bennett Cerf in
the summer of 1925 was surely the greatest single error in business
judgment that Horace ever made. For all practical purposes, the
ML was Horace's backlist. After publishing books for only eight
years, he needed the steady sales of his ML titles to stay afloat. The
sales of his B&L titles were much too erratic.

Cerf later believed, and it is widely supposed, that Horace was
driven to sell the ML in order to pay back Mr. Elsas the money he
had long owed him and, by so doing, to rid himself of Lucille.
That this cannot have been the case is revealed by the contract
Cerf signed. On this occasion, only Horace signed for the firm;
Lucille had vanished as the real owner of B&L.* It would appear,
then, that Horace had been able to obtain enough money to repay
Elsas sometime in 1924. Why, then, was he so desperate for cash
in the summer of 1925? We can't be certain, but it is more than
likely that the never-ending financial demands imposed by his
new career as a theatrical producer had much to do with his decision.

In later years Cerf and Donald Klopfer insisted that Horace had
never really been seriously interested in the ML and that he cared
little about its fate. They both saw Horace in the grip of his gambling and theatrical obsessions, so much so that he had long since
lost any interest in editorial matters that he might once have had.
They also claimed that he didn't care what kinds of books were
included in the series. This alleged indifference is allied to the

*The Liverights obtained their separation agreement in 1926 and were divorced in 1928.

mythical Horace Liveright who read few if any books. Even a casual examination of Horace's correspondence with writers as diverse as Hemingway, Gertrude Atherton, and Bertrand Russell reveals a Liveright with considerable editorial acumen. It is also evident as far back as his 1918 correspondence with William Dean Howells at the time when Howells was preparing for Horace the contents of his huge collection, *The Great American Stories*. As to what was (or was not) to be included in the ML, we possess strong evidence indicating Horace's concern.

Norman Douglas's sophisticated novel *South Wind* was first published in England in 1917 and almost immediately began to exert a strong influence on many of the younger writers, among them Ronald Firbank, Aldous Huxley, and Evelyn Waugh. The book is set on a Capri-like Mediterranean island called Nepenthe and its characters talk incessantly about art and sex. It still continues to charm as the century nears its end. In 1924 *South Wind* was a perfect title for inclusion in the Modern Library, but Frank Dodd of Dodd, Mead & Company, its U.S. publisher, would not license the reprint rights and refused to give a reason. It couldn't be that the book was selling *that* well; Horace became suspicious and investigated. He discovered that, because of its original lack of faith in the novel, Dodd, Mead had, in fact, destroyed Douglas's copyright by importing unbound British sheets of the book rather than having type set up for U.S. publication. This was a permissible procedure for U.S. houses that had reason to believe that a particular book would have a limited market here. However, once more than 1,500 copies had been imported into the United States, the book lost its copyright. By publishing the novel the way it had, Dodd, Mead had thrown *South Wind* into the public domain.* This fact was not a piece of information that Dodd, Mead wished Douglas to

---

*This situation prevailed again in the 1950s, when J. R. R. Tolkien's *Lord of the Rings* trilogy met the same fate.

discover; Horace's reprint offer had opened an issue that Frank Dodd wished to keep closed.

Once he had determined that *South Wind* was in the public domain, Horace offered to pay Dodd, Mead for the use of their plates for the proposed ML edition, but Frank Dodd refused to have any dealings whatsoever with Horace. At this point, Horace wrote to Douglas on Capri, offering him a standard royalty contract on all copies sold, despite the book's status. Douglas was delighted, telling Horace, "[It] strikes me as a very generous offer." When Horace relayed Douglas's pleasure in having his book included in the ML, Dodd replied that, in view of the fact that they were about to relaunch the book, Horace was guilty of unethical conduct, and that more would be heard from him. After receiving Dodd's angry letter, Horace wrote to Douglas:

> I feel that Mr. Dodd's very cold attitude is almost amusing. Legally, of course, I can include South Wind in the series and pay you royalties. I don't have to rent anyone's plates. I can set the book up by myself. How can Dodd Mead speak about their extensive plans for a selling campaign on South Wind when they are merely importing sheets from England?

With the parties deadlocked, Horace wrote again to Douglas:

> I am determined to put South Wind in the Modern Library unless Mr. Dodd can give me a much more convincing argument than he has up to date.

At this point, Dodd began to write a series of intimidating letters to Douglas that would persuade him to break off all relations with Horace. The firm was in a position to exert pressure because Douglas had signed a contract that gave them options on his next two novels. Once Douglas realized that he was endangering his relationship with his major American publisher, he began to back away from Horace's proposal. But Horace knew the magic note that had to be struck to bring Douglas around:

> Your letter of Oct 11th rather chilled me. I have said to Dodd Mead that you wanted very much to have me put South Wind in the ML, that if I seemed discourteous to their ethical point of view, I felt that the wishes of an author took precedence over everything else. It is, of course, distinctly in your interests to have the book in the ML. No sane person would think otherwise.
>
> Do write and make me feel that you really want the book in the ML. Naturally, if you even intimated that you didn't, I wouldn't put it there.

Douglas was persuaded. He gave Horace permission to proceed with publication and agreed to supply him with a new preface. Encouraged by his triumph, Horace tried to lure Douglas to come to America for a lecture tour and issued a standing invitation to stay with him in New Rochelle. Both invitations were politely rejected, but Horace had succeeded in accomplishing what he'd wanted. Publication of *South Wind* in the ML in 1925 established Douglas as a writer of consequence, just as had the appearance in the ML of books by Anderson, Dreiser, and O'Neill.

The facts about Horace's determination regarding *South Wind* would probably not have swayed Cerf in his feeling that Horace was not paying enough attention to the ML. There was only one way to nurture the series properly by his standards and that was to own it himself. Cerf had made offers to buy the ML and had been rebuffed, but he didn't give up hope. Only pure desperation would have persuaded Horace into parting with the ML. It was only a few months later that he found himself in just that position.

(3)

And so I'm off for bed after the most eventful day of my life.
I bought the Modern Library from Boni & Liveright after a
whirlwind conference—a step that will alter my entire
career.
                    —Bennett Cerf, May 20, 1925

CERF wrote these words in his cabin on the S.S. *Aquitania,* bound
for Southampton on the night of the very long day when he purchased the ML. It was the day on which Horace had suggested a
farewell lunch with him at Jack & Charlie's ("21" in later years).
Before leaving for the restaurant, Horace had done something
unusual for him, or so Cerf thought: He had gulped down two
quick drinks back at the office. At "J and C's" he continued to
drink, claiming that he was edgy about the continuing Elsas situation at B&L, as well as Lucille's part of the picture.* He concluded
his list of woes by exclaiming, "Oh, how I'd like to pay him off and
get rid of him." At this point Cerf responded by suggesting that he
buy the ML, an idea that had previously enraged Horace. Not this
time: Horace's answer was unequivocal: "What will you give me
for it?"

Why would Horace evoke the presence of Mr. Elsas when he
was already out of the picture? It may be that he was ashamed to
tell Bennett the truth—that he was in such dire need for immediate
cash because of the huge amounts he required to continue producing plays on Broadway. In any event, the price was agreed upon:
$150,000 in cash plus the $50,000 that Horace owed Cerf for the
unpaid loan and the B&L stock he owned. Determined to settle
matters at once (Bennett was sailing that night at ten), Horace suggested that he have his lawyer, Arthur Garfield Hays, come over to

*Cerf may have been recalling earlier talks with Horace about the Elsas situation.

the office and draw up the contract for their signature later that afternoon.

On their return to the office, Horace summoned Julian Messner and Arthur Pell to tell them the news. They were both horrified and outraged at the prospect of the firm's losing, without a word of warning, its chief asset and glory as well as its bulwark against future bad times. Under no circumstances could Horace do something so monstrous! When Hays arrived, all three of Horace's associates attempted to reason him out of the deal, but he remained adamant. Hays was the most outspoken, telling Horace, "Well, you're my client. I've given you my advice. If you don't want to listen to it, the hell with you."

Horace's version of what happened that afternoon, echoed in Komroff's memoirs, has a melodramatic, somewhat hard-to-believe quality. Their version adds a further element: As the wrangling continued, a disturbance could be heard in the reception area just outside Horace's office. Messner was dispatched to investigate. He informed Horace that "John," a literary agent as well as the jealous husband of one of Horace's young conquests, was waiting for him outside with a loaded pistol in his pocket. Horace's solution was for Messner to explain to John the gravity of the situation— the ML wasn't sold every day—and for the two of them to have a few drinks in the speakeasy just across the street. Horace would be glad to talk to John in just an hour or so. Messner obeyed; his departure thus weakened the most powerful opposition to the sale, for Horace valued his sales manager's view that the ML was the very heart of B&L. Messner's absence in the critical hours made it far easier to proceed with the preparation of the contract. John and his now–close friend Messner were last seen that evening weaving their way down Forty-eighth Street arm in arm. The Modern Library was now the property of Bennett Cerf and his as yet unaware partner to be, Donald Klopfer.

The purchase of the ML was probably the most important business event in Cerf's life. The present-day Random House was built
on the solid foundation of a series that became depression-proof in
the thirties and has been reactivated in the nineties. When Random
House began publishing its own first titles in 1927, the ML constituted a stable backlist for a new and venturesome house.

In the forty years that followed the purchase, Cerf told some
stories that had little or no reality to them about the 108 titles he'd
bought from Horace. He stated in his memoirs, *At Random,**
betraying his exasperation at some of Horace's unbusinesslike
methods:

> About nine or so were books that Liveright had added because of
> some whim or to please some author he was trying to sign up or to
> show off to somebody. If a girl he was trying to win said, "You
> ought to have this in Modern Library," and it meant a weekend at
> Atlantic City, he'd put the book in. We knew what we were going
> to do with Modern Library when we got our hands on it—throw
> those out immediately.

It is true that, over the years, Cerf and Klopfer dropped many
titles from the ML list, but they were books that had, either temporarily or lastingly, gone out of fashion. In the first category were
Stendhal's *Charterhouse of Parma* and Fitzgerald's *Great Gatsby,* while
in the second were five novels by Gabriele D'Annunzio and four
novels by Anatole France. The only title that remotely fits Cerf's
assertion was Ben Hecht's first novel, *Erik Dorn.* Hecht was a novelist whom Horace was anxious to please. *Dorn* continued to hold its
place in the series, however, until 1937. An examination of the ML
list does not indicate a single woman author of the variety conjured
up by Cerf. The only criterion for dropping books from the ML

---

*These memoirs were produced from Cerf's taped interviews. They were never reviewed by
Cerf before his death.

Left to right: Tommy Smith,
HBL, and Herman Liveright in
the mid-twenties at Ogonquit.
Lucy Wilson collection

Lucille and HBL on the beach at
Ogonquit in the early twenties.
Lucy Wilson collection

Left to right: Tommy Smith, HBL, and Lucy
Liveright at Ogonquit.
Lucy Wilson collection

remains the same as always—if a title doesn't sell a minimum number of copies per year it is dropped. Such was Cerf's painful decision in 1939, when he told Max Perkins, the Scribner's editor, that *The Great Gatsby* was selling only about 700 copies per year.

The sale of the Modern Library was the first in a series of major mistakes that eventually led to Horace's losing control of the company and his departure for Hollywood. In itself the sale was not a death blow, but it is more than likely that, had B&L been able to retain the series, it would have weathered the depression of the early 1930s.

(4)

> He [Komroff] continues to claim that he hired me on the basis that there must be something good in somebody who has been fired from three colleges: Harvard, Yale, and Princeton.
>
> —Donald Friede, 1948

WHEN Anthony Powell was nearing the end of his twelve-volume novel sequence, *A Dance to the Music of Time,* he introduced to his readers a new character, Louis Glober, an American Jew aged sixty whom the narrator, Nick Jenkins, had not encountered since the mid-twenties. Glober is portrayed as an ex-publisher, film producer, playboy-tycoon, and womanizer extraordinaire. He also collects works of art. In the 1920s, we are told, in pursuit of an Augustus John drawing, he had asked Nick to introduce him to its owner. Nick now learns that Glober seduced the owner in order to get the drawing. Tall and athletically built, Glober exudes the worldly charm of his prototype, Donald Friede, the young man who became the third major partner of Horace's, just a few months after the departure of Bennett Cerf.

After giving up on college, the restless Friede had taken on a number of beginners' jobs, including eight months of training to become a railway locomotive salesman. Like Horace and Bennett Cerf, Friede tried selling bonds but found that he was no more attracted to this line of endeavor than they. Among his early jobs was one in the stockroom of Alfred A. Knopf. From this ten-dollar-a-week position, he went on to the firm's accounting department; eventually he was transferred to H. L. Mencken's *American Mercury,* the monthly magazine that Knopf was backing. Friede's job was to sell advertising in the pages of the journal—a job that proved to be virtually impossible. But by this time Friede claimed that he had fallen in love with the publishing business, and it was not long before he turned to the most talked-about house in town.

Manuel Komroff hired Friede as his assistant in the production department of B&L despite the dire warning given him by Donald Klopfer, who, on a visit to his friend Cerf, had noticed Friede's unexpected appearance in the building. Klopfer told Komroff about the expulsions from Yale and Princeton, but these facts did not deter the author of *The Adventures of Marco Polo* from hiring Friede, who began an intensive course in the art and science of book production. The course was suddenly interrupted by the young trainee's decision to invest $110,000 of his family's money in B&L, thereby becoming an instant vice president. According to Friede, Komroff discovered the changed role of his pupil quite early one morning only a month or so after he'd been hired:

> "So when I wanted something done that morning I naturally asked Donald to do it. . . . And do you know what he said to me?" he asks. "He looked at me calmly and said 'I'm sorry, Man. You'll have to get somebody else to do that for you. You see, I'm vice president of the company now.' "

Friede's $110,000 investment gave him a "half-interest" in the firm or, in general terms, power equal to that of Horace. This power-sharing idea was nonsense, for neither Horace nor Friede was capable of working with an equal; it created a potentially explosive factor in the administration of the firm. Friede was not shy about displaying his new power; he ordered Julian Messner's sales department to seek out new and smaller quarters so that the new vice president might have an office as large as Horace's. From the moment of his arrival Friede threw his weight about in the editorial department; his enemies announced that he discovered a new genius at least once a week. He stuck by his opinions, for I once heard him say that the wisest editorial decision that he had ever made was his rejection of Thomas Wolfe's first novel, *Look Homeward, Angel!** Standing out in sharp isolation from just about everyone else at B&L (except Arthur Pell), Friede developed a warm friendship with Dreiser, a fact that probably did not endear him to Horace.

In his two years at B&L, Friede was responsible for placing some notable books on the list, especially Isadora Duncan's autobiography, *My Life,* which sold 33,000 copies. Those who have seen Karel Reisz's film *Isadora* may recall the young American editor who cajoles Isadora into telling him her life story. The incident is loosely based on Friede's visit to her, shortly before her accidental death.

While in Paris on a buying trip, he worked with Djuna Barnes in preparing her first novel, *Ryder,* for the press. The task included replacing all her forbidden four-letter words with asterisks. Also in Paris, he got along famously with Hemingway, who admitted he thought he'd given B&L a bum deal by going to Scribner's with *The Sun Also Rises* and promised to make it up to him someday.**

That same year in Paris (1928) Friede made overtures to James

---

*Presumably by his own firm, Covici-Friede.

**He did, seven years after Horace's death, by permitting Friede to be the agent who sold the movie rights to *For Whom the Bell Tolls* to Paramount for $100,000, then the highest price ever paid for a novel.

Joyce concerning the possible publication of *Ulysses* in America by B&L. Unfortunately, Friede wound up alienating Joyce, who believed (falsely) that Friede had attempted to cheat him of his rights concerning a small section of *Finnegans Wake* that Friede had arranged to publish for him in Holland in order to gain American copyright. As was the custom of the time, Friede had applied for *ad interim* copyright in his own name as claimant, thus necessitating its appearance on the copyright page of the thin little volume. Nothing Friede said in explanation served to placate Joyce, who was permanently convinced that he was dealing with a literary criminal. This failure concluded the second attempt of B&L to bring out *Ulysses* in America.

Because of his youthful travels with his father, Friede could both read and speak several languages—French, German, and Russian —and thus possessed a distinct advantage over the other B&L editors, Kronenberger excepted. It was probably this knowledge that enabled him to obtain the early works of two future winners of the Nobel Prize for Literature, François Mauriac (*Thérèse*) and Roger Martin du Gard (*The Thibaults*). These were certainly "Knopf-like" writers; in later years they would be published by Farrar, Straus and Giroux and the Viking Press. Publishing them in 1927 showed that, despite all the publicity about Dreiser and Anderson, B&L were continuing to publish the very best in modern Continental writing.

As the editorial vice president, Friede, it sometimes appeared, picked books for the B&L list solely for their singularity; he once confessed (truthfully?) that he had taken on a novel because the hero's name was Donald. In the area of taking risks, he may well have felt that he was in active competition with the man who had published Djuna Barnes's first volume of stories, *A Book*. It sold only 295 copies, although it established her as a respected member of the avant-garde. Friede delighted in displaying what was perhaps the most idiosyncratic taste of any of the B&L staff. One such book was touted as the worst novel ever written—a book so bad that those readers who can stick with it are reduced to "fits of giggles," as its English publisher, Peter Meynell, once remarked. This was *Irene Iddesleigh* by Amanda M'Kittrick Ros, an early-twentieth-century "romantic" Irish novel that Meynell, the founder of the famous Nonesuch Press in London, had decided to reprint in 1926, more or less as a joke. One reason he gave for reissuing the book was that he had been informed that D. H. Lawrence had professed to find a strange kind of merit in its pages. Friede came across a copy of the beautifully printed little volume (he haunted rare-book stores) and decided—all on his own, it would appear—that B&L should undertake its publication in America. To give the book a semblance of literary value, he commissioned Thomas Beer, a well-known critic of the time, to write a sardonic commentary on the text. It is difficult to convey the full flavor of *Irene Iddesleigh* in short quotations. Here is a sample of dialogue:

> "Speak! Irene! Wife! Woman! Do not sit in silence and allow the blood that now boils in my veins to ooze through cavities of unrestrained passion and trickle down to drench me with its crimson hue!"

Irene sold only 435 copies out of the 1,250 printed. The financial loss fueled Horace's increasing dissatisfaction with Donald Friede, who later ascribed Horace's feeling about him to the disparity in their talent for publishing. But another factor was surely at work—Friede resembled his senior partner in far too many ways for them ever to function as real partners. Friede's range of outside interests was just as wide as the founder's. If Horace became famous for producing plays on Broadway, Friede would become the producer/impresario for George Antheil's notorious 1925 musical work, *Ballet Méchanique,* which required eleven grand pianos, six xylophones, an airplane propeller to create wind effects, and a working fire siren. The premiere of the work was a total fiasco, with an Algonquin wit telling Friede, "Too bad, Donald. You tried to make a mountain out of an Antheil."

Money certainly played a major part in the rivalry: Friede had plenty of his own, while Horace required B&L funds to indulge his theatrical tastes. From reports of those who worked with them, Horace and Friede vied with one another in the tales about their various sexual adventures which they related at the weekly editorial meetings. Most of this sounds like boyish boasting, but it is clear that a distinct conflict began to prevail over the way the firm was being run. *Irene Iddesleigh,* Horace thought, was an example of Donald's enthusiasm running wild, especially when he had placed the book on the B&L list without going through the required protocol. Horace laid down the law to Friede by sending him a list of his sins, with *Irene* leading all the rest:

> There seems to be quite some difference of opinion between you and me regarding books on our list for which you are responsible financially under our agreement, which specifies that unless a book has been approved by the majority of the editorial committee . . . such books shall be the financial responsibility of either you or me, depending on which one of us has placed the book on the list.
>
> After going over the matter thoroughly with Julian Messner and T. R. Smith, we unanimously came to the conclusion that the following books were put on our list by you without any majority vote of the editorial committee.

Donald responded in kind on the following day by stating that he would soon "prove that none of them were my books." Some of them weren't, but, after a vigorous exchange of memos, Friede was forced to retreat on most of the contested titles. In a report to Horace, his most detailed defense of his titles was reserved for *Irene:*

I read a section of it to Julian [Messner] in his office, and then later
on, at an editorial meeting the same day, brought up the question
of publishing the book in this country. I had previously spoken to
T.R. [Smith] about it and also read him the same extract. I suggested it for our Spring list, saying it was very small and would not
be very expensive to produce, and the suggestion was concurred in
by T.R., who said he thought it would be an amusing thing to do.
. . . you were not particularly amused by my favorite extract, but
nevertheless said it was perfectly all right to go ahead. As a matter
of fact, the book was never brought to a formal vote, the acceptance being on the basis I have just mentioned.

Tommy Smith rejected Friede's assertions in a forthright manner that discouraged further discussion of *Irene:*

I must repudiate any responsibility, even so much as a suggestion
for the publication of this work in America. I was not consulted as
to its publication, and I have no recollection that it was taken up
editorially.

The memos continued to fly back and forth over who was
responsible for the contested titles. The following one from
Horace to Friede was, apparently, final:

I think we must agree that in determining this matter, we must
accept the evidence of the members of the editorial committee.
Inasmuch as no minutes were kept of the meetings at which any of
these matters may have been discussed, the evidence of Mr. Smith,
Mr. Messner, and myself is to be considered as overweighing that
of only one person, yourself.

With Horace's two chief executives supporting him this
strongly, Friede was left very much on the defensive. While in
London on a buying trip, Friede had received a cable from Horace

that began UNANIMOUSLY REJECT ALL BOOKS MENTIONED YOUR CABLE EVEN DATE FOR REASONS WILL EXPLAIN ON YOUR RETURN.

Manuel Komroff wrote an unpublished, hostile account of Friede's time at B&L, although he was present for very little of it (he had departed for Paris to take up a writing career shortly after Friede's arrival). But, using the testimony of Mary Gold, his former secretary, Komroff accuses Friede of stealing, on a regular basis, the corrected galleys of Eugene O'Neill's plays and selling them to rare-book dealers. When Horace learned of this, as Komroff tells it, relations between the partners grew even more difficult.

By the summer of 1927 Horace, not at all sure of his rights in the situation, wrote to his attorney, Arthur Garfield Hays, to determine what he might do about Friede's ever-growing independence:

> The only thing I want to know . . . from the legal point of view is whether or not I am empowered to insist on my part that Donald fulfills certain functions that shall be clearly defined . . . and that he shall quit interfering with the running of the business by its President unless the Board of Directors instruct otherwise. Naturally, the Board of Directors can't instruct this because it is evenly divided. Naturally, I shall tell Donald . . . that he must quit giving any instructions regarding the running of the business in any way at all . . . please telephone me on this.

Tommy Smith was not a member of the board of directors, but with Julian Messner always backing him, Horace was opposed by Friede and Arthur Pell, who had begun to buy shares in the company. The standoff did not continue for long; in just a month or two Friede had begun negotiations with Pascal Covici, a young Chicago-based publisher, about starting their own business.

After he left Horace, Donald Friede went off on his own to create a small, distinguished firm, Covici-Friede, which made literary history with such books as John Steinbeck's early novels *Tortilla Flat, In Dubious Battle,* and *Of Mice and Men,* e. e. cummings's *EIMI,* and Nathanael West's *A Cool Million.* Its first success was Radclyffe Hall's *The Well of Loneliness,* originally contracted for by Alfred Knopf, who feared criminal prosecution because of its lesbian theme.

At the beginning of 1928 Horace and Friede set up a buyback agreement under the terms of which B&L would reimburse Friede for the stock he had purchased, in quarterly payments of $9,000. Because of the firm's rapid decline after Horace's departure in 1930, Friede received very little of his money. At the time of the

Donald Friede about to embark for Boston where he had been fined $300 for selling a copy of Dreiser's *An American Tragedy*.
UPI/Bettman

bankruptcy in 1933, Friede still held his original 825 shares of pre-ferred stock; his common shares had melted down from 250 to 16. Immediately after Friede's departure, Horace had to begin looking for still new financing, to support his increasing theatrical activities.

In an October 1928 letter to Ezra Pound, Horace set forth his reasons for getting rid of the man whom Ezra had greatly admired, perhaps because of his passion for George Antheil:

What shall I write you about my little dear lamented, departed, unhonored and unsung business associate, Mr. Donald Friede? I can only say to you, not in any too particular confidence, although there is no use in stirring up a hornet's nest with a red-hot poker, that I don't like the gentleman, and don't trust him and never did, and what is more, never shall or will (whatever word should be used). If you ever do any business with him, strike me off your mailing list.

Two That Got Away:
Faulkner and Hemingway

About Faulkner: he's a peculiar man and my heart didn't
warm to him when I met him.
> —HBL to Sherwood Anderson, April 26, 1926

(1)

Young William Faulkner thought that Sherwood Anderson's
relaxed, easygoing way of life in the French Quarter of New
Orleans was a fine way to pass the time, commenting, "If this is
what it takes to be a novelist, then that's the life for me." In the
next few months he wrote his first novel and gave it to Anderson's
second wife, Elizabeth Prall, who informed him a few days later
that "Sherwood says he'll make a swap with you. He says that if he
doesn't have to read it, he'll tell Liveright to take it." As he related
the story, Faulkner made nothing of the slight about his work nor
did he mention that Anderson had recently declined to speak to
him. Apparently, Faulkner had done something "nasty" to him, or
so he claimed in a letter to Horace.

Nevertheless, Anderson wrote Horace about the novel he'd
soon be receiving. Horace replied by assuring him that he'd "read

Bill Falkner's [*sic*] May Day with much sympathy. And, by the way, the best story Scott Fitzgerald ever did was called May Day." (It may be that Horace's recalling the Fitzgerald story was the reason for the change of title.) A few weeks later Horace wrote Anderson that two of his readers had liked Faulkner's book but that one had not. Consequently Horace would read it himself. He liked it well enough to accept it for a $200 advance with the usual B&L option on the author's next two books. Faulkner was still in Paris on a walking trip through France when he received the check which he had considerable trouble getting cashed.

Soldiers' Pay received mostly good reviews, although Ernest Hemingway was unable to finish the novel, claiming that it was unreadable—or so he told Isador Schneider, who sent him copies of all the B&L books he thought he might like. (Louis Kronenberger wrote a favorable review for *The Literary Digest*—perhaps this helped him obtain his job at B&L.) It sold about 2,500 copies, a perfectly respectable sale then for a first novel. Although *Soldiers' Pay* lacked the freshness and sparkle of Fitzgerald's *This Side of Paradise* or Hemingway's *The Sun Also Rises,* Faulkner's novel-writing career was off to an excellent start.

When Anderson had first heard that Horace had bought Faulkner's book, he wrote him, "I am glad you are going to publish Faulkner's novel. I have a hunch this man is a comer. Will tell you a lot more about him in late October or November." By the time the book was published the following spring, Anderson was more specific in communicating his opinion about Faulkner to Horace:

I hope you will have sales enough of this novel to encourage both Faulkner and yourself. I do not like the man personally very much but . . . he is a man who will write the kind of novels that will sell. He is modern enough and not too modern, also he is smart. If I were you I would do what I could to encourage him to keep at work. If you want to do so why can't you write him a letter telling

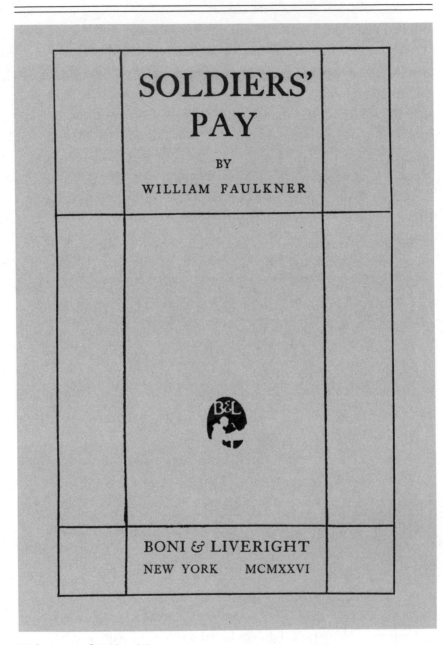

Title page of *Soldiers' Pay*.

him some of the things I have said about him as it may buck him up, particularly if this first novel does not have much sale. You see what I mean. He may be a little bit like a thoroughbred cold [sic] who needs a race or two before he can do his best. He was so nasty to me personally that I don't want to write him myself but would be glad if you were to do it in this indirect way as I surely think he is a good prospect.

Horace's reply was curious. After telling Anderson that his heart didn't "warm to him," Horace defended his attitude toward Faulkner:

This doesn't mean that we're not working very hard on his book and spending more in fact than we have on a first novel in a long time. But I don't want to write him a personal letter for a while. I want to wait until the sale gets to a certain point. Hang it all, he's not the man that I can write to frankly and intimately and whole-heartedly.

There is no way of determining why Horace felt the way he did. Perhaps Anderson had told him about Faulkner's lies about his war wounds and, out of loyalty, Horace was taking a stand against the man who had offended his friend. But this is unlikely: Horace stretched the truth as often and as vigorously as Faulkner. Perhaps, on the basis of their first meeting, Faulkner's notoriously long silences, coupled with his difficult-to-understand southern drawl, may have caused Horace's standoffishness.

Back in 1927 Faulkner had not been aware of Horace's doubts about him, even risking his wrath when he informed his publisher that he had taken drastic steps to improve his fiscal status:

Lost some money last week-end and I have drawn a draft on you. Turn it down, if it's no go. It will give temporary relief. Sorry to have the necessity. If you are inclined to pay it, you can charge it off against my next advance, the mss of which I shall send you by Sept. 1. I'm about half done. Draft is for two hundred.

A "draft," of course, is simply another way of saying "bad check," but Horace went along with honoring it, only chiding Faulkner by warning him not to do it again. Faulkner cashed his check at the local bank in Oxford, Mississippi; it survives and is of interest because of the name that appears as the endorser for the First National Bank: J. E. Avent, the chief cashier for the bank. The swarming Avent family was the prototype of Faulkner's famous Snopes clan, who run their rapacious way through a number of his books; in *Sartoris,* the old Colonel Sartoris loses his bank to a

Canceled forced draft drawn by Faulkner on B&L.
Liveright Publishing Corp., W. W. Norton Co.

Snopes—the very bank that honored a doubtful check drawn on a
New York publishing house two thousand miles away.

Six months earlier Horace had received another letter from
Faulkner that may have given him pause. When Faulkner had
returned the corrected galleys of his second novel, *Mosquitoes,* to
Forty-eighth Street, the firm owed him the rest of his advance.
When it hadn't arrived within a reasonable time, the financially
strapped author addressed Horace:

> Will you please jog Mr. Pell's elbow in a courteous but firm man-
> ner? For example life is beginning to pall on me, and my feet itch:
> nor have I had delirium tremens in almost a year, so if you'll per-
> suade Mr. Pell to send me the 400 advance, I'll take Bill Faulkner
> to New Orleans or Cuba or some place and show him a good time.

Horace's kindness in honoring Faulkner's bad check represented
the advance for his third novel, a book that has been published
twice in radically different versions. Faulkner's *Flags in the Dust,* his
first book to deal with the mythical Yoknapatawpha County,
arrived at Forty-eighth Street to be read by an unsympathetic audience. The consensus was that the book was unpublishable and that
Faulkner would do well to abandon it. The firm, however, was
willing to let him keep the advance for any other book he might
care to submit. Faulkner came up to New York for a rare visit; it
was Kronenberger who was delegated to explain more fully B&L's
decision to reject the book. He told about the moment in his memoirs:

> I remember we talked about it in a sort of summerhouse at the
> office where I used to read manuscripts in hot weather. Or, rather,
> I talked about it, with increasing embarrassment as Faulkner said
> nothing. . . . He simply sat on. I had, of course, given him upset-
> ting news; but he sat on and on, while I made an effort at small talk

or a pretense of reading a manuscript; sat on for what seemed hours, to get up at last, say very courteously "good-bye," and leave.

It is likely that Faulkner's visit to New York—a place he hated—was prompted by Horace's formal letter of rejection that began

> It is with sorrow in my heart that I write to tell you that three of us have read Flags in the Dust and don't believe that Boni & Liveright should publish it. Furthermore, as a firm deeply interested in your work, we don't believe that you should offer it for publication.

Horace continued the bad news by running over the good and bad points of *Soldiers' Pay* and *Mosquitoes,* pointing out that the second book showed

> little improvement in your spiritual development and I think none in your art of writing. Now comes Flags in the Dust and we're frankly disappointed in it. It is diffuse and non-integral with neither very much plot development nor character development. . . . The story really does not get anywhere and has a thousand loose ends. If the book had plot and structure, we might suggest shortening and revisions but it is so diffuse that I don't think it would be any use. My chief objection is that you don't seem to have any story to tell and I contend that a novel should tell a story and tell it well.

A letter couched in these terms and addressed to the writer who would become perhaps the most important American novelist of the century raises the obvious question: Is there any chance that Horace and his associates were right in 1927? Could *Flags in the Dust* have been that bad? Could it be, as Faulkner's friend Ben Wasson suggested, that *Flags* was not one novel but six, all struggling along simultaneously? The answer is yes, in part because the book that was published by Harcourt, Brace in 1929 as *Sartoris* differed sharply from the manuscript submitted to B&L. We know this because of the evidence indicating Faulkner's determined efforts to revise his manuscript over the span of at least a year. He wrote to his Aunt 'Bama in Mississippi in the spring of 1928, telling her:

> Every day or so I burn some of it up and rewrite it, and at present it is almost incoherent. So much so that I've got a little weary of it and I think that I shall put it away for a while and forget about it.

He soon returned to it, continuing to revise the manuscript to the point when he could resubmit it for publication. After a number of rejections, he placed the book in the hands of Ben Wasson, a fellow Mississippian who was beginning a brief career as a literary agent in New York. Wasson finally sold it to Harcourt, Brace with the contractual understanding that the book would be cut by one fourth—the cutting not to be undertaken by Faulkner. The result was *Sartoris* of 1929, not a terribly good book even after all the torturous process of revision, but nevertheless the novel that set Faulkner on the track he was to pursue for the next thirty years.

Anderson and Faulkner never really repaired their friendship until chance brought them together at the Algonquin Hotel in New York in 1937. Faulkner was then in the midst of what was surely his most disastrous drinking episode. The two had last met six years before at a cocktail party in New York at which Faulkner had tried to convince Anderson of his continued desire to maintain their friendship. Anderson may have felt the same way, because he paid numerous visits to Faulkner's room at the Algonquin in 1937 when the younger man was recuperating from agonizing third-degree burns suffered after falling asleep in a drunken stupor while on the toilet. He had fallen back onto the hot steam pipe directly behind the toilet bowl; his condition had made him temporarily insensible to the pain that he now had to endure. A doctor known to Anderson was called in to administer paraldehyde to get Faulkner over his monstrous hangover. Anderson's presence may well have meant much to him.

Faulkner had freed himself in late 1928 from his indebtedness to Horace. Harrison Smith, then an editor at Harcourt, Brace, agreed not only to publish *Flags* (as *Sartoris*) but to repay the $400 that B&L had advanced Faulkner for his next book, having turned down *Flags*. While awaiting word from Horace about *Flags,* Faulkner had begun his fourth novel, *The Sound and the Fury.* Although Faulkner thought of it as a book written solely for himself, Smith took it on while still working for Harcourt, Brace. He was in the process of leaving that firm to create his own—Jonathan Cape & Harrison Smith. *The Sound and the Fury* was on his first list. (The totally rewritten and radically cut *Flags* was published by Harcourt, Brace at the beginning of 1929.)

Accepted wisdom has it that Horace and his staff would have turned down *The Sound and the Fury,* but this is not necessarily so. The writing is far superior to anything in *Flags* or, for that matter, *Soldiers' Pay* and *Mosquitoes.* It was a modernist book, of some difficulty, but Horace had had no qualms about publishing Hart Crane's *White Buildings,* as well as Eliot's *The Waste Land.* He had been perfectly willing to proceed with Joyce's *Ulysses* until it was made clear that he would be prosecuted with probable success if he went through with his plans.

Faulkner had begun with warm feelings for Horace as a publisher when the firm was bringing out his first two novels; things cooled, understandably, after the rejection of *Flags.* Faulkner is reported at one point to have declared that Horace "should have been a stock broker or something,—anything but a purveyor of serious literature." There was another factor in his desire to leave

B&L, mentioned in a letter he wrote at this time to his Aunt 'Bama: "I'm going to be published by white folks now. Harcourt Brace & Co bought me from Liveright. Much, much nicer there." There is little doubt that Faulkner was alluding to the fact that he was leaving a Jewish publishing house for a Christian one.

(2)

If Liveright had been here he would have written a check."
—Ernest Hemingway to Gertrude Stein, ca. May 13, 1924

HEMINGWAY was attempting to cheer up Stein when no American publisher would take on her monumental work *The Making of Americans*. As Hemingway saw it, if Horace had been on the scene in Paris, he would have had no hesitation about Gertrude Stein or any other difficult writer. He was partially correct, for B&L was probably one of the few conceivable homes for the thousand-page work. Nevertheless, Horace and his associates turned down the work; Harcourt published an abridged edition in 1934. It is likely that Hemingway's feelings about Horace came to him from his good friend Ezra Pound, currently on Horace's payroll as his Paris scout. Pound liked to praise his "pearl among publishers."   .

At the time of this letter, Hemingway was not quite ready to make his debut before the American public. He had, however, published in Paris two little pamphlets (*Three Stories and Ten Poems* and *in our time*). Toward the end of 1924 Hemingway assembled two separate manuscripts which consisted of the stories in both these little volumes, now called *In Our Time,* and submitted one to his new friend in New York, the writer Donald Ogden Stewart, and the other to Leon. Fleischman, Horace's former partner, now working for him as still another scout in Paris. Hemingway had discovered Fleischman through his friendship with Harold Loeb, then editing the avant-garde magazine *Broom*. He had written a novel entitled *Doodab* that Fleischman had liked well enough to acquire for B&L.

Nothing significant came from the Stewart submission—his own publisher, Doran, liked the book but felt it could not be sold; Harcourt, Brace felt much the same way. Mencken promised that if he liked the collection he would recommend it to Knopf; he didn't, and Knopf never saw the manuscript. The situation seemed more hopeful in Paris when Harold Loeb approached his old friend from New York. Although *Doodab* was to sell only 579 copies, Leon respected Loeb's critical judgment and looked forward to meeting the young man Ezra Pound and Gertrude Stein were talking about in Montparnasse.

Not for many years did Loeb discover that in 1924 he was in precisely the same position in establishing Hemingway's publishing career in America as was F. Scott Fitzgerald, who naturally saw Hemingway as a writer who should be published by Scribner's; just as naturally, Loeb wanted Hemingway with him at B&L:

> I thought it would be wonderful if Hemingway would be published in the United States as I was. By putting together his stories and short pieces he could easily assemble a good-sized book. I scouted out Fleishman [sic] . . . I said I'd bring him [Hemingway] over for a drink.

Fleischman lived with his wife, Helen, in a luxuriously furnished apartment just off the Champs-Élysées, a far cry from "The Quarter," where Hemingway was living—or claiming to live—a Spartan existence. All accounts of the meeting that night agree that Hemingway was unusually reserved, hardly saying a word. It later appeared that Fleischman had stirred Hemingway's wrath (or envy?) by appearing in an expensive-looking velvet smoking jacket.

Feeling the tension, Loeb became terribly embarrassed by the conversation that took place about Hemingway's work: "I squirmed, I
seemed to be hearing Leon with Hemingway's ears, and everything
he said sounded particularly pretentious, supercilious, affected."
Hemingway believed that Fleischman was patronizing him when he
indicated that he'd be glad to read the stories and, if he liked them,
would send them on to Horace in New York. When Loeb and
Hemingway left the Fleischmans' apartment, Hemingway's rage
became uncontrollable. On the boulevard he began shouting
repeatedly that Fleischman was "a low-down kike." Loeb, a Jew,
may have been surprised by his friend's sudden outburst of anti-
Semitism, but he was in for far greater surprises only a year or so
later, when *The Sun Also Rises* appeared, which contained devastat-
ing portraits of Loeb and all his friends. He became Robert Cohcn.

Either Fleischman was slow in getting around to Hemingway's
stories or his report simply lay unread at West Forty-eighth Street,
for months passed without a word from B&L. By that time Loeb
had returned to New York and got himself invited to dinner at
Horace's place in New Rochelle to discuss his novel *Doodab*:

> Just the three of us: Liveright, his wife, a pleasant red-headed
> woman and myself. Though the dinner was excellent, I felt uneasy.
> Over brandy, Horace asked me about American writers in Europe,
> and that gave me a chance to put in a plug for Hemingway, whose
> manuscript Liveright finally admitted was in his office.

When Loeb paid a visit the next day to the B&L office, he discovered by chance that the Hemingway manuscript was in the
process of being mailed back to Fleischman in Paris. He was able
to prevent this by demanding that Horace speak with Beatrice
Kaufman, who much admired the stories. According to Loeb, her
impassioned account persuaded Horace to read the manuscript.
He sent off an immediate cabled offer to Paris which was sent on

to Hemingway where he was skiing in the Austrian Vorarlberg. When he received the news, his reply was an ecstatic DELIGHTED. ACCEPT.

Loeb's account of how Hemingway came to be published by Horace appears convincing, but there are areas where the evidence seems to cast doubt on the story that Loeb and Kaufman's joint enthusiasm was the only force that carried the day with Horace. On May 23, Hemingway wrote Sherwood Anderson:

> I certainly do appreciate your having put my book over with Liveright. I'm terribly glad about you going over to Liveright and I can't tell you how grateful I am for your getting my stuff published. It means such a hell of a lot and you have to get it published so you get it back of you and it means a lot in other ways.

Anderson always insisted that it was through his efforts with Horace that Hemingway first saw print in America. But there were other claimants: Leon Fleischman in Paris, whose reader's report Horace must have read at some point, as well as Hemingway's friends in New York, Donald Ogden Stewart and Henry "Mike" Strater, who both saw Horace on several occasions in their efforts to place the collection.

When his contract arrived, Hemingway read the usual one-page B&L letter of agreement that gave him an advance of $200 against the standard royalties (10 percent of the retail price of the first 2,500 copies). There was a further clause that gave B&L the option of publishing Hemingway's next three books, "one of which shall be a full-length novel." It also stated unequivocally that "unless we publish your second book, we relinquish our option to the third book." Hemingway signed the letter without asking for any changes. Horace wrote to him at the beginning of May, warning him not to be too optimistic about sales:

The book is unquestionably a peach, and with all the ballyhooing we're going to do for it, it may possibly sell a little better than most volumes of short stories. I'm sure that you will become a property and if I say it myself, as who should, you'll find that we're pretty good builders.

Hemingway liked Horace's concern about his future as a property: "I do not have to tell you how pleased I am to be published by Boni & Liveright and I hope I will become a property. That's up to both of us." He was jovial with his first American publisher: "We could have photographs taken—Hemingway—Before and After being grabbed off by Horace Liveright . . ."

The amiable feeling between the two had not been disturbed by Horace's insistence that Hemingway must remove the story "Up in Michigan" from the collection because of possible legal action. "Up in Michigan" was an outdoor sexual defloration tale, actually a rape story, that had its young victim expressing great fear about the hugeness of her seducer's organ. After the act is accomplished, the woman is in tears, unable to waken her drunken partner. This was very strong stuff for 1925. Gertrude Stein, whose voice can be heard clearly throughout the story, thought it was *"inaccrochable,"* or "like a picture that a painter paints and he cannot hang it when he has a show and nobody will buy it because they cannot hang it either." Hemingway made no protest and substituted a new (and far better) story, "The Battler." A few other changes were necessary, and Horace explained why:

I'm sorry to advise you that the fine old word son of a bitch, a fine word it is, may not be any longer under section 1171 of the Penal Code, but its inclusion in a book is enough to exclude it from the sales activities of Baker & Taylor or the American News Company, the two largest wholesale distributors, of course.

With a severe, all-type dust jacket adorned with short blurbs from Waldo Frank, Gilbert Seldes, Ford Madox Ford, Donald Ogden Stewart, and Sherwood Anderson, *In Our Time* appeared in the bookshops in September 1925. Horace ordered a printing of 1,300 copies, a figure that seems minuscule today. The sad fact is that a year and a half after the little book's publication (February 1927), only 1,083 copies had been sold, a large number of them *after* the success of *The Sun Also Rises* in October 1926. Horace had been right: collections of short stories by unknown writers were as hard to sell then as now, rave reviews notwithstanding.

Hemingway knew little or nothing about the sales picture on his first book as he finished his second, the little satire that caused his departure from B&L. *The Torrents of Spring* is a heavy-handed, not terribly funny, 28,000-word attack on the work of both Sherwood Anderson and Gertrude Stein, with Anderson bearing most of the onslaught. (Why Hemingway chose the title of a famous Turgenev work has never been explained.) The plot, if it can be called that, is based on Anderson's *Dark Laughter,* then a major success for Horace and B&L. Hemingway hated the book, as did Scott Fitzgerald and Faulkner and virtually everyone of prominence among the younger writers. It was felt that Anderson had embraced a form of literary primitivism that featured the superior wisdom of blacks and Indians, a kind of mumbo-jumbo mysticism that went against the grain of his real talent, so evident in *Winesburg, Ohio.* Some also felt that Anderson had taken on too many of the mannerisms of Gertrude Stein. Hemingway might well have been sensitive about this, since he, too, had been influenced by her in the creation of his own style. But since he had by this time broken with Stein, she became fair game.

Over the years, a body of legend has persisted that an ever-deceitful Hemingway deliberately wrote a nasty little book that abused Anderson just in order to break his option clause with B&L and join his friend Scott Fitzgerald over at the more traditional (and

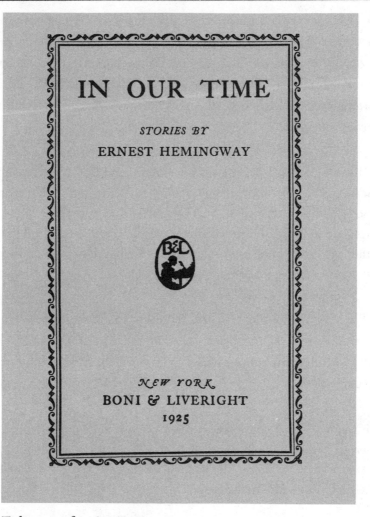

IN OUR TIME

STORIES BY
ERNEST HEMINGWAY

NEW YORK
BONI & LIVERIGHT
1925

Title page of *In Our Time*.
Author's collection

Christian) firm of Scribner's, but there is little evidence that this was Hemingway's intention. If one examines the sales pitch letter that Hemingway wrote Horace (as well as Fitzgerald's letter that followed), it is clear that Hemingway made every effort to convince his publisher that *Torrents* was a commercial book. He compared it with Donald Ogden Stewart's *Parody Outline of History*, which had been a best-seller the previous year, although he went out of his way to distance himself in this area: "The humor is not Lardner's, Stewart's or Benchley's either." Advising Horace that he should obtain the services of Ralph Barton (then nationally famous for his illustrations for *Gentlemen Prefer Blondes*), Hemingway got down to the central issue that would influence Horace's decision:

> The only reason I can conceive that you might not want to publish it would be for fear of offending Sherwood. I do not think that any-body with any stuff can be hurt by satire. In any event, it should be to your interest to differentiate between Sherwood and myself in the eyes of the public and you might as well have us both under the same roof and get it coming and going.

There was no plot to lure Hemingway away from Horace; everything was in the open, as evidenced by Fitzgerald's letter addressed to both Horace and Tommy Smith, in which he praised the parody:

> It might interest you to know that to one rather snooty reader, at least, it seems about the best comic book ever written by an American. It is simply devastating to about seven-eighths of the work of imitation Andersons.

Fitzgerald was quite candid with Horace and Smith, both of whom he admired and regarded as his friends:

> Frankly I hope you won't like it—because I am something of a bal-lyhoo man for Scribners and I'd like someday to see all my genera-tion (3)* that I admire rounded up in the same coop—but knowing

*That is, Ring Lardner, Hemingway, and himself.

my enthusiasm and his own trepidation Ernest agreed with me that such a statement of the former might break the ice for what is an extraordinary and unusual production.

Once he'd read the *Torrents* manuscript, Horace found himself in a dilemma created by two warring elements: his friendship with Anderson and the financial success that future Hemingway books would bring. No one at B&L thought the book had the slightest chance in the marketplace; here Horace agreed with his staff. But, if he can be believed, Horace was the only person there who had any liking for the satire. The problem for Horace was not any possible cash loss on the book but how much its publication might hurt Anderson. Thirty years after the event, Hemingway told Charles Poore that he had hoped that Horace would turn down *The Torrents of Spring*. At the same time he made it clear that "I did not write it to be turned down. I wrote it to be published." He also told Poore that he had left B&L because he did "not like him [Horace], nor did I trust him." It is worth noting that Hemingway had not at that time (spring 1925) ever met Horace, nor did he have any reason not to trust him.

Walker Gilmer points out that Horace's letter of rejection is "a model of firmness, restraint, and good sense." First he dealt with the probable sales: "There are too few people in our benighted land interested in intellectual travesty to assure you of a sale of more than 700 or 800 copies for *Torrents of Spring*." Horace then turned to the issue that counted most with him:

To get back to the Sherwood Anderson angle: it would be in extremely rotten taste, to say nothing of being horribly cruel, should we have wanted to publish it. Nevertheless, I feel that a publisher should keep an open forum and that it would be crueler to you not to publish a book we considered fine to protect one of our other authors. So you must understand that we are rejecting *Torrents of Spring* because we disagree with you and Scott Fitzgerald and Louis Bromfield and Dos Passos, that it is a fine and humorous American satire. We, of course, may be wrong, and when the book is published as possibly it will be by someone else, we may see how wrong we are.

When Hemingway had criticized the way *In Our Time* had been presented to the American public—in particular, the use of quotes on the jacket—Horace countered by asserting (correctly) that whatever sales the book had achieved had been obtained through this stratagem. He told Hemingway:

> [The American public] rejected *In Our Time* stupidly enough, but then they rejected Conrad for 10 or 15 years and . . . until we took over Sherwood Anderson, gave him a very luke warm support. *In Our Time* will sell some day—after your first successful novel. We published *In Our Time* because we, more than any other publishers in New York, play for the long future.

He then told Hemingway that he was cabling him his decision that day—the cable that has been reproduced many times: REJECTING TORRENTS OF SPRING PATIENTLY AWAITING SUN ALSO RISES WRITING FULLY.

Horace was bluffing, perfectly aware that his rejection had removed any obligation for Hemingway to send him the book that followed *Torrents*. When Hemingway arrived in New York to work out his contract with Scribner's, he paid a courtesy call at B&L. The meeting between the often truculent writer and Horace was quite friendly. Horace invited Hemingway out for some drinks at one of the many speakeasies that lined West Forty-eighth Street; they were on a first-name basis almost immediately: "Mr. Liveright or Horace—because we're Horace and Ernest now. . . ." In his letter to Bromfield, Hemingway asserted that he had actually "told him how sorry I was etc." Perhaps the sorrow was feigned, for he had written Fitzgerald that

> God it feels good to be out from Liveright with the disturbing reports I have had from Fleischman etc. Liveright is supposed to have dropped $50,000 on his last theatrical venture, has sold 1/2 business, sold Modern Library, etc.

Horace had lost any chance of further publishing Anderson's star pupil, who had clearly outdone his master. It may be that Horace comforted himself with the thought that his feeling for Anderson was worth the loss, a loss that was to take on an increased gravity as the years passed. At the time, the loss of Faulkner and Hemingway probably seemed to be of no particular financial import to Horace and his associates. Retaining Faulkner would only have added to the financial problems of the firm, for his books did not begin to sell in significant numbers until the 1950s. Hemingway, however, became an international best-seller as early as 1929 with A *Farewell to Arms*, a book that would have done much to avert the decline of the firm. It was ironic and tragic that Anderson later told Horace he would not at all have minded his publication of *Torrents*. Horace paid a high price for his loyalty.

Winning and Losing

> . . . we can't continue to kill each other this way. You must
> stop living your life only in mine.
>   —HBL to Lucille Liveright, ca. 1925

ORACE liked publishing the books of Bertrand Russell
because, among other things, he felt a kinship with him in their
ideas about sexual conduct. In late 1925, when Russell was completing his *Education and the Good Life,* a book for which Horace had
invented the title, Horace urged Russell to be more outspoken on
that subject than he'd been in the first draft. He then addressed a
series of questions to Russell:

> Do you, or don't you believe in absolute sex freedom? Do you or
> don't you believe that for some people sexual promiscuity is just as
> necessary as a change of air, scene or diet? Do you think that we
> should bring up our children to believe that the Lord made one
> man for one woman? Isn't a wife who continually nags her husband
> a great deal worse for him and society than she would be if she

treated him fairly decently and had an extra marital sex adventure,
etc. etc.

Horace is here attempting to have Russell confirm his own views
on sexual freedom. In 1926, when Russell had agreed to write a
book on this subject with his wife, Horace tried to state a credo for
Russell:

> 1, I believe in absolute sex freedom; 2, I believe some people are
> the better for promiscuity; 3, I think few men and women ought to
> attempt to be content with one partner for life—to my mind this
> credo makes the basis for a wonderful book.

But acting out this manifesto of promiscuity understandably placed
severe strains on his marriage, and by the early summer of 1926 he

HBL and Bertrand Russell in England, 1927.
Lucy Wilson collection

and Lucille were close to breaking up. Horace was constantly in the midst of love affairs, long and short, that became increasingly hard to disguise. Lucille eventually found his conduct intolerable, especially when accompanied by out-of-control drinking.

Horace's letters certainly indicate that he wished to go on with his family life in New Rochelle had Lucille not taken action. Despite their difficulties, Lucille and Horace had much to give each other, and Horace had proved to be a surprisingly good father for a man so taken up with work and play. Both Herman and Lucy Liveright express great fondness for the man who instilled in them a number of ethical principles. Besides, growing up with Horace around was fun. The house was often filled with guests, people like Hendrik Willem Van Loon, Tommy Smith, Waldo Frank, Sherwood Anderson, and Bennett Cerf. The Liveright children remember a loving father who held strong convictions about the world of politics. Herman recalls his father's passion for the Progressive cause the night that Robert LaFollette was reelected in Wisconsin. It was an evening when the Liveright family had been attending a film in New Rochelle. Horace suddenly vanished from the auditorium only to return in just a few minutes with the glad tidings (courtesy of the local radio shop) he'd been waiting to hear. Horace wanted to share his pleasure and bellowed the victory forth for the benefit of the entire audience.

The causes of the quarrels between Lucille and Horace ran deeper than adultery and alcoholism. Lucille suffered from low self-esteem despite her beauty, intelligence, and musical talent. She felt overshadowed by her sister Mary's singing career, and by Horace's flamboyant success. Horace thought that his wife tried to live *through* him, and this became a difficult burden. In a perverse and defensive letter of 1925 he wrote:

> What a fool I was (and am) not to have more faith in life & myself
> & not to get less cut-up about your bitterness & foolishness.—

Don't think I don't understand *every* bit of it, because I do.—I am a
symbol to you—of life—of love—of [eternity?].—You live in, on,
with me because you are you and *not* because I am I.—And I resent
this, not one-tenth so much for myself as I do for you. Because,
after all, I would rather make you entirely happy than accomplish
any of my other jobs (dreams—desires—call them what you will)
and I know perfectly well that I will lose, for you, that symbol-
ism—that something that in unconsciousness you've wanted since
you've been a girl. If I [quit?] being myself too much and become
what in your sanest conscious you think you want me to be—yes,
even about the drink question!!!!!

This is a mixed brew of attitudes, and it may well be that Horace
was not sober when he wrote this—it lacks his usual clearheaded-
ness. Significantly, his remarks about how Lucille regards him cul-
minate in "the drink question," which by 1925 was indeed
becoming *the* question.

In June 1926 Lucille closed down the house in New Rochelle
and sailed for Europe with the children for the summer. Effectively
it was the end of the marriage. Soon after her departure Horace
wrote his cousin Alfred Wallerstein: "Today is Lucille's birthday. I
wonder if you know how I feel about it all. I just sent her a wire
and heard from the boat that everything is going along beautifully."

Horace then rented a suite in a residence hotel near Central
Park, the first of many. His suite at 130 West Fifty-seventh Street
was a duplex, where Horace could entertain on a lavish scale and
even offer chosen guests his overnight hospitality. Lucille did not
bring formal divorce proceedings against Horace until March
1928, when she filed suit in New York, charging him with "mis-
conduct" at the Tumble Inn in Croton, N.Y., "with a person not
known to the plaintiff." Lucille sought "suitable alimony" and cus-
tody of Lucy; Herman was to remain with Horace. The children,
now teenagers, continued to see both parents. Horace remained

very close to Herman and Lucy. On May 11 Horace pleaded no
contest, and on May 29 the divorce was granted, to become effective in ninety days. A separation agreement preceding the divorce
had been signed on March 27 of that year, giving Lucille $8,000 a
year for support, a sum equivalent in mid-1990s money to more
than $100,000. Horace made a few of the quarterly payments but
could not keep them up, because by 1928 every penny that came
his way was tied up in the market or in the production of a show.
Lucille knew this and took no legal action; she had ample funds of
her own which made her independent of his support.

Horace was now free to indulge himself in the style of life he'd
been advocating for years and had managed to achieve only piecemeal while still keeping up the facade of his marriage to Lucille. He
was forty, still brimming with apparent self-confidence and vital-
ity; he became even more of a man-about-town than before.
Despising solitude, Horace usually had a house guest or two in residence at his duplex—people such as Bertrand Russell, Sherwood
Anderson, and Edwin Justus Mayer. But many of his guests at this
time were people connected with the Broadway theater—agents,
aspiring actors of both sexes, and backers who might be persuaded
to invest in one of Horace's productions if they could meet some of
the cast in close quarters.

It was about at this time that Horace's drinking, always heavy,
increased. Horace's problems with alcohol affected more than his
life with Lucille; drinking began to influence all his activities.
Those suffering from alcoholism differ in their capacity: there are
the so-called born drinkers who, at least initially, can consume
huge amounts of liquor, but there are also victims like F. Scott
Fitzgerald who get drunk on a small amount of alcohol. After two
or three drinks Horace often passed out. On other occasions, he
might drink all night with little memory of what had happened.
Louis Kronenberger observed that his normally affable employer
"could be at times a bad hand, not to say a boorish host." Horace

now began many of his days nursing what Hemingway once called "mastodon hangovers." He became irascible and less able to carry out the functions he'd been performing so brilliantly. Also, his memory suffered serious impairment after he'd consumed a certain amount. As the twenties drew to their close, Horace may have been aware that something was happening to him, something irreversible. In all good faith, he would occasionally "get on the wagon" and abstain for a few days or a week or two, only to return to the old routine—passing out, suffering brutal hangovers and the increasing need for the morning or restorative drink.

The working habits at 61 West Forty-eighth Street also made it next to impossible for Horace to do much about his alcohol problem. When not drinking on the premises, his staff was constantly coming and going to the dozens of speakeasies surrounding them. As mentioned earlier, one of the reasons that Eugene O'Neill avoided most of the B&L galas was the personal danger he felt at these affairs. O'Neill had only recently managed to give up drinking entirely. A ferocious drinker since his teens, he seemed an unlikely candidate for permanent sobriety, but he proved to be the only major American writer suffering from alcoholism in his generation to overcome its burden. Three factors contributed to his ability to abstain: awareness of his family's vulnerability to alcohol, fear that his talent would vanish, and an amazingly short series of psychotherapy sessions with a Dr. Hamilton. Horace had none of these forces working for him and would probably have found a life without booze unendurable.

In the twenties and for at least another five decades to come, men who openly confessed their difficulties with alcohol and then stopped drinking often felt their manhood to be impugned. Others believed they were in the grip of a fearful neurosis that drove them to drink. In short, alcoholism was still seen as a moral or psychological problem rather than as a disease. Hemingway formulated perfectly certain aspects of the prevailing wisdom of the day when he claimed that drinking was a skill that one mastered early in life: You *trained* yourself to drink correctly. If, by chance, you did not succeed in learning the correct drinking techniques, you would become one of his frequently cited "rummies": James Joyce, F. Scott Fitzgerald, and Faulkner. He told a friend that "rummies are rummies and can't help themselves and shouldn't drink." In this he was correct, but he subscribed to the end to the idea that he himself had graduated with high marks from the school of drinking and that it was therefore impossible for him to become an alcoholic. His belief was ill founded.

Horace's increased drinking certainly had an effect on the way he was perceived by his staff and by his authors, such as Waldo Frank. Although Frank was never a commercial writer in any sense of the word, Horace continued to publish him as a sort of duty to the future of American writing. In actuality, Frank's greatest contribution to B&L was bringing the work of Hart Crane to Horace's attention. Although Horace really didn't *like* Frank's experimental novels, he did like their author and developed a warm relationship with him. But their friendship was severely damaged in May of 1928, when Frank attempted to see Horace on an urgent matter concerning his latest book. By this time Horace had begun to conduct some of the firm's business from his duplex and he had invited Frank to drop over on a Thursday afternoon. When Frank arrived, he discovered that Horace was tied up with two houseguests; the appointment was rescheduled for the following morning at 11:00. On the next day, Horace finally greeted his friend at 11:50 to tell him that the appointment would again have to be postponed. Frank left in a huff and wrote Horace a grievance letter:

At 11:50 you come in, and I find you once more with the two guests who had been at your house the day before. You let me go without even suggesting that (as a last resort) you might see me in the afternoon. You are fully aware, all this time, that I live out of town, that the matter in question is important. . . . At its simplest, your action was discourteous.

Horace had never been a stickler about getting to work on time, but at least one of his younger employees began to emulate him. By the end of his second week at B&L Louis Kronenberger had discovered that "certain members of the staff often arrived after lunch, by which time others might have left for the day." Since punctuality seemed to have no priority at B&L, young Kronenberger was just finishing breakfast on the Tuesday of his third week at twenty minutes before noon. The place was the drugstore located just around the corner from B&L, and before long,

> In walked Mr. Liveright. He looked at me as at someone he ought to know, and very soon he did, winning me over for life with the most engaging of snubs: "This," he said with a well-trained smile, "is a hell of a time for me to be coming to work!"

Maybe it was, at least for the future of B&L, but by 1926 Horace Liveright was a man whose new lifestyle included frequently staying up until the very small hours.

If challenged about his tardiness about getting to work or criticized for spending less of his energies on creating the B&L list, Horace would probably have laughed. He might have told you in some detail about what we now think of as the glory years for B&L. In the three-year period from 1925 through 1927, the firm published two of the best-selling books of the decade: Emil Ludwig's *Napoleon* and Anita Loos's *Gentlemen Prefer Blondes*. Of all B&L's publications, from a purely classical point of view, *The Complete Works of Stendhal*, which began with *The Red and the Black* and *The Charterhouse of Parma*, were perhaps the ones with the most significant, long-reaching effect on modern taste besides the work of Eliot and Pound. The literary careers of Faulkner and Hemingway were launched with Faulkner's *Soldiers' Pay* and *Mosquitoes* and Hemingway's first book of stories, *In Our Time.* In modern poetry, B&L held the lead by far. Henry Holt had Robert Frost and Knopf had Wallace Stevens, but Horace, in this short period, published Pound's *Personae,* Hart Crane's *White Buildings,* e. e. cummings's *Is 5,* Robinson Jeffers's *Roan Stallion* and *The Women at Point Sur,* Edgar Lee Masters's *The New Spoon River,* and *The Complete Poems of H.D.* Horace also published the first of Dorothy Parker's collections, *Enough Rope,* which proved that poetry could sell. The Parker volume sold 42,000 copies, a figure surpassed only by Samuel Hoffenstein's collection, *Poems in Praise of Practically Nothing,* which sold 60,000.

Committed to publishing all of O'Neill, Horace brought out three of his plays in this period, *The Great God Brown, Lazarus Laughed,* and *Marco Millions.* Arguably among his worst, they nevertheless sold 16,000 each. Nineteen twenty-five was, of course, the year of vindication and triumph for both Dreiser and Anderson with *An American Tragedy* and *Dark Laughter.* The nonfiction list also included several titles that are still read today: Isadora Duncan's *My Life,* Bertrand Russell's *Education and the Good Life,* and Lewis Mumford's critical work *The Golden Day.*

These three years constituted an astounding performance for a firm that had been in business for less than a decade—its general level has never been equaled. With its concentration on writers like Dreiser, Anderson, Faulkner, Hemingway, Pound, cummings, and Crane, it can be said truly that Horace was publishing a good part of what has become the basic canon of modern American literature. The list also included Jean Toomer's *Cane,* the first purely literary book written by an American black. All these writers had several things in common when Horace began publishing them: they were pariahs because of their subject matter, their obscurity, and the fact that nearly all of the U.S. book trade thought there was no market for these books; Horace proved it to be right in the short

HBL and John J. McGraw with a copy of his *My Thirty Years in Baseball*,
published by B&L in 1927.
UPI/Bettman

run but not the long. Which meant, of course, that B&L produced
minuscule profits in the period of its literary greatness. It took a
Napoleon or a book of its proportions to offset Pound, cummings,
and Crane and, in particular, a writer like Djuna Barnes, whose
first two collections of stories, *A Book* and *A Night Among the Horses*,

Dorothy Parker, 1928.
Warder Collection, W. W. Norton Co.

sold only 295 and 375 copies, respectively. Although she was convinced that her first novel, *Ryder,* of 1928, would be a best-seller, it
sold only 3,700 copies. Nevertheless, Horace was convinced that
her work would eventually find readers and gave Barnes a contract
for a novel that for years was entitled *Bow Down;* it was finally published as *Nightwood* in 1936. He was equally convinced of Katherine

Anne Porter's talent and kept giving her advances on a biography of Cotton Mather that she eventually abandoned in order to write the stories that appeared in *Flowering Judas* in 1930. Since Porter had never returned her B&L advances, Arthur Pell was still threatening dire actions against her and her new publisher, Harcourt, Brace, for several years after Horace's death.

Although B&L remained unchallengeable in the area of American writing, its triumphs in European books, although respectable, were less certain. While Knopf, Horace's greatest rival, was publishing Thomas Mann, Sigrid Undset, and André Gide, Horace responded with Jakob Wassermann and Hermann

Title page for *Ryder*, 1928.
Author's collection.

Katherine Anne Porter, 1929.
Warder Collection, W. W. Norton Co.

Sudermann from the modern German writers and, from the French, Roger Martin du Gard, François Mauriac, and Paul Morand. Both Nobel Prize winners, Undset and Gide have faded now, but Wassermann, Sudermann, and Morand perhaps more so. Although Mauriac and Martin du Gard went on to win the Nobel

Prize, it was obvious that Horace and his staff were not as thoroughly attuned to Continental writing as they were to American. They made up for this shortcoming, however, by publishing the Stendhal novels, as well as the six-volume set of Zola's best novels, complete and unexpurgated for the first time in America.

By 1927, on purely literary grounds, Knopf excepted, B&L was second to no publishing firm in America. It was obvious, however, that unless B&L could manage to produce at least two or three huge best-sellers each year, books that would sell at least 150,000 copies each, the minuscule profits mentioned earlier would become serious deficits. As the twenties drew to a close, only Francis Hackett's biography *Henry the Eighth* performed in this way by selling a total of 160,000 copies, making it the number two best-selling book of nonfiction in 1929. But even here there was a major drawback: 64,000 of these were published by the Book-of-the-Month Club, which paid the publisher much less than the bookstores, thus generating far smaller revenues for B&L at a time when the firm needed them most.

As for Horace, he soon found himself obliged to use B&L funds to support his increasingly disastrous stock market dealings, made under the guidance of Otto Kahn. The great financier had taken on the role of Horace's chief investment adviser—a role in which he failed dismally. The borrowing could be repaid from the proceeds of a hit play, when Horace took up theatrical production, or the books at least balanced by the unexpectedly large amount of money earned in 1928 by the publication of O'Neill's *Strange Interlude,* which sold 107,000 copies, an unprecedented sale for a then unproduced play.

Horace's solution to his problems was to borrow money, not from the banks, which wouldn't lend him a dime, but from money-lenders who charged exorbitant rates of interest. Paying back these people resulted in his having to borrow still more. There were apparently no further Bennett Cerfs or Donald Friedes around to

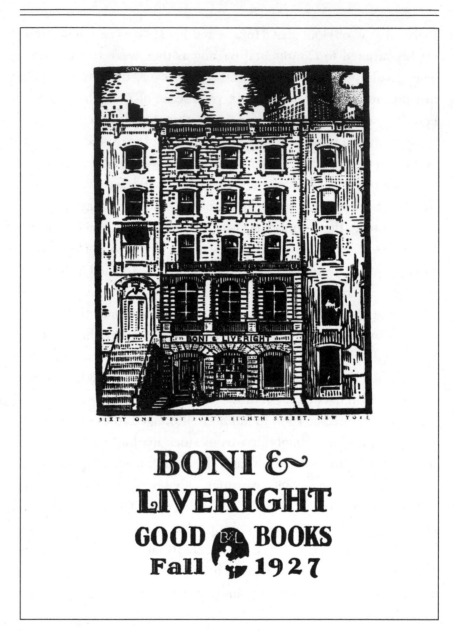

61 West Forty-eighth Street, 1927.

Liveright Publishing Corp., W. W. Norton Co.

become vice presidents and bail him out. Horace was led to the expedient of borrowing from the moneylenders by Arthur Pell, who exerted an ever-stronger influence on the direction of the firm. About this time Pell began to buy some of Horace's shares in the company, first a few, then more, to cover some of the unpaid loans. If Horace's plays kept running, if his books kept selling well, and if the bottom didn't drop out of the stock market, Horace might just survive the financial disaster that loomed. A failure in any of these areas might easily result in disaster both for him personally and for the survival of the firm.

"I Am . . . Dracula"

I SAW WITH UNDERSTANDING THE BEHAVIOR OF YOU AND YOUR
WOMEN AT THE REHEARSAL I WAS DIRECTING LAST NIGHT AND
NOW I KNOW THE NECESSITY OF ARABS NOT ONLY IN THE OLD
JERUSALEM BUT IN THE NEW.
      —John D. Williams to HBL, September 14, 1929

(1)

THE mid-twenties were the most exciting period in the history
of the American theater. Horace found the theatrical climate of this
period irresistible. With seventy-six theaters putting on more than
two hundred new plays and revues each year—a staggering number by today's standards—there was something for every taste. On
the lighter side were Florenz Ziegfeld, and his perennial *Follies*,
twenty-four of them from 1907 through 1931, filled with feathers
and rhinestones, beautiful girls, and comedians such as W. C.
Fields, Eddie Cantor, Fanny Brice, and Will Rogers. There were
also the George Gershwin musicals *Oh, Kay!* and *Funny Face*, and
Jerome Kern's *Show Boat*, which outran almost everything else produced in the decade. The early Noël Coward and Cole Porter
musicals were just beginning to appear; Horace missed none of
them.

Among the dramas, there was a new Eugene O'Neill play performed nearly every year—plays such as *All God's Chillun Got
Wings, The Hairy Ape,* and *Desire Under the Elms.* Horace had the plea-
sure and profit of publishing them, although all production rights
were retained by O'Neill and the Theatre Guild. Major assaults
were being made on the traditional American drama by Maxwell
Anderson and Laurence Stallings's *What Price Glory?,* Sidney
Howard's *They Knew What They Wanted,* and Elmer Rice's *Street
Scene.* Horace published two of the better comedies of the period,
George S. Kaufman's *Beggar on Horseback* and *The Butter and Egg
Man,* as well as Ferenc Molnár's *Liliom,* the source of *Carousel.*

The richness of the theatrical offerings stimulated a corresponding array of reviewing talent. Theatergoers who paid attention to
the reviews in the newspapers and magazines of the day could read
what Alexander Woollcott, Stark Young, Robert Benchley, and
George Jean Nathan had to say about the latest opening. No single
critic could make or break a play, since eleven of them were writing daily reviews. With such riches as these, audiences flocked to
the theater as they never have again. It truly was a golden age.

Although it may have been Horace's intention to enter theatrical
production from his earliest days, he held back until he became
friends with Edwin Justus Mayer in 1923. Mayer had written a
charmingly premature autobiography, *A Preface to Life,* which
Horace published simply because he liked both the book and its
author. *A Preface* was a failure, selling only 532 copies, but Horace
and Mayer remained close friends for life. They had much in common besides their passion for theater—a taste for poetry and beautiful women, and a fierce appetite for liquor. When most of
Horace's friends had long given up on him, Mayer continued his
vain attempts to assist the man who had launched his successful
career as both a playwright and, far more lucrative, as a Hollywood
screenwriter. It was a chance meeting with F. Scott Fitzgerald in
Horace's office that precipitated Mayer's career as a playwright. In

recalling this encounter later, Mayer noted that Fitzgerald had been "light, airy, golden with talent . . . so successful that he made me feel dirty." He expressed his envy to Horace, who began to ask him what his current interests were. Mayer was then in love with *The Autobiography of Benvenuto Cellini* and informed Horace that he believed he could write a successful play about the Renaissance sculptor's amatory adventures. He thought that a six-month stay in Italy would furnish him with the necessary background to write about the court intrigues of the time.

Predictably, Horace advanced Mayer the money necessary for his researches; the result was *The Firebrand,* the first of Horace's Broadway productions. Opening on October 15, 1924, with a cast that included Edward G. Robinson and Joseph Schildkraut, the play received superb reviews and ran for 287 performances. Samuel Goldwyn bought the movie rights and made a silent version that was followed by the more familiar 1934 *The Affairs of Cellini,* starring Fredric March. (The work took on a new but brief life as *The Firebrand of Florence,* a 1945 musical version with lyrics by Ira Gershwin and a score by Kurt Weill.) Few Broadway producers have begun with a comparable success, one that only encouraged Horace to broaden his theatrical interests. It was at this time that the wall in his office on Forty-eighth Street was broken down and additional space was secured in the building next door to accommodate the flow of people bent on dealing with Horace Liveright Productions, Inc.

Having the by-now-celebrated Mary Ellis as his sister-in-law was still another reason for Horace to become involved with the theater. Lucille and Horace saw much of Mary, who had begun her singing career at the Metropolitan Opera Company in 1918. After leaving the Met in 1922, because she could not imagine herself there in major roles, Mary sang the lead in a number of the operettas of the day—*Rose-Marie* was written for her. When not singing onstage, Mary starred in many major Broadway plays, including a translation of Shloime Ansky's Yiddish play *The Dybbuk*.

After her marriage to the actor Basil Sydney (who played the title role in Horace's 1926 modern-dress production of *Hamlet*), Mary spent most of her time in London, where she triumphed in several West End productions starring Ivor Novello. Her immense success in London was followed by starring roles in several musical films produced by Paramount in the mid-1930s. In later years she appeared in many English productions of O'Neill and Terence Rattigan plays and in her nineties played Mrs. Hudson, Sherlock Holmes's landlady, in the British TV series about life in Baker Street. She remembers Horace as being infatuated with everything about the theater and found it inevitable that he would enter that world the moment it became financially feasible.

Besides Eddie Mayer and Mary Ellis, the Liverights were on close terms with Aline Bernstein, the famous costume designer for many Broadway productions. Bernstein became Thomas Wolfe's lover and, in later years, a writer of consequence. Horace commissioned her to design the contemporary costumes in his *Hamlet*. As Horace's involvement with Broadway deepened, more and more theatrical people began appearing at his parties, thus causing some of his old friends to believe that he had lost his taste for books. Horace denied this charge in a letter to a young novelist, Mildred Gilman, who had complained that Horace was not devoting enough time to promoting her new book:

> You really amuse me! Where do you get the feeling that producing is so much more important to me than publishing will always remain a deep and dark mystery. You should know me well enough and closely enough to know that this is absolutely a joke. To say that I spend one-tenth of my working time and energies on producing as against nine-tenths on publishing would be an overstate-

ment. Really, considering the fact that I never take vacations, I am entitled to produce a play every other year.

There is considerable denial here about the reality of Horace's daily life in the late twenties. He fails to tell Gilman just how much of his time was actually going into play production. Production is a taxing enterprise, often entailing rehearsals that go on long past midnight, at least some of them accompanied by the erotic side effects mentioned by producer John Williams in his venomous telegram to Horace. But time is only one aspect of play produc-tion—the most troubling perhaps is the terrible financial risk that beclouds nearly every play opening on Broadway. Horace soon found that the success of *The Firebrand* was no guarantee that it would be repeated.

It is likely that Horace contemplated giving up book publishing for stage production, for it was certain he could not pursue both with equal vigor. His letters to his wealthy cousin Alfred Wallerstein describe the divided path he was now pursuing. Always worried about money, he told Wallerstein in August 1927:

> Since I saw you last, Bennett Cerf and Dick Simon asked me to put a price on the business, Bennett having offered me $250,000 and I believe that he could be gotten to pay $300,000. I wrestled with my soul a good deal and I have come to the definite conclusion that publishing is a pretty fine vocation . . . and that with proper man-agement, while we won't make a fortune, I should have a good steady safe income here. I am getting no younger and if I cut adrift from publishing, it might not have a good spiritual effect on my life. I've let everyone around the office know that and I'll see that the publishing world at large learns it too.

Horace went on to conclude, almost absentmindedly, that "of course, the theatre does occupy some of my time and thoughts.

When you get back I'll tell you about an idea I have for you becoming a director of the company." Horace's idea took a full year to realize, and then only when there was not much choice. Despite his resolves about publishing, he found the Broadway life intoxicating; it fulfilled an image of himself he'd had since boyhood and his near success with his own musical, *John Smith.*

Horace's second venture, undertaken with Donald Friede in 1925, was *Black Boy,* a play by Jim Tully and Frank Dazey about a young black boxer in the toils of crooked New York fight promoters—perhaps the *ur* play on this subject, which has had hundreds of imitators. Paul Robeson, then only twenty-two, starred. The day that Horace and Donald invited Robeson over to sign his contract seemed the right time to have lunch with the young actor-singer and his wife. But where? In the year 1926 every restaurant and speakeasy within walking distance of the B&L office informed Horace and Friede that the skin color of their guests made it impossible to serve them. The dining room at the Algonquin temporized: If the diners wouldn't mind sitting in a private room, they would be served gladly—an offer that was declined. Friede finally avoided the problem by taking the Robesons to his mother's town house on the East River.

Black Boy received mixed reviews and ran for only thirty-seven performances. A month or so afterward, Horace presented what was perhaps his most ambitious effort. This was the first modern-dress version of *Hamlet,* directed by Jimmy Light, Eugene O'Neill's friend from Provincetown days. It starred Mary Ellis's husband, Basil Sydney. This November 1925 production contained a number of novelties: Hamlet smoked continuously during his soliloquies; he killed Polonius with a pistol. Queen Gertrude appeared with the bobbed hair that was currently the rage, inspired by Louise Brooks and Colleen Moore. Aline Bernstein's high-fashion costumes were esteemed by the critics, as was much else about the production, but the public took to it rather tepidly.

At least one of Horace's authors had no qualms about his publisher's involvement with Broadway. In *The New Yorker*'s 1926 profile of Horace ("One Hundred Per Cent American"), Waldo Frank noted his presence in the *Hamlet* production:

> The hero of the Liveright show was neither the Dane nor the Bard, but Horace Liveright. This was not his conscious doing. He did not know it himself. He simply couldn't help it. The words were Shakespeare's, the act was Basil Sydney, the stage was Jimmy Light's. But the nervous, pelting, hectic, breathless lyric lilt of the thing was HBL. The wonder is that he did not go into the theater long ago.

Horace's production of *An American Tragedy* opened in New York in October 1926, less than a year after the novel's publication. With Miriam Hopkins in the role of Sondra Finchley, the play had a very good run of 216 performances. As mentioned earlier, the film rights were sold to Paramount for a record sum, but no film production was undertaken at that time. The depressing nature of the story discouraged the Paramount executives. Not until 1930, when Horace was working in Hollywood at Paramount, did production actually begin.

It was Horace's next play, however, that became his greatest success on Broadway and a theatrical gold mine that has continued, unabated, into the 1990s. This was *Dracula,* based on Bram Stoker's famous Victorian horror novel, which has been the source for scores of other vampire novels and films. Dorothy Peterson, the principal woman in Horace's life after 1927, costarred. *Dracula* was the play that helped him obtain his contract with Paramount Pictures in Hollywood; it was the only one of his stage presentations that kept him alive when all other sources of income had dried up.

ARISTOPHANES
THE ELEVEN COMEDIES

LITERALLY AND COMPLETELY TRANSLATED
FROM THE GREEK TONGUE INTO ENGLISH
WITH TRANSLATOR'S FOREWORD, AN
INTRODUCTION TO EACH COMEDY
AND ELUCIDATORY NOTES

ILLUSTRATIONS IN COLOUR AND BLACK AND WHITE
BY
JEAN DE BOSSCHERE

NEW YORK
PUBLISHED FOR SUBSCRIBERS ONLY BY
HORACE LIVERIGHT
1928

Liveright brochure for Aristophanes' *Eleven Comedies*.
Liveright Publishing Corp., W. W. Norton Co.

(2)

DEAR ALFRED TOMORROW NIGHT I WILL BE ON THE AQUITANIA
AWAY FOR ENGLAND . . . STOP YOU WILL BE GLAD TO KNOW
THAT I AM POSITIVELY AND ABSOLUTELY AND IRREVOCABLY
COMMITTED TO THE STRICTEST KIND OF TEMPERANCE DUE TO

DR. PHILIP'S MINISTRATIONS CAN'T SAY I ENJOY IT AT ALL BUT I
HAVE NO CHOICE.
        —HBL to Alfred Wallerstein, March 17, 1927

I'LL ADMIT I HAVE BEEN A VERY BAD BOY SINCE YOU'VE BEEN
AWAY STOP HAVE HAD SO MANY COMPLICATING THINGS IN MY
LIFE THAT I FELL OFF WAGON STOP DRACULA DOING VERY WELL
MAKING NET PROFIT EACH WEEK OF OVER TWENTY FIVE
HUNDRED.
        —HBL to Alfred Wallerstein, November 18, 1927

HORACE told an interviewer that he'd seen the original British production of *Dracula* four times during his two-week stay in London:
"Although it was badly produced, I got a kick out of it each time."
What he saw in London was not what he produced on Broadway
that October. The London version of *Dracula* was the work of
actor-manager Hamilton Deane, who had apparently no talent for
writing natural dialogue. His characters spoke in a halting, awkward English heard nowhere else in the world. By all accounts,
what Horace witnessed was a travesty, a play poorly constructed
and shockingly bad by ordinary standards. Despite everything that
was wrong about the London *Dracula,* Horace felt there was a
deeply rooted appeal in a work that had the potential of being, as
David Skal, author of *Hollywood Gothic,* has commented, "A censor-
proof way to present outrageous themes of oral sexuality, insanity,
and borderline necrophilia (what after all was the kiss of Dracula if
not sex with a walking corpse?)"

A total rewrite was in order, and Horace commissioned playwright John L. Balderston to carry it out. Balderston is best known
for his dramatization of Henry James's *The Sense of the Past* as
Berkeley Square, but he agreed to share the writer's credit with
Hamilton Deane. Horace had difficulties in clearing the rights to
the property with Bram Stoker's widow, Florence. She disliked
Horace on sight—David Skal claims that she thought of him as a
"flashy American . . . [who] seemed to *be* Dracula in some unde-

fined and unsavory way." When Horace drew up the contract with
Mrs. Stoker, he was unable to acquire the film rights to the property. Horace's 1927 failure to obtain these rights was costly in the
coming years.

The English actor Raymond Huntley rejected Horace's offer of
$125 per week to star as the bloodthirsty count. Accounts differ as
to how Horace hired Bela Lugosi, the Hungarian actor who played
the vampire role with which he became identified for the rest of his
life. One version has Horace encountering a rival producer at the
Harvard Club who had finally given up in his own efforts to bring
Dracula to Broadway, but who had chosen Lugosi for the leading
role. He recommended Lugosi so strongly that Horace auditioned
the Hungarian and gave him the part the same day. But an immediate difficulty arose when Lugosi, whose English was poor, revealed
that he had made it his practice to learn all his roles in English pho-
netically and proposed repeating the process for *Dracula;* one
account says that he had to be directed in French. Whatever the
truth of the matter, Lugosi's measured, slow-spoken, heavily
accented tones were exactly right in suggesting the eerie nature of
the living dead.

It may well have been Lugosi's performance that prompted
Alexander Woollcott's famous quip about the play: "Ye who have
fits, prepare to throw them now." To build up the atmosphere of
fear, Horace repeated the London practice of having a uniformed
nurse in attendance for every performance to minister to the faint-
hearted should they become overwhelmed by the free-flowing
blood onstage. The reviews were mixed, but word of mouth
attracted long lines at the box office. At least one daily reviewer
noted the apparent incongruity of a publisher of Horace's eminence producing *Dracula:* "The count . . . in a sort of dinner clothes
cut from what looked to be the polar bear rug in the Boni and
Liveright anteroom." The taunted rug was immediately and permanently removed from the production.

Dracula became the talk of New York—it ran for 241 performances, and road companies were still on tour in places like Hoboken, New Jersey, and the Bronx as late as 1931. Newspapers reported that Horace had made a profit of more than a million dollars on the play—surely an exaggeration—but in estimating his wealth they failed to note that Horace had money invested in other plays that failed miserably, plays undertaken by his rivals. Nor could they have known about Horace's erratic ups and downs on Wall Street.

Horace and Dorothy Peterson, whom he cast as Lucy in *Dracula,* became lovers in late 1926. Young, redheaded Dorothy was from Chicago. She had achieved considerable success playing ingenue roles in a series of Broadway hits, among them Owen Davis's *Icebound* and O'Neill's *All God's Chillun Got Wings.* Edwin Justus Mayer's son, Paul, recalls Dorothy's wit and intelligence, especially her sharp outspokenness on the issues of the day. She had a personality that usually made her the center of attraction in rooms where many more traditionally beautiful women were present. A talented woman, firmly embarked on her stage career, Dorothy Peterson became the central romantic interest for Horace after the breakup with Lucille. Dorothy and Horace continued their affair when they both went out to Hollywood in 1930, Dorothy to begin a film career that would span seventeen years.

Horace's main production for 1928 was *The Dagger and the Rose,* a lavish musical comedy version of Eddie Mayer's *Firebrand,* and a work that he felt couldn't fail to be a hit. Directed by the young George Cukor, and with a cast that included Frank Morgan, the Wizard in MGM's *The Wizard of Oz* film of 1939, *The Dagger* proved to be the most expensive of all Horace's shows to mount—an enormous amount of time and money went into endless rehearsals. The out-of-town opening in Atlantic City was postponed several times. Shortly before it, Horace fell from a fast-moving open car

Dorothy Peterson, 1927.
Culver Pictures

after a late-hour party, breaking his arm. It was excruciatingly painful; he had to wear a sling for months. When the great night arrived, the local critics were decidedly cool. Horace and his associates decided that the play still wasn't ready to suffer the undoubtedly even more savage attacks it might receive from the New York critics. Scores of expensive costumes were placed in storage vaults for the hoped-for Broadway opening, which never occurred. The New Jersey failure of *Dagger* placed a severe drain on Horace Liveright Productions—a blow from which it never really recovered. By the time *Dagger* would have been ready for its second life, Horace's worsening financial condition made it impossible to proceed.

With a woman as young and attractive as Dorothy on his arm every night at the opera or concerts or play openings, as well as at the endless round of parties to which they were invited, Horace had every reason to feel good about himself. At forty-three he was the producer of one of Broadway's most profitable plays; he was the founder and president of the most-talked-about publishing house in America. Certainly, there were money worries, but didn't everyone have them? Most men would have felt that their ambitions had been realized and that things might never get any better. But this was not the case with Horace—in him there was always something else in the distance, just out of sight, that something that Scott Fitzgerald once called "bluer skies somewhere," some further challenge to his ambitions, his intelligence, and his luck.

On the Edge

God it's terribly late 5 minutes to 6, and I don't see how I'll
do all I have to do including shave and get to the heiress's on
time.

—HBL to Julie Lasden, July 7, 1927

(1)

THE heiress was Delphine Dodge Cromwell, the young woman
who would inherit the immense fortune of the Dodge Brothers
Motor Car Corporation. Horace indicated to his London friend
Julie Lasden that he was taking the young woman out for dinner
and a play that night simply to obtain from her some desperately
needed cash for his new Broadway production. But there is evidence that he was seriously interested in marrying her.

Some information about Horace's brief courtship of Delphine
comes from a novel, *The Years of Indiscretion* by Maurice Hanline, a
young poet from Baltimore who was hired by Horace in 1925 on
the recommendation of Hendrik Willem Van Loon for services
that were never defined. Manuel Komroff described him as having
"dark curly hair and a complexion that was as dark as Julian
Messner's. All in all he looked like a Jewish Edgar Allan Poe."

Kronenberger thought of him as a "minister without portfolio." Hanline shared many of the same tastes as Horace: beautiful young women, alcohol, raucous parties, and the literary life. For a year or so Hanline shared living quarters with Horace in his expensive duplex on West Fifty-seventh Street. Some thought of Hanline as Horace's principal drinking companion and also as a panderer with a talent for finding girls for Horace and his friends. In 1928 Hanline was dispatched to London to supervise the Liveright office there, an enterprise that lasted only a year. After that Horace and Hanline had a serious falling-out when both men were drunk; blows were struck, and Hanline was fired for good after many earlier terminations that had been forgiven.

He had his revenge, if it can be called that, in his curious, amateurishly written, melodramatic book published the year after Horace's death. Although it is a venomous portrait of Horace and the atmosphere at B&L, many details of the book ring true. Horace's plans to marry Miss Cromwell went awry when she discovered that her prospective husband had a serious drinking problem. At the time of his involvement with Delphine, Horace was in one of his short-lived periods of comparative sobriety. His resolve not to drink didn't involve complete abstinence, as can be seen when he informed Julie Lasden about Delphine and the evening before him:

> I think she's got millions or more but she's very intelligent and shrewd and it would be hard to get her to back any play; that's my game tonight. If I were drinking, which I'm not except very moderately, I could face tonight with more equanimity.

That night Horace had fueled himself with "a very weak gin and gingerale" at Dorothy Peterson's apartment before getting ready to meet the woman who might lift his ever-present financial burdens. It is clear that he was now depending more than ever on alcohol to see him through potentially difficult situations. One of the defining characteristics of alcoholism is loss of control. Horace's feeble attempts to cut back on his drinking at this time were in vain: alcoholics almost always relapse after such brief respites, often with a greater thirst than ever.

His relationship with Delphine didn't last long. Once Horace was convinced of Delphine's loss of interest, he resumed his relationship with Dorothy Peterson, although they did not live together until he was granted his divorce from Lucille in 1928. Dorothy became, in Herman Liveright's words, "the great love of his life," and they remained together until Horace's return from Hollywood in the summer of 1931.

Horace's troubles with alcohol, however, only got worse after 1927. He confessed to his cousin Alfred Wallerstein, an old and trusted friend, all about them, in letters that reveal much about his rationale for drinking. He was crossing what many alcoholics refer to as the "invisible line" distinguishing the heavy social drinker from the alcoholic. In one letter he described an incident involving Otto Kahn, the internationally famous financier and till then a regular guest at all the B&L social functions. Kahn had subjected his friend to a "20 minute lecture" about his behavior:

> I saw that he was really very fond of me and that he had been hurt at what he considered my drunken rottenness. Of course I gave him my reasons for it, and while I was very decent about it, I didn't hesitate to tell him again how he spoiled parties. . . . We parted only fairly good friends.

Horace, of course, took for granted that his friend Alfred would readily understand that he, Horace, had good "reasons" for his drunken behavior. Wallerstein "understood" all right and became concerned about Horace's worsening condition. He had ample reason: In the same letter Horace went on to tell him that his quarrel with Kahn had now been patched up and that his critic had requested him to throw a big party at the apartment to celebrate Kahn's departure for Europe. But in the next-to-last paragraph, Horace delivered the news that Alfred may well have anticipated:

> Now for a little confession: I'm not on the wagon. Don't think that this means I'm really drinking. But I find that when I sit around all night with a crowd that is drinking, until I take one or two gin and gingerales, I seem to give nothing; but with a drink or two I'm much more my real self. This may sound like an awful bit of sophistry to you. It's really true. . . . Since you've left I've been an angel, so don't worry that the occasional drink is going to develop into anything more. I'm simply lost when I feel that I can't do something.

This is the confession of an addict who can safely tell an old friend that he no longer feels comfortable without alcohol.* In the few years left to him. Horace repeatedly vowed to give up drinking entirely, especially after a particularly disastrous episode. But he couldn't embrace total abstinence; living a fast-paced life in Manhattan's Prohibition atmosphere made sobriety, for him, almost impossible. Most of the people he knew were alcoholics or close to it. Actually, Horace loved being at the center of all the many social (and business) events that involved liquor; as he tells Wallerstein:

> I have really not been quite as good as I should be since I saw you last. I have been mixing up a little too much with Delphine Dodge's Long Island crowd, and they are pretty heavy drinkers and

---

*Horace's letters to Wallerstein at this time about his absolute need to continue drinking are eerily similar to those F. Scott Fitzgerald wrote to many of his closest friends just a few years later, in the early 1930s.

I have been having too many parties at my apartment and at their places. If it weren't for the lure of the game which even ascetic[ically] you may understand, I'd cut them all out and I guess I will soon. Of course it's possible that I may be shot or beaten up before I decide to quit . . . this weekend I'm taking a crowd down to Otto Kahn's [Long Island estate]: Heywood Broun, Tom Smith . . . Dorothy and some girls you don't know.

By November 1927 he had resumed drinking. It made no difference whether things were going well or badly for Horace—any kind of news became the motivating or "complicating factor" that justified what he liked to call his periods of "hard drinking." All through 1928 and 1929 Horace kept reassuring close friends that his on-and-off stance about drinking was quite acceptable and that they had no occasion to worry. In June 1929 he told Wallerstein's daughter, Betsy, that he had reassumed control of things on Forty-eighth Street while Julian Messner was away on his honeymoon trip with Kitty Carne:

And in spite of Alfred's doubts, misgivings, premonitions—call them what you will,—with the exception of two weeks of real hard serious drinking, starting in Chicago where I went with Julian and Kitty . . . I've been fairly temperate and since Julian's good-bye party, have had nothing at all and don't intend to until he gets back. By that time I suppose I will pretty much have lost my taste for demon rum in a large way.

Not large enough: Horace's drinking episodes steadily increased in severity, and the time involved in recovering from them increased as well. He would have agreed with at least two of his younger writers, Hemingway and Faulkner, that a life without alcohol was no life at all. All through 1929 Horace continued to hedge his bets about his resolve to remain sober. Late that summer

he wired Wallerstein in Paris that he was WORKING TERRIBLY HARD
AM ON WATER WAGON NOW FOR TWO MONTHS AND PROBABLY FOR
GOOD STOP.

(2)

> The stock market as you know has been simply terrible. Otto
> Kahn has loaned me $12,000 on a year's note with all my
> Boni and Liveright stock as collateral . . . he seems to be as
> much at sea regarding the market as any of us. He certainly
> has been dead wrong up to date and has cost me $35,000.
> —HBL to T. R. Smith, April 5, 1926

THE $35,000 loss was only one in a long series of losses in the Wall
Street market, most traceable to the advice given Horace by Otto
Kahn, falsely believed to have clairvoyant powers in matters financial. Nevertheless, the losses did not shake Horace's faith in Kahn,
whose judgment was sometimes brilliantly right. Then Horace's
fortunes would bloom, but almost predictably Kahn would offer
suggestions that often led to disaster. Horace would then be forced
to seek further loans to back up his stock purchases—loans hur-
riedly obtained at relatively high rates of interest. Many of them
were secured by Horace's treasurer, the wily Arthur Pell, who
sometimes made them from his own funds, with Horace's B&L
stock as collateral. This growing obsession with Wall Street resembled Horace's behavior back in the Hocking Coal and Iron
Company days of his youth. This time the stock that continued to
fascinate Horace was Mexican Seaboard, a volatile security that
never fulfilled its early promise. For a year or so he was able to
withstand the huge losses he suffered in the market because of the
unexpected revenues produced by Dracula in 1927–28. But Dracula

was unique; after 1928 Horace's play productions were costly failures.

He also invested heavily in the Stutz Corporation, the auto makers, and by August 1929 confessed to his wealthy young friend Leonard Amster that he was feeling the intense pressure of the market and desperately needed help. At the beginning of the 1920s Amster had worked briefly for him as a reader. In his letter, Horace brought up the subject of Amster's returning to the publishing world in, as Horace put it, "a rather big way. . . . I think what Arthur Pell and I might be able to say would interest you and your father." Horace's attempt to get Amster's father to invest in B&L was simply another of his efforts to stave off his creditors.

By July 1928 B&L was in extremely poor shape financially, despite the fact that this was the month that the firm had five of the ten titles on *Publishers Weekly*'s best-seller list—a record that few trade publishers had ever accomplished. A unique aspect of the list was that two of the titles were in verse—Dorothy Parker's *Sunset Gun* and Samuel Hoffenstein's *Poems in Praise of Practically Nothing*— while one was a play, O'Neill's *Strange Interlude*. The remaining two were both by Emil Ludwig, *Napoleon* and *Son of Man*. The best-seller list compiled by *The Retail Bookseller* (The Baker and Taylor Company) was even rosier, with six of the top ten sellers going to B&L. Their list contained the same titles by Parker, Hoffenstein, and O'Neill but added "Warner Fabian" 's *Unforbidden Fruit,* Maxwell Bodenheim's *Georgie May,* and Anita Loos's *But Gentlemen Marry Brunettes.* Although B&L sold more than a million books that year, its cash position was so precarious that measures had to be taken to curb Horace's constant draining of incoming funds to subsidize his losses in the market and on Broadway. Unearned advances and lavish parties were also contributing factors.

On the basis of the available evidence, we can conclude that it was Horace's idea to bring in his cousin Alfred Wallerstein to take over some but not all of the responsibility for turning the company around. Wallerstein, the man who had introduced Horace to Albert Boni back in 1917, was persuaded by him to invest in B&L by buying a substantial number of Horace's shares. Nominally, Horace would continue to run the company but his loss of shares would mean that he now had people around him who might over-see his expenditures. This purchase cost Horace loss of control over the company. Losing some financial control to his cousin would not have been so bad, but the day-to-day running of the company was now to be in the hands of the firm's dour treasurer, Arthur Pell, as the other new investor. Under a three-way agree-ment signed on July 19, 1928, Horace agreed (or was forced to agree) to sell 250 shares of his preferred stock, nearly all he owned, and 100 of the common to the Wallerstein/Pell team. Pell bought 91 shares of the preferred and 38 of the common, while Wallerstein became the owner of 159 shares of preferred and 52 of the common. Wallerstein paid $25,000 for his shares and Pell $15,000, thus netting Horace $40,000 with which to extricate himself from the weight of debt all around him.

It would appear that Wallerstein's participation in the reorga-nized company would be purely financial; he was to be a silent partner despite his relationship to Horace. In his new role as investor/treasurer of the renamed company—it was now Horace Liveright Inc.—Arthur Pell increased his own salary to $10,000 for 1929 and $11,000 for 1930. Horace did not fare as well; the new arrangements placed a ceiling on how much he could earn as the firm's president—the agreement expressly limited his salary to $25,000 per year; only the written approval of Arthur Pell could produce an increase. The documentation concerning Pell's gaining control of the company—outside the agreement itself—is scanty. It may be useful to turn again to Hanline's novel to fill in some of the picture. The climactic scene occurs at the moment when Jason

Pertinax (Horace) attempts to fire McPhail (Pell). McPhail's reply, addressed to the assembled board of directors, is unexpected:

> You can't fire a majority owner in the business . . . I repeat . . . you can't fire me. I and some others own most of this business. Personally, I own you, lock, stock, and barrel . . . I haven't been idle these years, while I've been handling the finances of this madhouse. . . .
>
> Friends have loaned us money, personal friends of mine, I mean. They've discounted your notes and they've been inclined to listen to me when I rediscounted them. . . . It's been very easy for you to say, I need five thousand dollars, you've got to get it for me. Then you signed a note, and I've done the same thing, week after week, and month after month, until I've got quite a stack of them in my safety deposit box.
>
> You've had easy talking, very easy talking. I'm talking now, Jason, money talk, and all of you have got to listen.

How much of this corresponds to the truth is unknown. It is revealing, however, that in Edith Stern's memoir of Horace, she does have the words "You have easy talking, Horace" coming from Arthur Pell's mouth.

It wasn't for lack of effort that B&L was in such bad shape. The previous year had seen the launching of a new series of classics, the Black and Gold Library, which Horace thought might replace the loss of the Modern Library. These were larger, far more expensively produced books, bound in shiny black cloth adorned with gold stamping. Nearly all the titles were obtained from the B&L backlist, including the *Satyricon* of Petronius, *The Golden Ass* of Apuleius, Honoré de Balzac's *Droll Stories,* and Boccaccio's *Decameron,* these last two with the Ralph Barton illustrations. Many in the publishing world regarded these books as high-class erotica, but other titles in the series became the favorites of university professors: *The Dialogues of Plato,* Laurence Sterne's *Tristram Shandy,* and *The Shorter Novels of Herman Melville,* which contained the first U.S. printing of *Billy Budd.* It was an innovative line; most of the titles remained in print for decades, but it was clear that the Black and Gold Library could never replace the Modern Library. The relatively high retail price of the books ($2.50) relegated them to a small place in the overall business picture of a firm with a huge overhead and an ever-growing load of debt.

There was much talk at this time about certain policy changes in the running of the firm—changes that might reverse B&L's misfortunes. Economies were in order and efforts were made in this direction, but with little effect. For the first time in the history of the firm, the year 1929 produced no raises or bonuses for the staff. Another change was the editorial decision to publish more cheap, sexy fiction, with Maxwell Bodenheim's books serving as a model. Bodenheim was turning out at least one of these each year—his *Georgie May* sold 23,000 copies. Tommy Smith, Messner, and Hanline began to search for manuscripts that could be published for a quick profit. They succeeded only once: Carmen Dee Barnes had written *School Girl,* a first novel which purported to portray life, mostly sexual, at a private school in the deep South. Miss Barnes was only seventeen and attractive; her lively presence at press interviews helped produce a sale of 25,000 copies. Her next novel, however, sold only 5,000. Barnes was clearly a temporary aberration; her books constituted only a small part of the firm's list in the last year of Horace's editorial control.

In June 1929 Horace wrote a five-page, single-spaced letter to Wallerstein. He began it by stating his concern about the firm, especially its financial woes. He blamed most of the trouble on the general state of the U.S. book market, telling his cousin that

I'm pretty badly worried, Alfred, about our situation. We have always been undercapitalized and have made the mistake when we

HBL and Carmen Dee Barnes, 1929.
UPI/Bettman

have had money, of always drawing it out. So far this year, our sales are about $150,000 shy of last year. This is in spite of Henry VIII [by Francis Hackett] being a book-of-the-month, and apart from that, the best-selling book in the country for about six weeks.

What Horace failed to tell his new partner was that, to operate
at a profit, the firm would have needed at least three such titles.
But it lacked them, and the losses were predictable considering the
company's crushing overhead and the large number of titles which
were published at a loss. The cruel truth was that far too many of
Horace's books were published in this manner, and that method,
plus the extravagant way he conducted his business, was surely
leading to collapse.

(3)

> Dear Horace, you have always had a genius for being a
> gambler in talent, and in developing the new and unknown
> writer of promise. . . . I feel as if I am about to be discovered
> by someone. How about it? Will you add me to your list of
> trophies?
> —Mike [Michael] Gold to HBL, 1929

HORACE obliged, and Mike Gold became one of the last writers
that he launched. Gold, the literary editor of *The New Masses,* would
become the intellectual voice of the American Communist Party in
the 1930s, as well as its most polemical in the war against bour-
geois values; his famous 1930 attack on Thornton Wilder's *The
Woman of Andros* attracted national attention. He was regarded as
the spiritual father of the American proletarian writers of the
time—and certainly the most militant. Now, in 1929, he had written *Jews Without Money,* one of the first truly working-class books to
appear in this country. Half novel, half autobiography, *Jews Without
Money* presented a picture of impoverished Jewish life on the
Lower East Side of Manhattan that most readers had never encountered before. Publishing a book like this at the very outset of the
depression that was to grip the country for the decade seems oddly
appropriate for a house that prided itself on always being in the

vanguard. *Jews Without Money* was certainly a "bad times" book, but it sold more than *13,000* copies in its first year.

Horace may have admired Mike Gold for what he believed were his socialist convictions, but at the very same time he introduced a number of *New Yorker* contributors who showed no such concerns. As the decade drew to a close, Horace published the first two col-

S. J. Perelman, *1929*.
Warder Collection, W. W. Norton Co.

lections of Dorothy Parker's poems, *Enough Rope* and *Sunset Gun*. These early books displayed none of the deeply felt left-wing political convictions of her later career. A second *New Yorker* writer—the magazine was then in its fourth year—was S. J. Perelman, who made his debut with *Dawn Ginsburgh's Revenge* and (in collaboration with Quentin Reynolds) *Parlor, Bedroom and Bath,* thus beginning a forty-year writing career. Decades later, Perelman satirized a number of Liveright's publications, including *Replenishing Jessica, Flaming Youth,* and *Black Oxen,* in his famous "Cloudland Revisited" series. Taking on Perelman at this time ultimately led to the firm's acquiring its most notable new novel to be published in the last days of its decline: Nathanael West's *Miss Lonelyhearts.*

Almost everyone in publishing in the late *1920*s knew that cartoon collections could not be sold. Peter Arno's first two collections, *Peter Arno's Parade* and *Hullabaloo,* proved them wrong with sales of *16,000* and *19,000* copies. Horace and his editors seemed to know that the public would flock to the creator of the little girl at the dinner table who made her views about food plainly known: "I say it's spinach and I say the hell with it."

Horace sent a copy of Arno's *Parade* to Bertrand Russell, then running his Beacon Hill School in Wales. Russell thanked him for "the delicious book of pictures by Peter Arno, which I regret to say I have not been able to keep out of the hands of the female members of my staff, damaging as I feel that it must be to their moral influence." Beacon Hill was an experimental school for small children.

As far back as *1919* Horace had felt that he had much in common with the great English philosopher, especially in the area of sexual conduct. Considering the difficulty and seriousness of much of Russell's writings, it may seem strange for him to have appeared on Horace's list with three best-selling books, but Russell had, unlike nearly everyone else in his field, an unsurpassed ability to produce

Peter Arno,
1929.
Warder Collection,
W. W. Norton Co.

Liveright ad for *Peter Arno's Parade,* 1929.
Warder Collection, W. W. Norton Co.

very readable prose on the most abstruse subjects. This talent extended to works like his 1912 volume *The Problems of Philosophy,* which is still being used as a basic text for undergraduate courses in philosophy. Horace began to court Russell in 1919 when he wrote him to inquire about the chances of his writing a little treatise on education for a projected series. But Russell couldn't, and neither could Freud or John Dewey; the series never materialized. The two men did not meet until Horace's second visit to London at the end of 1923. Russell then agreed to write, for a $750 advance, a full-length general book on education that would be ready for publication in the autumn of 1925.

By 1923 and for several years after this, Russell had been forced to rely on his writing talents to remain afloat after dismissal from his professorship at Trinity College, Cambridge, because of his antiwar views; four years after the Armistice he was still an unpopular teacher whom no institution would hire. His publishing relation with Horace was unusual; the three books he produced for the firm were all commissioned. They were books that Horace was convinced could be sold and that Russell was obviously the best man to write.

While awaiting the manuscript of the education book, Horace sent Russell a Christmas gift in 1924 of a beautiful edition of *Alice in Wonderland* he'd recently published. Russell's thank-you note informed Horace that he'd been "brought up on the first edition. (Unfortunately it did not belong to me.) The small boy [John Russell], aged 3, has already derived much pleasure from it, though I do not allow him to touch it."

When the first portion of the education book arrived in the fall of 1925, Horace wrote Russell:

> I would be an ungrateful publisher and a more ungrateful human being if I didn't write you at once to tell you how pleased I am with

the book so far. It is not only on Education, it is a book, to use your own words, on the good life, and I suggest the title Education and the Good Life.

Russell was delighted, and the book, still in print, sold nearly 25,000 copies in its first year. It was the beginning of a warm relationship between two men who had in common an immense talent for shocking the world about them. Horace had much to do with arranging Russell's successful lecture tours of the United States, the first in 1927.

This was not Russell's first visit to the United States, but it was quite unlike those he'd made in the years preceding the First World War. Those had been exclusively devoted to lecturing to academic audiences at Harvard and Bryn Mawr. Russell's agent arranged a coast-to-coast schedule of appearances for Russell at civic auditoriums and town halls. It was again his chronic shortage of funds that prompted Russell to set out on such an exhausting tour. While in New York, Russell was Horace's houseguest at the duplex on West Fifty-seventh Street—not really the place for an aging British philosopher to prepare himself for the task ahead. As has been mentioned earlier, Horace greeted his guest with a party on the day of his arrival; a few days later Russell endured his memorable evening with the B&L crowd up in Harlem. Horace couldn't spend enough time with his guest, keeping him up late for endless discussions. As for Russell, Horace's guided trips through New York society were startling and thought-provoking. As the visit drew to its close, Russell promised Horace that he'd return to the apartment on his next American tour.

When Russell returned to New York in the autumn of 1929, Horace again offered his hospitality. His guest was delighted: "I do not see how you could make me more comfortable than you did last time. The visions of sybaritic luxury conjured up by this

promise are most enticing." Things had changed in the two-year
interval between visits. This time Russell discovered that the
atmosphere at Horace's apartment was far more frenetic. As
Waldo Frank had noted, people appeared to be coming and going
at all hours; daily life at Horace's now resembled a permanent
party. It was all too much for Russell, and after a few days he left
the duplex for the quiet of the Gramercy Park Hotel. His departure did not significantly alter Horace's determination to see as
much as he could of the writer on his list whom—aside from
Sherwood Anderson—he admired most. He introduced the
always needy Russell to Otto Kahn in the hope that the philanthropist might come through with some funding for the philosopher's ailing Beacon Hill School, but to no avail. With Dorothy
Peterson in tow, Horace engaged him in a wide spectrum of social
activity: Everyone wanted to see and talk with the author of
Marriage and Morals, the second book of Russell's to be published
by the firm.

When Horace had written Russell that the Book-of-the-Month
Club might select *Marriage and Morals,* its author doubted they
would but indicated his willingness to make revisions if necessary.
"You will find me reasonable; but I am not prepared to conceal my
hostility to Christianity, & more particularly Catholicism." It was
at this time that Horace requested Russell to include a paragraph of
commendation for his publisher who had done so much for free
speech; early editions of *Marriage and Morals* contain this endorse-
ment. Asking for such "praise to the face" was not all that surprising: he wanted to be admired and didn't mind asking people to go
on record to say they did.

Horace and Russell had their final meeting at the Beacon Hill
School in Wales when Horace made his next trip to Europe in the
spring of 1930. During this meeting, Russell agreed to abandon
Horace's idea of a book about extroversion in favor of a more

attractive subject: *The Conquest of Happiness,* which was published at the end of that year. The diminished sales figures for this volume demonstrate what had happened to the U.S. book trade within only a year into the depression. *Conquest* sold just 13,000 copies, as compared with 25,000 for his two previous books.

(4)

I don't know exactly how long I'll be away.
—HBL to Bertrand Russell, July 7, 1930

DESPITE the few excursions into the Bodenheim/Carmen Barnes territory, Horace stuck to his risky editorial policies even when he was aware that they now appeared even more out of place in a bad time for the book business in general and an especially bad one for his firm's financial stability. It was his decision, for instance, to go on publishing Hart Crane in 1929, when the poet was completing *The Bridge.* In the summer of 1929 Crane had written to Horace, inquiring about the sales figures on his first book, *White Buildings,* and, since it appeared to be out of print, asked about the chance of reprinting it. When Julian Messner informed Horace that the sales amounted to 378 copies, Horace delayed answering Crane for some weeks—Messner's reply to his note about the possibility of reprinting had been terse: "Certainly not."

Crane wrote again, claiming that at least three universities were using the book in poetry classes. Horace, after some research, replied that

I cannot understand how the book can be on the students' pre-scribed reading list in at least three universities without our receiving some class orders, which he [Julian Messner] says have never come in.

At this point Horace made the characteristic gesture that made Pound call him the "pearl among the publishers": "However I have given instructions to reprint an edition and you will get a copy of the new edition as soon as it is ready."

A week or so later Horace had lunch with his young editor from Tennessee, Leane Zugsmith, who told him how much she admired the sections of *The Bridge* that Crane had recently shown her. Horace promptly wrote Crane about her enthusiasm: "Let me tell you that . . . we both had lots of nice things to say about you. She tells me that your new poem The Bridge is wonderful. I am awfully eager to see it." Despite the fact that the poem was going to be published first in Paris by Harry and Caresse Crosby and some copies would appear in New York bookstores, Horace contracted for the rights to the American edition and published it in the spring of 1930. *The Bridge* sold 700 copies in its first year, a sale that came as no surprise to Horace, who still felt it was his duty to publish such works.

Pell and Wallerstein may have felt that Horace did not always have his mind on what was happening on West Forty-eighth Street as 1929 drew to a close. The 700-copy sale of *The Bridge* was only a minor ripple in a sea of disasters: Dreiser and Anderson continued to produce their lesser works, which usually sold only about three or four thousand copies. Bertrand Russell, Peter Arno, and Eugene O'Neill were the only relatively bright spots on the autumn 1929 list. The firm had no big books on that list and nothing on the horizon promised any relief. As for Pell and Wallerstein, they must surely have noticed a story in their morning *Times* about Horace having spent an evening as the judge in a "Beauty Versus Brains" contest at Hunter College in Manhattan. Horace could almost never say no to an invitation, and he did not miss this opportunity

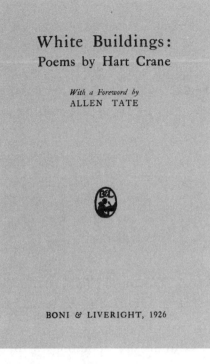

White Buildings:
Poems by Hart Crane

With a Foreword by
ALLEN TATE

BONI & LIVERIGHT, 1926

Title page for *White Buildings*.
Author's collection.

Hart Crane in the twenties.
Warder Collection, W. W. Norton Co.

to see confirmed that "brains" (the students) were indeed superior
to "beauty" (Broadway chorus girls)—the students won easily with
504 votes to the Broadway beauties' score of 326.

Horace's stock market losses were disastrous even in the months
just preceding the stock market crash in October, as he indicates in
this letter of August 29, written to Leonard Amster:

> The stock market has been disastrous for me. I'm a stubborn fool
> and realize it. I have nothing but Stutz and Mexican Seaboard and
> I'm out about $100,000 on these two stocks when other people
> have been making fortunes on good ones. I assure you I'm not
> blaming fate but only myself.

Horace's financial plight, nearly always the same as that of his firm,
was severe, with little to hope for in the first few tense months of
the Great Depression.

With all signs pointing to the imminent collapse of the firm,
Horace decided that it was time for an extended European buying
trip in the desperate hope that he might unearth some books to
turn the tide. He had told Wallerstein that he'd missed out on
Erich Maria Remarque's *All Quiet on the Western Front* by only a day
or so. Perhaps being on the scene might prevent such a loss in the
future. Just before his departure in March 1930 on the *Bremen,*
Horace told interviewers that he was arranging to see Mussolini,
Kemal Atatürk, and Stalin in order, he stated, to obtain books not
about war or the approach of war but about peace. He left New
York in mid-March and did not return until late May—the longest
of all his trips, but unfortunately not the most fruitful.

Horace left his old friend Fred Hummel in charge of daily oper-
ations in his absence. Although well known as a writer of commercial fiction (published by Horace), Hummel also had considerable
business experience. Horace hired him on a contingency basis to

raise capital for the company as well as to try to find a suitable buyer for the brownstone on West Forty-eighth Street. This was a wrenching decision for everyone in the firm, but there was no choice. With absolutely no cash reserves available, No. 61 represented the firm's chief salable asset. Things were now so bad that the semiannual royalties could not be paid. Selective decisions had to be made: Eugene O'Neill was the one author on the list who could not be slighted. He could easily void his contract if he could demonstrate the firm's inability to pay him. Unfortunately, the firm owed O'Neill more than any other author on the list. That spring the amount was $19,000 and was raised by combining the money received from the sale of Hendrik Willem Van Loon's *Rembrandt* to the Literary Guild plus a $10,000 "loan" from Wallerstein. Many in the firm must have wondered how long they could survive under such circumstances. But Hummel was sanguine, writing almost daily to Horace, telling him to relax:

> I, personally, don't give a damn whether you bring back a single contract. I know perfectly well that your trip regardless of that possibility will be of immense value to us as a publishing concern. And so far as I am concerned, I look on your trip to Europe with respect to its effect as a whole upon us rather than for any particular thing you might bump into.

Horace took him at his word and did relax.

None of Horace's planned interviews took place, and he brought back very few publishable books. He paid an extravagant $5,000 advance for an obscure Scandinavian novel, *Two Living and One Dead,* by Sigurd Christianson, a book that sold fewer than 4,000 copies. He had a pleasant time in Paris, where he lunched (separately) with Ezra Pound and Eugene O'Neill, neither of whom he had seen for years. A chatty visit to George Moore on

Ebury Street, London, was obligatory, as was a visit to Bertrand Russell's school in Wales. He hired Otto Theis to be the firm's chief European scout. He also ran up a series of very high hotel and entertainment bills that may have made his associates in New York wonder what to do.

Besides London and Paris, Horace's itinerary covered Berlin as well. In all these cities Horace made new friends and acquaintances, including Charles Gordon, a would-be screenwriter then working in Berlin. In the later part of Horace's trip, Gordon introduced him to Lena Bernstein, a young American aviatrix, as they were then called, who specialized in ferrying wealthy passengers across the English Channel. She flew Gordon and Horace to London and back to Paris at least once, when Horace paid her the substantial sum of 4,000 francs, which he appears to have thought was an advance on her unwritten memoirs. Alcohol had contributed to the misunderstanding—Miss Bernstein had to write Horace a note at the Hôtel Crillon in Paris to make it clear that half the 4,000 francs was payment for his friend Gordon's trip, while the other half covered his own. Accompanied by Gordon's friend Dick, the three men roared through a tour of European nightlife in Paris, London, and Berlin. There was even a side trip to Oslo. All the documentation about Horace's profligacy in his European wanderings wound up in the personal files of Arthur Pell, who was now in a position to use it for his own purposes.

Traveling around Europe with Lena Bernstein as one's flying chauffeur was exhilarating, as Gordon told Horace after his return to New York:

Dick had the good sense to stay sober on the return trip with dear Lena—but I didn't. So . . . I nearly froze to death flying back without any liquor and without a coat—the dear girl kept her windows open as usual. Of course, on the way over we didn't know whether

the windows were open or closed. . . . I wonder if you have the
marvelous memories of the delightful hours we spent together . . .
the trip to Oslo and dear sweet Lena.

Back in New York Hummel and the others (Pell and Messner)
vetoed spending any money on Lena's search for fame under the
Liveright imprint.

When Horace returned to New York in late May 1930, he had little to show for his ten weeks abroad. On his arrival he encountered
a publishing industry convulsed by what became known as the
"book war." With little or nothing selling widely in the stores,
Doubleday and three other major houses began to wage a price war
in which they published most of their new spring fiction at the
price of one dollar; nonfiction titles were reduced by about 40 percent. The draconian move terrified most of the book trade, especially Liveright. Cutting prices was impossible for a firm close to
going under. In addition, there was a tremendous feeling of uncer-
tainty in all areas of business in the wake of the very recent stock
market crash—the mood captured so well by John O'Hara in
Appointment in Samarra. With the panic produced by the book war,
it is likely that the huge expenses incurred by Horace on his
European jaunt, and its nearly fruitless results, made his departure
from the firm an absolute necessity for its survival. Horace
Liveright Inc. could no longer afford Horace, his high living, his
high salary, or his habit of writing checks for advances on books to
be published far in the future. Whether Horace was fired by Pell
and his associates or simply resigned can only be guessed at. When
the story leaked out that he was leaving the firm he had created in
1917, Horace preferred to view it as only a temporary move. In all
the letters he wrote to his favorite writers about the situation, he
made the same point. He wrote Bertrand Russell:

HBL standing in front of
61 West Forty-eighth
Street, spring 1930.
Lucy Wilson collection

It will interest you to know that I am going to the Pacific Coast in
two or three weeks to see two or three authors who are out there
and who have been begging me for a long time to visit them and
also to work on the filming of two or three books in which we are
interested. I don't know exactly how long I'll be away.

Horace was unable to face the naked truth that he had no choice
but to leave for California. He became a little more specific with
Eugene O'Neill, assuring him that he "hadn't sold myself down the
river." He told the playwright that he had worked out a plan for his

new job with Otto Kahn, who had banking connections with Paramount: "I am to spend two or three months in carefully going over our entire list of books from the time we started publishing and attempt to find two or three really outstanding publications for the talkies." In a sad postscript to his letter to O'Neill, who was living in Paris, Horace appeared fully aware that the dramatist had certainly read the news of his departure in the *Paris Tribune*. He addressed the issue by saying, "Of course the idea of my divorcing myself from my true love is utterly ridiculous."

It was indeed ridiculous but at the same time obvious that Horace was leaving publishing against his wishes. But he told hardly anybody that he had persuaded Paramount Publix—itself a company not far from bankruptcy—into hiring him at $500 a week for a trial period of six months. Horace's publishing career, perhaps the brightest of the century, was finished.

Eisenstein and Hollywood

EVERYTHING HERE IS MOVING ALONG BEAUTIFULLY AND I LIKE IT
IMMENSELY.

     —HBL to Arthur Pell, August 14, 1930

(1)

HORACE was being less than candid. While things were decidedly tense in the world of New York book publishing, they were
equally if not more so in Hollywood in the summer of 1930 when
Horace first began working at Paramount. The transition to sound
films was complete by the end of 1929, but the expense of wiring
thousands of theaters throughout the country had been—and continued to be—gigantic. It was only during 1930 that the Warner
Brothers Vitaphone system (sound on phonograph record) was
replaced by both the RCA Photophone system and Fox Movietone
(sound on film), which became standard for the industry.
Enormous sums of money had been spent on the installation of
sound equipment at the moment when revenues from film rentals
began an irreversible plunge because of the growing depression.

Near panic, the industry became extremely cost conscious in all areas of film production.

The sound revolution left many basic esthetic questions unanswered. The talkies were certainly here to stay, but how was the element of sound going to influence the kind of movies that were to be made? Only two kinds of pictures seemed surefire: musical comedies or operettas and adaptations of successful Broadway plays. In the musical comedy area, although they were expensive to make, things started well with the enormous success of MGM's *Broadway Melody* of 1929, which produced a profit of $1.5 million. But the market had become glutted very quickly, with more than a hundred musicals produced within a single year. As for the filmed plays, they remained just that: self-conscious actors addressing their lines to the sound equipment. As late as the beginning of 1931, many actors were convinced that working in the talkies meant speaking in a special way; speech schools that guaranteed students a voice that would qualify them for employment as speaking actors had mushroomed all over Hollywood. Virtually all the dialogue in the early sound films has a slow, leaden pace in which every syllable can be clearly heard. There was uncertainty about the way dialogue should be spoken. For example, what were the studios to do with the great silent comics of the twenties—Charlie Chaplin, Buster Keaton, and Harold Lloyd? If they had to talk, what were they going to say and how would they say it? All in all, it was a terrible time for Horace to enter an industry about which he knew nothing and in which even the greatest were having problems.

The position of Cecil B. DeMille at this time is indicative of what Horace encountered on his arrival at Paramount. Along with Jesse Lasky and Adolph Zukor, DeMille had been one of the three founders of Paramount. His status as a maker of hugely successful historical spectaculars like the 1927 *King of Kings* was unsurpassed.

HBL at his desk at Paramount, August 1930.
Culver Pictures

But in 1929 his conservative colleagues at the studio refused to support him in his efforts to make any more such films. In frustration, DeMille left Paramount to accept a three-picture deal from Irving Thalberg at MGM. Thalberg, however, was suffering from the same cost-consciousness as Lasky and Zukor. DeMille made three pictures for MGM (on subjects chosen for him by the studio), all three financial disasters. One of them, *Madame Satan* (a musical), tops some people's lists of the campiest films ever made. Shattered by what had happened to him at MGM, DeMille wrote to a friend:

> I cannot find any inspiration at all in the type of pictures that producers want me to make. They are in a state of panic and chaos. . . . I cannot find a producer who is willing to do anything but follow the mad rush for destruction.

If DeMille had met defeat, what could Horace hope for in such a climate?

When he'd told Eugene O'Neill that he'd been able to obtain his Paramount job through the influence of Otto Kahn, Horace wasn't telling the entire truth. It had been Jesse Lasky, then head of production at Paramount, who had hired Horace in New York. The two men had remained friendly ever since the coffee-throwing incident with Dreiser, and a peculiar kind of bond had grown between them. In the last year or so of his command over the firm, Horace had thoughtfully published two collections of verse by members of Lasky's family: Bessie Lasky's collection *And I Shall Have Music* and Jesse Jr.'s *Songs from the Heart of a Boy.* The sales figures for these little books were not good—105 copies for Bessie and 345 for Jessie Jr.—but the sales possibilities had not been the deciding factor in publishing them. It was clear that Lasky was in Horace's debt, and one way to pay it was to hire him as an "executive supervisor." Horace's $500-a-week contract for six months was the result.

There is nothing of interest concerning Horace in Paramount's production or legal files. With a single exception, none of his ideas was taken up by the studio. Horace had little to offer the executives of Paramount. Although he'd told his friends in the East that he would be going over the Liveright list to see if certain properties could be made into films, this was old hat to the people at Paramount. All the novels Horace now discussed with them had been offered to them previously and had been turned down for a variety of reasons. Once the Liveright backlist had been examined and rejected, Horace had good reason to wonder how he was going to earn his salary.

There was, however, a single exception on the list of projects: Dreiser's *An American Tragedy,* which Horace had sold to the studio four years earlier and which, because of the nature of the story, had never been placed in production. On this single occasion, Horace's enthusiasm for a book produced a positive response from the executive board, or at least from one member of it (Lasky), who believed that he had recently hired in Europe a man who might successfully write and direct a powerful film based on Dreiser's book. This was Sergei M. Eisenstein, the great Russian director whose *Battleship Potemkin* had created a worldwide sensation in the mid-twenties. By 1930 his name was magic in all advanced film circles. The Soviet government had given its most famous filmmaker a one- or even two-year leave of absence to tour the West in order to obtain information about the competing sound systems in the countries he visited. In his various stopovers in London, Berlin, and Paris, Eisenstein had lectured on the future of the film with great success. His English was fluent, and it is easy to see why Jesse Lasky, with the future of sound films very much in doubt, might hire Eisenstein to write and direct films for Paramount. He gave the Russian a six-month trial contract very much like Horace's— except for the money.

Paramount agreed to pay Eisenstein and his two associates, Grigori Alexandrov and Edward Tissé, a total of a thousand dollars a week to come up with film projects. Arriving just six weeks before Horace, the Russians settled down in a rented house in

Sergei Eisenstein at Paramount, July 1930.
Condé Nast

Coldwater Canyon. The threesome was accompanied by the young British Marxist critic Ivor Montagu and his wife; Montague idolized Eisenstein and hoped to assist him in the land of the capitalists. Within a few weeks they submitted their first effort, "Sutter's Gold," but it was deemed too expensive to produce. Things were

at a standstill until the beginning of August when Horace arrived
with his ideas about filming Dreiser.

When Eisenstein and Montagu discovered that Horace had convinced the studio to produce *An American Tragedy* and that they were
to be assigned the project, with Horace as their supervisor, they
were dumbfounded. Eisenstein had read the book and knew that an
honest version of its contents would be financially disastrous for
Paramount and his team as well. Dreiser's book was, Eisenstein
thought, far too critical of American society to succeed as a popular
film—strange news coming from the lips of a Soviet "people's filmmaker." But he would not entertain the idea of weakening the story
with a happy ending. And so Eisenstein's team reluctantly began
work on a project they considered doomed from the start. Part of
their bitterness arose from the distrust they felt toward Horace,
whose interests, they believed, were certainly not theirs.

Knowing that Horace was behind the Dreiser project, it is perhaps not surprising that Eisenstein appears to have been cool
toward Horace from the onset of their brief time together. He
described his work as a publisher thus:

> It makes no difference whether his books are political, social,
> morally risqué, or simply amoral. They are always sensational. A
> court case. A ban. . . . The public campaign against the court's
> decision. Apart from the ancient erotica and the extreme thereti-
> cians of psychology, Horace publishes with much fuss and publicity
> the early Dreiser.

Eisenstein seemed particularly incensed that Horace had a reputation as a publisher of erotica, a forbidden subject for dedicated
Communists. As for Horace, he had little choice in the matter. If
all they could do at Paramount was to assign him to supervise an
unpredictable, strong-willed director, he would just do that. The
prospects for success in making the film were dim; Ivor Montagu

was convinced that Jesse Lasky had never read Dreiser's book and had no idea of what he was leading his firm into. Once he found out, there was bound to be trouble.

Horace was also caught in the power struggle then in progress between his sponsor, Lasky, and the chief executive who challenged his power, B. P. Schulberg. Horace liked to think of Paramount's hierarchy as consisting of tiny Adolph Zukor as the Father, Lasky as the Son, and Walter Wanger in New York as the Holy Ghost. Within two months after Horace's arrival in Hollywood, the cast of characters changed, with Schulberg becoming the Holy Ghost and Wanger suddenly being dumped. With box-office receipts dropping to all-time lows, what was to be the fate of such a daring enterprise as *An American Tragedy?*

(2)

Today on the Paramount "white sheets" my production assignments were reduced from four to two and not a word was said to me about it, so I haven't much work to do.
—HBL to Dorothy Peterson, autumn 1930

[In 1931] the pride was breaking . . . the more he drank the more we talked of those days, not so many years before.
—Lillian Hellman, 1969

HORACE had sublet the home of the actor Eugene O'Brien, located on Whitley Heights, about twelve miles from the ocean. He chose that location because Dorothy Peterson had an apartment nearby. They resumed the relationship that had been suddenly interrupted in New York when Dorothy had been offered a short-term contract at Warner Brothers. After her initial appearance in a tearjerker called *Mother's Cry,* Dorothy settled down into a solid career as a featured player typecast as a sympathetic nurse or as the understanding older sister of the leading lady (or man). Despite her youth and physical attractiveness, Dorothy played these roles so well that she was never able to escape them. She appeared in a number of famous films, including *Payment Deferred, I'm No Angel, Dark Victory, Saboteur, Air Force,* and *The Woman in the Window.* Unlike most young players of the time, Dorothy refused the safety of long-term contracts and worked on a freelance basis for virtually every studio in Hollywood.

The first few months of working for Paramount were pleasant for Horace. With Dorothy accompanying him nearly everywhere, he was invited to dozens of parties in Hollywood. Many people were eager to renew their acquaintance with the man who had revolutionized American publishing or curious because they had heard of him from afar. Among his older friends, Horace saw much of Eddie Mayer and his wife, Herman and Sara Mankiewicz, the historian Herbert Asbury, the novelist Jim Tully, Lillian Hellman, the playwright Samson Raphaelson, Upton Sinclair, and the Gershwin brothers, George and Ira. A particular joy lay in renewing his friendship with the pianist José Iturbi, whom Horace had originally met in London through the good offices of his friend Julie Lasden. Horace had heard Iturbi play at Aeolian Hall and urged the Spanish musician to try his luck in America. After his great success in New York, Iturbi would introduce Horace as "his Columbus." Horace recalled that his first recital at Carnegie Hall "was one of the greatest triumphs I have ever witnessed. . . . After the final encore, Dorothy and I unashamedly threw our arms around each other and clung together in an ecstatic embrace. We felt that it was my triumph as well as Iturbi's." Now, here in California, was "Meester Eetoorbi" on the phone, calling from Tucson, Arizona, and wondering if Horace and Dorothy could put him up until he found a place of his own.

Horace was delighted to oblige and before the distinguished

musician's departure for New York they had heard his entire concert repertory. In the morning, he and Dorothy would listen to
Iturbi, the hosts dressed in lounging pajamas in what Horace called
the "heavenly California sunshine." At night, after one of his concerts, "Dorothy and [he] would come back to my home for some
scrambled eggs and champagne." Iturbi did not like large parties
and permitted Horace to give only one in his honor. Iturbi liked
Hollywood so much that he returned in the 1940s to launch a long
screen-acting career in a number of musicals. Music was always
one of Horace's passions, and having Iturbi around day and night
made his problems at Paramount easier to bear.

With Dorothy as a willing pupil, Horace began a series of joint
readings in modern literature that oddly anticipate Sheilah Gra-
ham's famous *College of One,* in which F. Scott Fitzgerald attempted
to broaden the cultural perspectives of his young lover. Together,
Horace and Dorothy read H. G. Wells's *Outline of History,* Aldous
Huxley's *Point Counter Point,* Virginia Woolf's *Orlando,* Julien
Green's *Dark Journey,* James Joyce's *Portrait of the Artist as a Young
Man,* Dostoyevsky's *Crime and Punishment,* and Proust's *Swann's
Way.* Many of the books were read at the beach at Santa Monica. At
this time Horace was apparently attempting to control his drinking
and went out of his way to mention that he and Dorothy would
"drink an occasional gin-ricky."

The script for *An American Tragedy,* written almost entirely by
Eisenstein himself, was completed by October and (according to
Montagu) was found extraordinarily good by both Schulberg and
Lasky. Schulberg was quoted as saying that it was "the best scenario
Paramount ever had." The picture was to be placed into immediate
production; the Eisenstein team was asked to leave for New York,
where some of the exteriors were to be shot. When the threesome
reported to Lasky's office in New York a few days later, they were

shocked to be told: "Gentlemen, it is over. Our agreement is at an end." Once the dramatics were over, the truth was plain enough. Lasky explained that Paramount had been under attack all summer by Major Frank Pease, a self-styled patriot who was the president of an obscure organization called the Hollywood Technical Directors Institute. Pease had been firing off attacks for months about Paramount's perfidy for having brought the "cut-throat Red dog, Eisenstein" to the United States to make films that would undermine the American way of life. Some of Pease's press remarks about "the Moscow Jew, Eisenstein" were blatantly anti-Semitic. Major Pease was so extreme that his attacks would not have caused all that much damage, but the issue was then taken up by Congressman Hamilton Fish from New York, who was attempting to create what Martin Dies succeeded in doing in the late 1930s: a House Un-American Activities Committee.

David O. Selznick, then on Paramount's payroll as a junior producer, had this to say about the script for *An American Tragedy* and the effect that its production might have on "happy-minded Americans":

> It was for me a memorable experience; the most moving script I have ever read. It was so effective, that I wanted to reach for the bourbon bottle. As entertainment, I don't think it has one chance in a hundred. . . . I should like to suggest that we have the courage not to make the picture, but to take whatever rap is coming to us for not supporting Eisenstein the artist (as he proves himself to be with this script), with a million or more of the stockholders' cash.

Selznick's memo was addressed to his boss, B. P. Schulberg, and it may well be that this was the decisive factor which forced Lasky to abandon production plans as well as terminate Eisenstein's contract. The situation was extremely awkward for Horace, because the Dreiser project was the only one with which he had been associated since his arrival at the studio. Now that it was dead, how was he to justify Paramount's keeping him on salary?

One other factor that had been rankling the Paramount executives about the project was Horace's (and Dreiser's) insistence that they were entitled to an additional share for the talkie rights to the book, claiming that the studio had only bought the rights to make a silent film. The studio, eager to proceed, reluctantly decided to pay them what they wanted. There was then a new dispute between Dreiser and Horace, which remained unresolved. Dreiser refused to give Horace any of his share. Paramount finally settled the issue by giving Horace $4,000, but the bitterness the issue had created was very likely to have been in the minds of those who were to determine Horace's future at the studio. By early January 1931 the decision was made: On Horace's employment record, in the space where contract renewals were to be entered, appears the curt notation "NO—Lew." After only six months Horace was again out of a job.

(3)

> Well, Liveright . . . I know all the trouble you had over at Paramount. . . . You were sent out here from the East and you didn't have a chance with Schulberg from the minute you put your foot on the train in New York. He heard you had brains and guts.
> —Charles Rogers to HBL, 1931

THE speaker was the head of production at Pathé Studios, one of the nine major film-producing firms in 1931. In business for twenty years, the Pathé production facilities at Culver City were the main attraction when the newly created RKO Radio Pictures Corporation bought the organization later that year. Fortunately,

Horace's agent managed to obtain for him at Pathé very much the
same kind of position he'd held at Paramount: "production supervisor." The salary was the same, $500 a week, and again it was for
six months. But working conditions would be much tougher for
him there than at Paramount:

> I was put on the spot in two studios,—in a mild fashion by the
> more civilized Paramount organization but in a way that would
> have been humiliating to one who could not afford to laugh at it, by
> the over-lords of the Pathé studio.

In their initial meeting, Rogers had been blunt why he was hiring Horace:

> I know all the trouble you had over at Paramount . . . but I knew
> what you were up against. . . . You're the sort of man we want
> around here to give the place tone. . . . It would be nice to have a
> man like you sit at a table with us when we eat because I'll bet you
> know how to use a knife and fork!

Being hired to lend "class" to the studio was probably unexpected, but Horace dutifully began attending the daily story con-
ferences and screenings. When he suggested to the Pathé board
that they buy the rights to O'Neill's *Strange Interlude,* they weren't
interested. Irving Thalberg at MGM did buy it the following year
for his wife, Norma Shearer, and Clark Gable, whose star power
sold enough tickets to produce a modest profit of $90,000. It may
be that Pathé's decision was the right one for them: They had no
Gables.

Shortly after joining Pathé, Horace had an unpleasant altercation
at a large party with Leonore Gershwin, who was supported by her
husband, Ira, and his brother, George. Probably Horace's drinking

was responsible for whatever happened. George and Ira were then
working at Fox Films on the songs for the new Janet Gaynor film,
Delicious; it was for this film that George Gershwin wrote what
became his *Second Rhapsody.* The confrontation was so severe that
news of it flew back to New York, where Tommy Smith and Julian
Messner were in regular touch with their old boss. When Smith
wrote Horace asking for details about the incident, Horace went
on the offensive in his reply:

> Poor, poor deluded mid-Victorian! So you believed all the stories,
> didn't you? Good lord, if I was stupid enough to write to you about
> all the stories that are brought out here regarding your conduct . . .
> why I would take the first aeroplane east to attend your funeral.
> . . . The Gershwin thing is easily understood and shows once more
> what venom is in so many people. The only time I saw George
> Gershwin except to nod to him at lunch . . . was at a party which he
> and his brother and sister-in-law gave. I went with Eddie Mayer
> . . . [who] can testify to my grace, wit, charm, sobriety and ele-
> gance of demeanor that evening. Since you mention George
> Gershwin's name, I must insist you see him and demand an expla-
> nation. I think you will find that his sister-in-law plays a big part in
> it all. She was lightly spiffed at a party at Sam's [Hoffenstein] and
> told me that both her husband and George were both dull idiots,
> particularly George. I flirted with her rather mildly, promised to
> call her up for tea the next day and promptly forgot all about her
> until Eddie took me to the party.

Horace is blustering here, but he follows this with strongly felt
claims about his sobriety:

> As a matter of fact, my dear friend, I have never done less drinking
> in public since I have been fifteen or sixteen years old than I have
> done in the last seven months out here. I was tight at exactly one

HBL in a Dracula-like pose at RKO, spring 1931.
Billy Rose Collection, New York Public Library

party, which is almost a record out here for anyone who drinks at all; and once again, at this party I was unfortunate enough to annoy the beautiful Alice Glazer by flirting with her there and absolutely dropping her afterward. She has made the most of it, but it doesn't bother me in the least.

But Horace's behavior at these parties probably did bother the people at Pathé, who heard more reliable accounts than did Tommy and Julian in New York. It may be safe to say that at forty-seven, Horace could not now predict what he might do when drinking. This loss of control, plus an increasing denial that anything is wrong, are sure signs of advanced alcoholism. In a letter written two months later to Smith and Messner, Horace casually mentions that he is "commencing to feel myself again, but I had two rotten weeks in bed and one week of anything but comfortable convalescence." Three weeks "out sick" coupled with the stories about his behavior at parties surely weakened his position at Pathé.

But there were bright moments during his tenure at Pathé. Horace had told Bertrand Russell and Eugene O'Neill that he would be visiting a number of his authors in California and he now kept his promise. Accompanied by Dorothy, Horace visited the writer in San Francisco who had given him his first major fiction best-seller back in 1923. Gertrude Atherton, the *grande dame* of California writers, took Horace to task for what "she termed my desertion from the field of publishing. She kindly told me that she knew no one who could immediately take my place in it." He attempted to reassure her that her editorial needs would be taken care of by Tommy Smith.

Although he had published *Roan Stallion*—the book that made Robinson Jeffers famous—in 1925, Horace had never met the shy, withdrawn poet who continued to produce a series of long narratives about violent people and deeds on the rugged Pacific coast around Carmel and Point Sur. Eliot, Pound, Crane, and cummings all had their partisans at 61 West Forty-eighth Street, but the favorite of Horace, Bennett Cerf, and Donald Friede was always Jeffers. Cerf thought so much of Jeffers that when he had a chance to buy some of the assets of Horace's firm, he acquired the work of only two writers, Eugene O'Neill and Jeffers.

There had been no invitation from Jeffers: Horace had simply wired the poet from Hollywood, asking if he and Dorothy could pay a visit. The poet was widely known for his love of solitude in the wilderness surrounding his famous stone house, but he responded favorably and waited patiently for the arrival of his ex-publisher. When Dorothy and Horace located the Jeffers place, they were briefly dismayed to find a sign reading "Away for three days," but this announcement proved to be due to Jeffers's absent-mindedness: he had simply forgotten to take the sign down after the family's last motor trip. The visitors were greeted by the poet's wife, Una, and their twin fourteen-year-old boys, Garth and Donnan. Jeffers showed them around their home, called Tor House, built by the poet himself out of stones found in the imme-diate area. He also showed them his Hawk Tower, the smaller building where he wrote. Horace's magnetism was still effective: although not usually given to talk, Jeffers stayed up conversing with his guests long past midnight. The following day he took them for a two-hour drive along the Pacific coast that he had made famous in *The Women at Point Sur* and *Thurso's Landing*.

When the subject of Horace's departure from publishing arose, his reply to Jeffers's question about the matter was a bit mysteri-ous. He told the poet that "my love for books had largely motivated my desire," which told him nothing. The two men spent hours talking about writing and the few people they knew in common, with Horace informing Jeffers that he was having a much better time now because "we were two men together rather than an author and publisher." Jeffers was amused by Horace's account of his single meeting with Joseph Conrad during which Conrad had spoken of his dread of publishers:

Mr. Liveright . . . when they get here Friday afternoon, the first two hours aren't so bad, discussing sales figures, methods of exploitation, and ideas for future books, but from then until

Monday morning it is such a terrible, terrible ordeal. After that we have so little to say, largely, I am sure, because we are just a bit afraid of each other.

The two days spent with Jeffers and his family filled Horace with a feeling that the thirteen years he had spent in publishing books had been "stultifying." He may have been trying to cheer himself up—the time he spent with Mrs. Atherton and Jeffers could only remind Horace of his great days on West Forty-eighth Street. His new life of daily board meetings at Pathé, where his role was to furnish "tone" to the proceedings, was no substitute.

Lillian Hellman, who was now working as a reader for Sam Goldwyn, ran into Horace at a number of Hollywood parties. She caught a glimpse of what her old boss was really feeling in his new role of studio executive:

Some of the old glamour was there, where his name was famous, and his recent history not yet fully understood. But every time I saw him—not many times, perhaps five or six . . . I knew, for a simple reason, that the pride was breaking: he would, immediately, cross the room to sit beside me because I alone in the room was the respectful young girl who had known him in the great days, and the more he drank the more we talked of those days, not so many years before.

As if to demonstrate that book publishing was never far from his thoughts, Horace came up with an idea for a little book to be called *Yes Man's World,* which would contain the distilled wit and humor of the countless stories about life in the big studios. He passed the idea on to Tay Garnett, later to become famous as the director of *Slave Ship* and *The Postman Always Rings Twice,* and Tom Buckingham, a colleague at Pathé. Once Garnett and Buckingham had taken to Horace's idea, he wrote Tommy Smith and Julian Messner requesting a contract and a small advance. Horace was convinced that the little book (to be priced at a dollar) would have a sale of at least 10,000 copies. Just in case Smith and Messner had any reservations about the project, Horace attempted to quiet them by sending them a long collect wire that actually included the selling copy for the book to be included in the upcoming fall Liveright catalog. He gave a sample of the volume's contents by concluding his telegram with IN THE WORDS OF THE MOST IMPORTANT TALKIE EXECUTIVE I'LL GIVE YOU THE ANSWER IN TWO WORDS IM POSSIBLE, an ancient Sam Goldwynism that should have alerted Smith and Messner to the fact that nearly everyone knew these stories and that several publishers had already lost money by publishing them. It is perhaps significant that Horace's telegram was sent collect and that it was addressed not to 61 West Forty-eighth Street but to 31 West Forty-seventh Street, the firm's new address. Fred Hummel had finally sold No. 61, and the newly reorganized firm was occupying far cheaper space in an office building just off Fifth Avenue. The old Liveright ambiance (and perhaps the magic) was now gone for good—Tay Garnett's little book sold less than 4,000 copies.

When Horace claimed that both Paramount and Pathé had put him "on the spot," he probably meant that he was in an untenable position, because they would never accept any of his ideas about making films. Indeed, Horace's Pathé contract was not renewed at the end of the summer, and since his reputation as a nonproducing producer who drank heavily was established, it was unlikely that he could obtain another job in Hollywood. In addition, since economic conditions in the industry were far worse than they had been on his arrival, there was little point in hanging on. He wanted to have Dorothy accompany him back to New York, but she refused (perhaps wisely), and they quarreled over the issue.

When Horace was writing his autobiography in the summer of 1933, it had been two years since he had last seen Dorothy. When he mentioned their final parting in Hollywood two years earlier, he appeared to have little hope of ever seeing her again. But he could not close the door completely:

> Dorothy and Eddie drove me to the train and as I held Dorothy in my arms and kissed her good-bye it seemed to be good-bye indeed, and not merely au revoir. Of course, one never knows.

The Light Fades

As you stay on in a given place, things and people go to
pieces around you and start to stink for your own special
benefit.
              —Louis-Ferdinand Céline, 1932

[HBL] could be found tapping his long cigarette holder
nervously at a table at the Algonquin, a mere shadow of his
former jaunty self.
              —Bennett Cerf, 1933

(1)

HORACE had met defeat in California, a confrontation that he
had not experienced as sharply since the day he'd discovered that
John Smith was not going to be staged. He had taken on the
Hollywood jobs partly in desperation but also because there
appeared to be no future in any of the things that mattered to him
in New York. Book publishing had been out of the question then,
and it continued to be so now. Horace Liveright was a luxury that
publishers in New York could not afford even if they had wished to
do so. His high salary and even grander spending habits had priced
him out of the market. In addition, everyone knew that Horace
could never work successfully under someone else's direction. Or,
as Louis Kronenberger put it: "Horace could scarcely work any-
where at all. . . . Horace had to sit at the head of the table, and
carve—it was the *role* that mattered." His only hope now lay in

returning to his first love, the Broadway stage, where, however, the future appeared as cloudy as book publishing, a situation brought about by the ever-increasing pressures of the Depression. Whatever productions Horace chose to mount would have to be financed in the same old way—finding investors willing to gamble twenty or thirty thousand dollars against enormous odds. But he had no choice, and for the next two years Horace was involved in the nearly hopeless struggle to obtain funds to produce plays in 1932 and 1933.

The New York that Horace had left in August 1930 was not the same as the one he returned to a year later. One of the most dramatic changes appeared now every evening only a few blocks away from his apartment at the Hotel Salisbury on West Fifty-seventh Street. At nearby Columbus Circle, thousands of unemployed men lined up to receive their allotment of coffee and doughnuts, or soup, or sometimes even stew, a gift of the Hearst newspaper chain. Another venue for free food was located off Times Square, a fact deplored by theater managers, who feared that so much open misery could be bad for business. These long breadlines were located all over New York; many people stayed alive by going from one to another during the course of the day. All over the city, the employment agencies had lines stretching around the block. Some local movie admissions had dropped to as low as a dime; the best seats at the Roxy now cost fifty-five cents. Men selling apples for a nickel were everywhere. Pay cuts had become standard procedure in most businesses. Only some of the wealthy remained unaffected by the Depression, which worsened every day.

For the moment at least, Horace continued to live on in the high style to which he was accustomed. He had managed to save a few thousand dollars from his Pathé checks, and this money would have to last until the tide turned in his favor. He spent the first few weeks in getting reacquainted with many of the hundreds of friends he hadn't seen for over a year. He saw a good deal of his children,

Herman and Lucy. Herman was now studying at Carnegie Tech in Pittsburgh, while Lucy, after attending a series of schools in France, spent much of her time with her mother in Westchester. Both children had liked Dorothy Peterson and undoubtedly wondered what had happened to the woman their father had called "the love of my life."

Horace continued to think about Dorothy and her life apart from him in Hollywood. A mutual friend, Helen Woodward, attests to the number of their late phone calls, some of which were filled with accusations and recriminations. Helen also kept up a regular correspondence with Eddie Mayer in Hollywood, who was always glad to hear news about Horace. When Mayer inquired about Horace's drinking, Helen replied:

> Mostly Horace has been sober when I've seen him. But from what other people say I gather that was for my benefit. When I did see him tight, he had only one subject of conversation. Dorothy. Why doesn't she write? Why has she phoned him so often at two in the morning? Did we think you [Mayer and Dorothy] were consoling each other—[the] last repeated till we had to answer it seriously but I know so much on the subject, and he was so upset, that I told him that if Dorothy was angry it was about time. That she'd delayed the moment for years.

Horace had not, predictably, taken up celibacy. He had become involved with Elise Bartlett, a pretty young ingenue whom he may have first met the previous year in Hollywood, where she appeared in a small role in the Universal production of *Show Boat*. Elise had then been married to the film's star, the well-known Broadway actor Joseph Schildkraut. The Schildkrauts had maintained a jealousy-ridden, stormy marriage that ended in 1930. Now, a year later, Elise and Horace were about to be married. This union with a woman he scarcely knew can be regarded as a "spite marriage," in which Horace was telling Dorothy, "All right, if you won't return to New York to marry me, I'll just marry Elise." At least Helen Woodward thought so, telling Mayer, "Tommy Smith and I think it's [the wedding] for Dorothy's benefit. But Dorothy's adjusted and getting along so well. For God's sake don't tell her so."

Helen also told him that "the party for the wedding had been a horror" but spared him the details of what happened at the reception held in a penthouse apartment at 148 East Forty-eighth Street. Many of Horace's closest friends were there: Julian Messner and his wife, Kitty, Tommy Smith, Horace's attorney Arthur Hays, Hendrik Willem Van Loon, Otto Kahn, Condé Nast, and Dorothy Day. Hetty Liveright, his mother, was there, as well as his sisters, Ada and Carrie. Young Lucy and Herman attended, and film stars Edmund Lowe and Lilyan Tashman. Lillian Hellman and Dashiell Hammett were invited, but Lillian did not care to go. Hammett, who didn't know Horace well, talked her into going to the reception. It proved to be a tawdry, drunken affair at which Horace spent most of the afternoon and early evening passed out in one of the bedrooms. His bride, visibly drunk, lurched around the apartment, demanding a divorce because of the black eye she had received from her husband, although Hellman noted that her eyes were "beautiful and clear." Louis Kronenberger recalled that Horace and Elise had invited "a great many people, people oddly familiar, people weirdly anonymous, at length such a mongrel crowd as only the prohibition era could assemble." The reception was a strange gathering of Horace's literary friends and Broadway types, a mixture so unpleasant to some that Hendrik Willem Van Loon left almost immediately, as did some of Horace's oldest friends.

One report has it that Horace had been assaulted in the early afternoon by two thugs employed by Schildkraut to revenge himself on the man he thought had stolen her affections. The bride's mother was reported telling whoever would listen to her, "She's a bitch. This marriage won't last any longer than the last one." This was the melee that Hellman and Hammett encountered on their arrival at Horace's reception. She wanted to leave immediately but Hammett restrained her by saying, "No. Wait for him, the poor bastard." The two sat uneasily on a couch, drinking little while holding desultory conversations with strangers. Hellman stayed only because of her loyalty to the man she had once admired so much:

> I think I must have dozed, because I remember being surprised to see Hammett on his feet as Horace came through the door. The fine clothes were crumpled, the strong handsome face was set as if it had been arranged before a mirror. . . . Horace said, "You don't have to rise to greet me, nobody does anymore."

After Horace told them that he needed a drink, he asked, "Lilly, were you the only one to come today?" She told him that all his friends had been there earlier (mostly, but not entirely, true) and that they had departed only when they couldn't find him. His instant reply was unsettling: "I've been resting." His next question, "Where's the bride?" was followed by his departure to search for Elise. When Hellman and Hammett left the apartment soon after their brief interchange, they could hear Horace and Elise shouting furiously at one another in the next room. It was the last time that Hellman saw Horace.

Through his correspondence with Helen Woodward and Julian Messner, Eddie Mayer heard a good deal about Horace's continued jealousy over Dorothy Peterson. Mayer resented his old friend's insinuations about their activities in California: "It's a little trying to have him associate Dorothy's name and mine in public places . . . that of course, being another of his alcoholic fantasies." Mayer was so incensed by Horace's behavior that he did not even send him a congratulatory wire when he married Elise. Nevertheless, by the spring of 1932, when it became apparent that Horace was having no luck whatever in his Broadway play production plans, Mayer offered him the most significant help he could—the chance to produce his latest play, *The Last Mask*. The combined track record of Liveright and Mayer as a team made it very likely that the play might be financed. "I gave it to him at the time that he needed something to interest him in New York which would prevent him going off on a 'bust.' " But Horace was already embarked on one, as Mayer told Woodward:

> When I arrived in New York and Horace thought he was going to have money to produce the play, we started to cast one day. I arrived at Horace's apartment at 2:30 in the afternoon, where I found about fifty actors and actresses and in their midst, Horace, in a condition which you can imagine. I felt then that I was under no further obligation to let him keep the play since, after all, I had a right to protect my property. . . . I haven't got anything in the world against Horace. I don't think he can be held responsible for any of his actions during the last few years.

Mayer concluded by telling her that, "I wish him luck, but I don't want to do business with him again or get mixed up in his personal affairs." Mayer asserted that Horace had become furious with him over withdrawing the rights to the play, and that he had denounced Mayer to all his friends.

By the beginning of 1932 Horace had sold for quick cash whatever remaining share of the production rights to *Dracula* he still retained. This sale, combined with that of the last of his rights to *An American Tragedy* to Paramount, left him with little else to fall back upon.

A sizable amount of whatever money came Horace's way in 1932 and 1933 was spent optioning plays for which he was unable to secure the necessary funding. The constant drain on his limited resources left him virtually penniless. Despite his quarrel with Mayer, Horace attempted to secure his participation in obtaining the rights to a play he and Maurice Hanline thought might enjoy success. Having no money, he wired Mayer, who was on board the *Europa* en route to Europe:

> GOLDSMITH HANLINE AGREE I HAVE CINCH BET NEW ONE
> SET PLAY SURE PICTURE MATERIAL BEG YOU ARRANGE
> LOAN FIVE HUNDRED OFFERED LAST WEEK TO OBTAIN
> OPTION RIGHTS CABLE ANSWER LIVERIGHT NY.

Even after all he'd told Helen Woodward, Mayer couldn't say no to Horace and wired the money to Arthur Pell, who was taking care of his financial matters in New York. It is not certain that Horace used the five hundred to secure his option. By this time he was borrowing heavily from nearly everyone he knew and may well have had to use Mayer's money to keep afloat. Mayer lent Horace still another two hundred in March 1933, but this loan, like all the others, was simply not enough to cover Horace's style of life. On March 23, 1932, Horace signed an agreement with Pell that denied him any chance of receiving "any obligation for salary or other obligations" that he still might be entitled to under a prior agreement he had reached with the new directors of the firm in July 1930. In effect, this was a general release which meant that whatever money Pell deigned to give Horace from now on was strictly charity.

But Arthur Pell did continue to dole out sums to Horace every week or so in 1932, varying from as low as twenty-five dollars to two hundred. Included among these dozens of checks were ones made out to Mount Sinai Hospital as payment for Horace's hospital bills. Since the grand total of these checks for 1932 far exceeded the five hundred due him from Mayer, it seems clear that Horace's former bookkeeper was now his chief means of financial support. It is also clear that the dole came from Pell's own funds and not from those of the Liveright concern of which he was now the chief director.

Horace's final year in New York is a sad story of professional failure, financial embarassment, and steady drinking. There were many humiliations. He ran up large hotel bills at several residence hotels on both the East and West sides of Manhattan. At one of them he was not allowed to take his personal property with him at the time he was evicted for nonpayment of rent, thereby losing most of his wardrobe. The image of the usually sartorially splendid Horace reduced to a single dark blue suit was painful to his friends. One among them was the filmmaker Nathan Kroll, who recalled for me a lunch he had with Horace at this time when everything was going badly in his life. A friend of Tommy Smith and Manuel Komroff, Kroll was then a young musician whom Horace engaged to play the piano at the B&L parties in the heyday years of the late twenties. In 1992 Kroll had not lost his great admiration for Horace, remembering him as unfailingly energetic and charming. A phone call from Horace in early 1933 had surprised Kroll because the two men had lost touch since his friend's departure for California. HBL called to say that their mutual friend José Iturbi was in town for a concert and to suggest, for old times' sake, a luncheon together. Kroll was happy to oblige, and the threesome met at a midtown restaurant.

Kroll was dismayed to discover that Horace had been wearing his expensive suit for so long now that it had become shiny. Far worse, he noticed that Horace had clumsily dyed the fraying edges of his suit cuffs with blue ink so that the wear would not show. Despite these outward signs of poverty, Horace refused to even intimate that things were going badly for him—it was as if the nearly three years since he had left publishing had never happened.

Except for the fact of his not picking up the check, Horace appeared to be in every way the same man that Kroll had known previously—still absolutely radiant in his enthusiasm for everything about life. After Horace had left them for an appointment uptown, Kroll and Iturbi discussed what they called the "heart-breaking" situation in which Horace now found himself.

Horace's fierce pride in denying that he had any financial problems possibly cost him several thousand dollars that he needed at this time. The money might have been obtained from his old friend/enemy, the screenwriter Ben Hecht. Although Horace had published several of the writer's novels in the mid-1920s, the two had quarreled over an asserted slight on Horace's part about Hecht's wife, Rose. She frequently claimed to have read books that she had not, and once Horace decided to challenge her about one of her favorite authors, Henry James. She said that she never went to sleep at night without reading a chapter of James, an assertion that Horace thought preposterous. He asked her, "Don't you love the character of the potter in *The Golden Bowl?*" Rose took the bait, not realizing that there is no such character in James's novel. When Horace revealed this fact, Rose stomped off to her husband, telling him that Horace had made offensive overtures to her. Hecht believed her story and never got around to repaying the two thousand dollars he had borrowed from Horace—a personal loan unconnected with B&L. He also left the firm for Donald Friede's new house. Now in 1933, with Horace close to destitution, Tommy Smith intervened to ask the now-affluent writer to pay his debt and, surprisingly, Hecht agreed. He visited Horace, who promptly struck a positive note:

> He told me that he had contracted for three Broadway productions. Three. I had a check in my pocket but, hell, anyone who is putting on three Broadway plays certainly does not need my lousy two thousand dollars.

Hecht left with the check in his pocket. All of Smith's remonstrances that the two thousand dollars were rightfully Horace's and not Hecht's were in vain.

In 1933 Frank Heller was Herman Liveright's roommate at Carnegie Tech. He later became widely known as a radio and television director. Herman had introduced Heller to his father a year or so before Horace's plight became acute. Young Heller was fascinated by Horace's talk about literature and the stage. He recalls spending an evening with Horace at one of the residence hotels on the West Side—probably the Hotel Meurice. Accompanied by two of his school friends, Heller, at Herman's urging, visited Horace's penthouse suite and discovered that his host had filled the living room with scores of autographed books. Here were titles by George Moore, Ezra Pound, Dreiser, Eugene O'Neill, Bertrand Russell, and Sherwood Anderson, all of them with dedications to the man who had published them. Toward the end of the evening, Horace informed his guests that, since he was going to be evicted from the premises on the following day, they might take with them as many volumes as they could carry undetected. All three boys loaded themselves up with books to their taste. Sixty years after that night, Heller could still recall Horace's absolutely perfect diction and the fact that he listened to you very carefully; he spoke with intensity at all times.

By the spring of 1933 Horace's downward course seemed irreversible. It was no comfort to him to notice that America itself was at its lowest ebb. The newly elected President Franklin D. Roosevelt closed the banks briefly to protect what was left in them. There was certainly no cash around to invest in plays, as Horace kept discovering with each miserable turndown.

Another thing that went very badly for Horace that year of national disaster was his physical health. At forty-nine, his constant drinking and smoking now began to have predictable effects.

Always bone thin, Horace had worn himself out; his physical resilience was very low. The 1932 Mount Sinai Hospital visits may have been for his alcoholism. The most immediate threat to his life, however, was the condition of his lungs. When he was admitted to Roosevelt Hospital in January 1933 for pneumonia, it was discovered that he also had emphysema.

(2)

All summer long they drank his scotch.
—Madeline Bazel, 1933

MANUEL Komroff had seen little of Horace since he had quit his job as production manager of B&L in early 1926 to begin a career in Paris as a professional writer. By 1930 he had succeeded in achieving fame as the author of *Coronet,* a major book club selection, and then wrote several screenplays in Hollywood. In an unpublished memoir, Komroff indicates how much luck had to do with their getting together again. A chance meeting in a midtown restaurant with a Broadway theatrical agent, Madeline Bazel, led to Komroff's beginning anew his old friendship with a radically changed Horace. Miss Bazel, who specialized in booking acrobats throughout the nation, said she was acquainted with Horace Liveright and that he lived only two blocks from where they were eating. Would Mr. Komroff like to see Horace's penthouse with its beautiful view of the Manhattan skyline? He would, and the two set out for what may have been the Hotel Meurice on West Fifty-eighth Street.

At the desk they discovered that Horace had checked out the previous day. By intimidating the desk clerk, Miss Bazel obtained the key to Horace's suite, and she and Komroff went up to inspect the premises. There they found a scene of near-total destruction:

all of Horace's favorite photos of the authors he had published over the years were lying torn to bits or trampled on the floor. Their frames had been smashed; broken glass littered the floor. Nearly all the furniture in the suite had been destroyed.

Komroff found the scene unbearable, surrounded as he was in this shabby, littered hotel suite by all the reminders of Horace's great days: "There was the picture of John Reed in his fleece-lined trench coat wearing a Russian fur hat and of Bertrand Russell smoking his pipe." These pictures had meant so much to Horace that he always put them up in any location he found himself in. What could have been responsible for such destruction? Miss Bazel had a simple explanation of what had happened in the past few days and before that:

> All summer long his goddam friends were sitting around talking about the plays they would be writing or directing or producing and using the phone to call Hollywood on the slightest pretext . . . long distance all over the U.S. And he let them do just what they liked. Half the time he was potted . . . They [the hotel management] must have put him out and he could not take them [the pictures] with him. . . . So I guess he and maybe one or two cronies got good and plastered and smashed what they could not take with them. All summer long they drank his scotch.

Within a couple of days Komroff had tracked down Horace's whereabouts through the help of Julian Messner. After his eviction, Horace had relocated in a two-room suite in a small residence hotel on West Fifty-first Street, in the area where the construction of Rockefeller Center was under way. The din of the explosions required for the excavations was unnerving, but the two old friends talked on for hours. Horace spoke of his impending Broadway productions, all of which seemed unreal to Komroff.

Feeling distinctly uneasy about Horace and his situation, Komroff called Tommy Smith, who promised that he, too, would soon visit his old boss. It was at this point that Komroff had the idea he thought might save Horace from going under completely. This was for him to write his autobiography, a notion that Horace accepted with some hesitation. Only after Arthur Pell had agreed to release his correspondence files did he consent. Komroff would have Messner supply a stenographer who would take down Horace's dictation. Horace would then revise the rough draft. As for a publisher, Komroff thought Simon and Schuster would be the right house, a feeling fortunately shared by Dick Simon. The advance was $2,000, a sum that might keep Horace afloat for some months.

In what was probably a far more positive mood than he'd been in before Komroff reached him, Horace began dictating at the beginning of July. He kept a close count of the number of words he produced each day, as well as noting the amount of time involved in the work. On August 18, the thirty-sixth day, he had dictated 58,000 words. Reliving his life this way threw him into a self-challenging mood in which he questioned much about the way he had managed his life:

> Why have I gambled and drunk too much throughout my life? Why have I so frequently through the years attempted achievements that have overtaxed my strength and abilities? Why, when I have attained what seemed to me almost impossible goals, have I been unwilling to believe that I have scored a touchdown and unconsciously and sometimes deliberately fumbled the ball?

Horace interrupted his self-questioning to reveal to his imagined readers that he would have much preferred to have been the headmaster of a glorious school for boys that would have included on its faculty people as diverse as Bertrand Russell, Ezra Pound, Gilbert Murray, Mies van der Rohe, Max Eastman, John Dewey, Edmund Wilson, Willa Cather, Rose Macaulay, and Leopold Stokowski,

From the final list, spring 1933: title page for *Miss Lonelyhearts*.
Author's collection

among many other luminaries. It was all a fantasy, but it indicates how much Horace had wanted to change the world and his genuine passion for education.

Tommy Smith had told Sherwood Anderson where Horace was living, and the novelist paid a visit. Although it was midmorning, Horace was dressed in black pajamas, surrounded by a group of his new "friends," who appeared to have been left over from the guests at the previous night's party. As Anderson recalled it, Horace's friends all shared a theatrical background and a taste for strong drink. To Anderson, Horace appeared to be both sick and ashamed of his condition: "He arose and went with me into a hallway. . . . 'Well, what the hell, Sherwood, I've sunk,' he said."

Horace pretended that he would be playing a role in the newly reorganized Liveright Publishing Corporation, but doubted that he could take an active part because of all his other pressing interests.

> "I'll just be chairman of the board," he said and then with a bitter little laugh and knowing that I knew what I knew he turned and walked away.
>
> As for myself I took the elevator down out of that apartment and walked in the street below with tears blinding my eyes.

This was Anderson's final meeting with Horace.

Since he lived only four or five blocks from the relocated Liveright firm on West Forty-seventh Street, Horace often came round to see people he was close to there: Messner, Smith, Zugsmith, and Kronenberger. Sometime in late 1932, Arthur Pell decided that he had enough of Horace's visits. In a voice that could be heard by everyone in the reception area, the new president of Liveright told the man who had first hired him, "Horace, I don't think you'd better come in anymore; it doesn't look good for business." Horace never returned.

Komroff had wanted to see Horace through the writing of his book, but Paramount offered him a short-term contract to write an original screenplay for Marlene Dietrich in Hollywood. Although worried about Horace, Komroff accepted the assignment, promising to keep in touch with him by letter.

Late in August, Komroff received news from Horace that was not cheering:

> There is nothing for me to tell you and if there were I could hardly make the effort to tell it. I have been in bed for three days with a temperature that hangs around 104 and the doctors—yes, I'm very swanky and have two, neither of whom will take any pay from me—think I have a heavy attack of bronchitis or another unimportant pneumonia . . . you will forgive me for making this so short— I feel pretty lousy.

For emphysema victims there are no "unimportant pneumonias." All such onslaughts are potentially fatal, and Horace had been weakened still further by his obsessive drinking and smoking.

After his discharge from the hospital, Horace resumed his daily dictation until he noticed that some of the literary material he thought he had brought with him from Hollywood had apparently been left behind. In a letter to Eddie Mayer, asking for his aid (and Dorothy Peterson's) to recover the missing files from the Bekins warehouse in Los Angeles, he included this bit of news:

> It was pneumonia again and it seems that my two recurrent attacks were caused by liquid in my lungs which was never drawn off. I was "needled" several times during this attack and though the recovery is maddeningly slow, it should be sure this time. Maybe I'll be able to get out in the fresh air next week. I've been trying to work on my book this week and it's not gone badly. If I get well and strong pronto the book will be absolutely finished on contract time.

Horace died three days later, on September 25. Herman was away at school, but Lucy had just returned from Europe with her mother and was at his bedside, as were Julian Messner and Alfred Wallerstein.

It could be argued that Horace's life was over when he left the publishing scene in 1930. His death marked the end of an era when a complete outsider such as Horace Liveright could undertake to publish authors on hunches, or with the feeling that certain books *had* to be published or that it might just be fun to do it. The age of the firebrand was over.

There was a grandeur, a warmth of generosity about Horace Liveright in his relationship to books and writers that has never been equaled. He had a passion for finding an audience for those new writers whose message was obscure, a challenge to society, or deemed unpublishable by the rest of the book trade. He transformed the staid, self-satisfied atmosphere of American publishing into an exciting, pulsing forum in which contemporary American writing could come of age. He couldn't resist his many temptations and was proud of the fact, an attitude that has unduly influenced our feeling about him. Perhaps he belongs in the company of men like Oliver Goldsmith, whom Samuel Johnson eulogized in these words:

> He had raised money and squandered it, by every artifice of acquisition, and folly of expense. But let not his frailties be remembered; he was a very great man.

Aftermath

I_N addition to the immediate members of his family, at least
three of Horace's major authors attended the funeral held at the
Universal Chapel on Lexington Avenue: Theodore Dreiser, Upton
Sinclair, and Sherwood Anderson. So, too, did Bennett Cerf,
Tommy Smith, and Julian Messner. It was Horace's old Socialist
comrade, Sinclair, who delivered the eulogy.

The Liveright firm was placed into involuntary bankruptcy in
May 1933. Despite strong efforts, Bennett Cerf was unable to
acquire the firm's assets for Random House. Arthur Pell, working
behind the scenes, managed to buy them for $18,500 in cash by
using a "dummy," or phony buyer, to make the purchase. A new
firm was then created on the ruins of the old: Liveright Publishing
Corporation. Pell's financing for this maneuver was so precarious
that he was forced to sell the publication rights to all the works of

O'Neill and Jeffers. Cerf bought them and continued to publish both writers for decades. Despite the bankruptcy, Pell refused to revert the publishing rights of the old Liveright titles to their authors unless they agreed to pay him the original costs of the plates. After a series of lawsuits, Dreiser finally obtained his rights (and plates) in 1938, but not until he had repaid Pell $16,383 of his unearned advances. On the other hand, Dorothy Parker dared the lightning and, ignoring Pell's warnings, sold her rights to Viking Press.

Pell continued to eke out a living from Horace's backlist for several decades. In the 1960s he sold the firm to Gilbert Harrison, who attempted to invigorate it as the New Liveright. Harrison then sold it to W. W. Norton, the firm that continues to bring out some of the old titles that Horace made famous in the 1920s. The Liveright corporate name appears on the glass doors of their offices in New York.

Tommy Smith never got another full-time job in book publishing. He died in poverty at Bellevue Hospital in 1942. He had supported himself in his last years by selling off, one by one, his collection of first editions and signed copies of the books he had worked on for a thirty-year period.

Starting with only a single B&L writer, Frances Parkinson Keyes, and at probably the worst time in American history to begin a new business venture, Julian Messner and his wife, Kitty, began publishing under his name in the fall of 1933. Donald Friede's firm was placed in bankruptcy in 1938. Several years earlier, he went to Hollywood where he courted Jean Harlow and became a successful agent. In the 1950s he returned to New York and worked for Doubleday and World Publishing as a senior editor. In these later years, Friede married M.F.K. Fisher and then Eleanor Kask. He died in 1966.

Louis Kronenberger became internationally famous as a scholar and writer. He also worked for *Fortune* and *PM* as well as becoming a professor at Brandeis University. He edited or wrote more than a score of books.

The Boni brothers continued to publish books until 1937. By that time they had sold most of their major properties to other houses in order to keep going—Proust to Random House and D. H. Lawrence to Viking. Albert then undertook a completely new career in the science of micro–photo reduction techniques.

Lucille Liveright remarried. Lucy and Herman survive her, and both treasure the memory of their father far more than this book can suggest.

Bibliography

Anderson, Sherwood. *Sherwood Anderson's Memoirs: A Critical Edition,* ed. Ray Lewis White (Chapel Hill: University of North Carolina Press, 1969).

Bernays, Edward L. *Biography of an Idea: Memoirs of Public Relations Counsel Edward L. Bernays* (New York: Simon and Schuster, 1965).

Blotner, Joseph. *Faulkner: A Biography* (1-vol. ed.) (New York: Random House, 1984).

————. *Faulkner: A Biography* (2 vols.) (New York: Random House, 1974).

Boswell, James. *Boswell's Life of Johnson,* ed. G. B. Hill and L. F. Powell (Oxford: The Clarendon Press, 1934).

Boyer, Paul S. *Purity in Print* (New York: Charles Scribner's Sons, 1968).

Carver, Raymond. *No Heroics Please* (New York: Vintage Books, 1988).

Céline, Louis-Ferdinand. *Journey to the End of the Night,* John H. P. Marks, trans. (Boston: Little, Brown, 1934).

Cerf, Bennett. *At Random: The Reminiscences of Bennett Cerf* (New York: Random House, 1977).

Cleaton, Irene and Allen. *Books and Battles: American Literature, 1920–1930* (Boston: Houghton Mifflin, 1937).

Dardis, Tom. *The Thirsty Muse: Alcohol and the American Writer* (New York: Ticknor and Fields, 1989).

de Grazia, Edward. *Girls Lean Back Everywhere: The Law of Obscenity and the Assault on Genius* (New York: Random House, 1992).

DeMille, Cecil B. *Autobiography* (Englewood Cliffs, N.J.: Prentice-Hall, 1963).

Donald, David Herbert. *Look Homeward: A Life of Thomas Wolfe* (Boston: Little, Brown, 1987).

Dreiser, Theodore. *Letters of Theodore Dreiser,* ed. Robert H. Elias (3 vols.) (Philadelphia: University of Pennsylvania Press, 1959).

Dreiser–Mencken Letters: The Correspondence of Theodore Dreiser and H. L. Mencken, 1907–1945, ed. Thomas P. Riggio (Philadelphia: University of Pennsylvania Press, 1986).

Eisenstein, Sergei. *Immoral Memories: An Autobiography* (Boston: Houghton Mifflin, 1983).

Eliot, T. S. *The Letters of T. S. Eliot,* Vol. 1: *1898–1922,* ed. Valerie Eliot (New York: Harcourt Brace Jovanovich, 1988).

Ellis, Mary. *Those Dancing Years* (London: John Murray, 1981).

Faulkner, William. *Essays, Speeches and Public Letters,* ed. James Meriweather (New York: Random House, 1965).

———. *Selected Letters,* ed. Joseph Blotner (New York: Random House, 1977).

Fitzgerald, F. Scott. *Correspondence of F. Scott Fitzgerald,* ed. Matthew Broccoli and Margaret M. Duggan (New York: Random House, 1980).

Frank, Waldo. *Time Exposures* (New York: Boni and Liveright, 1926).

Friede, Donald. *The Mechanical Angel* (New York: Alfred A. Knopf, 1948).

Gilmer, Walker. *Horace Liveright, Publisher of the Twenties* (New York: David Lewis, 1970).

Hanline, Maurice. *The Years of Indiscretion* (New York: The Macaulay Company, 1934).

Hays, Arthur Garfield. *City Lawyer* (New York: Simon and Schuster, 1942).

———. *Let Freedom Ring* (New York: Boni and Liveright, 1928).

Hecht, Ben. *A Jew in Love* (New York: Covici-Friede, 1930).

Hellman, Lillian. *An Unfinished Woman: A Memoir* (Boston: Little, Brown, 1969).

Hemingway, Ernest. *A Moveable Feast* (New York: Charles Scribner's Sons, 1964).

———. *Selected Letters,* ed. Carlos Baker (New York: Charles Scribner's Sons, 1981).

Howard, Michael S. *Jonathan Cape: Publisher* (London: Jonathan Cape, 1971).

Howe, Irving. *Sherwood Anderson* (New York: William Sloane Associates, 1951).

Kronenberger, Louis. *No Whippings, No Gold Watches* (Boston: Little, Brown, 1970).

Langner, Lawrence. *The Magic Curtain* (New York: E. P. Dutton, 1951).

Lewis, Sinclair. *From Main Street to Stockholm* (New York: Harcourt, Brace, 1952).

Lingeman, Richard. *Theodore Dreiser,* Vol. 1: *At the Gates of the City, 1891–1917* (New York: G. P. Putnam's Sons, 1990).

Liveright, Horace B. "The Absurdity of Censorship," *The Independent,* 110:3838 (March 17, 1923), pp. 192–193.

Loeb, Harold. *The Way It Was* (New York: Criterion Books, 1959).

Maddox, Brenda. *Nora: The Real Life of Molly Bloom* (Boston: Houghton Mifflin, 1988).

Mayer, Edwin Justus. *A Preface to Life* (New York: Boni and Liveright, 1923).

Mencken, H. L. *The American Scene: A Reader,* ed. Huntington Cairns (New York: Alfred A. Knopf, 1963).

———. *H. L. Mencken's Smart Set Criticism* (Chicago: Gateway Editions, 1987).

———. *My Life as Author and Editor,* ed. Jonathan Yardley (New York: Alfred A. Knopf, 1993).

Montagu, Ivor. *With Eisenstein in Hollywood* (Berlin: Seven Seas, 1968).

Oberwager, Charles. "Decision . . . Dismissing the Complaint of the New York Society for the Suppression of Vice" (privately printed, 1922).

Pound, Ezra. *The Cantos* (New York: New Directions, 1948).

Pound/Ford Letters, ed. Brita Lindberg Seuersted (New York: New Directions, 1982).

Pound/Lewis Letters, ed. Timothy Materer (New York: New Directions, 1985).

Rainey, Lawrence. "The Price of Modernism: Publishing *The Waste Land,*" in *T. S. Eliot: The Modernist in History,* ed. Ronald Bush (New York: Cambridge University Press, 1991).

Rascoe, Burton. *We Were Interrupted* (New York: Doubleday, 1947).

Reid, B. L. *The Man from New York: John Quinn and His Friends* (New York: Oxford University Press, 1968).

Selznick, David O. *Memo from David O. Selznick* (New York: The Viking Press, 1972).

Seton, Marie. *Sergei M. Eisenstein.* London: Dennis Dobson, 1978.

Skal, David J. *Hollywood Gothic* (New York: W. W. Norton, 1990).

Smith, Constance. *Rose Macaulay.* London: Collins, 1972.

Steel, Ronald. *Walter Lippmann and the American Century* (Boston: Atlantic Monthly Press, 1980).

Stern, Edith. "The Man Who Was Unafraid," *Saturday Review of Literature,* June
    28, 1941, pp. 14ff.
Swanberg, W. A. *Dreiser* (New York: Charles Scribner's Sons, 1963).
Townsend, Kim. *Sherwood Anderson: A Biography* (Boston: Houghton Mifflin,
    1987).
Turnbull, Andrew. *F. Scott Fitzgerald: A Biography* (New York: Charles
    Scribner's Sons, 1962).
Weeks, Edward. *My Green Age* (Boston: Atlantic Monthly Press, 1971).
Wolfe, Thomas. *The Web and the Rock* (New York: Harper & Brothers, 1939).

Sources

Abbreviations of frequently cited works, archives, and people:

APC   Arthur Pell papers, Gary Giddins, New York City
BC   The Berg Collection, New York Public Library
BRC   Bertrand Russell Collection, McMaster Library, McMaster University
CU   Oral History Collection, Columbia University
EHC   Ernest Hemingway Correspondence, Princeton Library, Princeton University
EPC   Ezra Pound Collection, Beinecke Library, Yale University
GMC   George Moore Correspondence, Houghton Library, Harvard University
HBL   Horace B. Liveright
HLC   Horace Liveright Collection, Van Pelt Library, University of Pennsylvania
JQC   John Quinn Collection, New York Public Library
LWC   Lucy Wilson personal collection
SAC   Sherwood Anderson Collection, Newberry Library, Chicago Public Library

TD   Theodore Dreiser

TY   "The Turbulent Years." Unpublished autobiography of HBL.

USC   Upton Sinclair Collection, Lilly Library, University of Indiana

WWN   W. W. Norton company files

Chapter 1: New York Bound

p. 3   "Dear God, bless": TY, p. 9

p. 4   "The company deducted": ibid., p. 1.

p. 9   "If the . . . Green": ibid., p. 12.

p. 10   "And when Charlotte": ibid., p. 12.

p. 14   "You ought to": ibid., p. 49.

p. 15   "Don't you fret": ibid., p. 45.

p. 15   "Your cablegram came": Marcus Lewin to HBL, March 9, 1901, LWC.

p. 16   "There is much": TY, p. 76.

p. 17   "The chief, the": ibid., p. 86.

p. 18   "Don't worry about": ibid., p. 83.

p. 18   "[it] brought more": ibid., p. 84.

p. 19   "Hooray, hooray, hooray": ibid., p. 87.

p. 19   "RICE IS NO": Wire, B. Fleisher to HBL, July 21, 1902, LWC.

p. 20   "I am pleased": Edward Rice to HBL, July 23, 1901, TY, p. 89.

p. 21   "horrible, sordid, and": ibid., p. 36.

p. 22   "Col Newcombe presents": Henry Liveright to HBL, ibid., p. 49.

p. 22   "A working man": LWC.

Chapter 2: "I Believe in My Destiny"

p. 25   "I usually wore": TY, p. 64.

p. 26   "This is my": ibid., p. 112.

p. 28   "I did not": ibid., p. 38.

p. 28   "had had a": ibid.

p. 30   "You're a gambler": ibid., p. 109.

p. 31   "with the pot": ibid., p. 169.

p. 32   "I bragged about": ibid., p. 171.

p. 33   "For the first": ibid., p. 176.

p. 33   "If you sold": ibid., p. 190.

p. 36   "You believe that": Ronald Steel, *Walter Lippmann and the American Century,* p. 31.

p. 36   "Mr. and Mrs.": LWC.

p. 37   "refused to kiss": Steel, p. 56.

p. 37   "her *père* is": mock after-dinner speech by HBL, LWC.

p. 37   "had been living": Interview with Mary Ellis, London, March 1992.

p. 39   "I believe in": HBL to LL, "Thursday night," 1914, LWC.

p. 40   "—all I need": HBL to LL, October 14, 1914, LWC.

p. 40   "By the time": HBL to LL, "Monday morning," 1914, LWC.

p. 40   "I am terribly": HBL to LL, no date, LWC.

p. 40   "As you know": HBL to LL, August 1914, LWC.

p. 41   "Hope you slept": HBL to LL, no date, LWC.

p. 41   "You upset me": HBL to LL, no date, LWC.

p. 42   "I feel well": HBL to LL, October 1914, LWC.

p. 42   "Starting my new": HBL to LL, no date, LWC.

p. 42   "—then if I die": ibid.

p. 43   "I have to": HBL to LL, July 15, 1915, LWC.

Chapter 3: "Let's Call It the Modern Library!"

p. 45   "[Liveright] was a": Lawrence Langner, *The Magic Curtain*, p. 75.

p. 49   "When I go": Alex Baskin interview with Albert Boni, October 20, 1972, Tamiment Library, New York University, pp. 15–16.

p. 50   "No, Horace Liveright": Langner, *The Magic Curtain*, p. 199.

p. 50   "Publishing had the": interview with Max Schuster, 1964, p. 58, CU.

p. 51   "Most of the": H. L. Mencken, *H. L. Mencken's Smart Set Criticism*, p. 105.

p. 56   "Ten years later": TY, p. 163.

p. 57   "Injurious to the": Walker Gilmer, *Horace Liveright: Publisher of the Twenties*, p. 16.

p. 57   "Albert, what the": Manuel Komroff, "The Liveright Story" (unpublished ms.), special collections, Columbia University Library, p. 36.

p. 58   "In view of": George Creel to HBL, August 21, 1918, WWN.

p. 58   "Use my letter": George Creel to HBL, September 18, 1918, ibid.

p. 58   "Tell Horace that": Gilmer, *Horace Liveright*, p. 21.

p. 60   "as well as": HBL to LL, no date, LWC.

p. 60   "was a terrible": HBL to LL, no date, LWC.

p. 60   "—hell, I'm glad": HBL to LL, no date, LWC.

p. 63   "could bring it": HBL to Upton Sinclair, January 17, 1926, LWC.

p. 64   "I have been": Upton Sinclair to HBL, November 6, 1926, USC.

p. 64   "Let me say": Upton Sinclair to HBL, November 12, 1926, USC.

p. 66   "Albert is positively": HBL to LL, October 8, 1918.

p. 66   "a couple of": TY, p. 160.

p. 66   "We have offered": HBL to LL, March 27, 1918, LWC.

p. 67   "I will thank": HBL to LL, May 8, 1918, LWC.

p. 68   "ravishingly beautiful lady": B. L. Reid, *The Man From New York: John Quinn and His Friends*, p. 592.

p. 68   "an admirable business": ibid.

p. 68   "It's funny how": HBL to LL, no date, LWC.

p. 70   "certain English intonations": H. L. Mencken, *My Life as Author and Editor*, p. 327.

p. 70   "curious": ibid.

Chapter 4: Putting Up with Theodore Dreiser

p. 73   "I sometimes think": TD to H. L. Mencken, *Dreiser–Mencken Letters*, p. 65.

p. 74   "Ever since 1909": H. L. Mencken, *My Life as Author and Editor*, pp. 127–28.

p. 74   "the best American": ibid., p. 132.

p. 74   "My second reading": ibid.

p. 77   "And I was": ibid., p. 133

p. 77   "Always thinking that": Bennett Cerf, *At Random*, p. 36.

p. 78   "Our printers advise": HBL to TD, June 24, 1918, HLC.

p. 78   "Where on earth": HBL to TD, June 27, 1918, HLC.

p. 79   "I was always": H. L. Mencken to TD, *Dreiser–Mencken Letters*, p. 385.

p. 82   "Liveright . . . is insane": TD to H. L. Mencken, December 6, 1920, *Dreiser–Mencken Letters*, p. 413.

p. 82   "The burden of": TD to HBL, November 20, 1920, HLC.

p. 83   "[I] called him": TD to H. L. Mencken, September 20, 1921, *Dreiser–Mencken Letters*, p. 392.

p. 84   " 'The Genius,' coming": H. L. Mencken, *The American Scene: A Reader*, p. 142.

p. 84   "groping toward a": ibid., p. 156.

p. 84   "He is driving": ibid.

Chapter 5: "Going Toward the Light" with Pound and Eliot

p. 86   "Horace . . . is a": Ezra Pound to John Quinn, JQC.

p. 86   "I have written": T. S. Eliot to John Quinn, *Letters of T. S. Eliot*, p. 530.

p. 87   "I have a": HBL to LL, December 17, 1921, LWC.

p. 87   "While the 60": Ezra Pound, *The Cantos*, No. 80, 83.

p. 88   "long poem of": T. S. Eliot to Quinn, *Letters of T. S. Eliot*, p. 530.

p. 90   "Liveright . . . offered to": Ezra Pound to John Quinn, February 21, 1922, JQC.

p. 92   "What would *Vanity*": Lawrence Rainey, "The Price of Modernism: Publishing *The Waste Land*," p. 98, letter of March 5, 1922.

p. 93   "I wish to": Ezra Pound to Scofield Thayer, March 9–10, 1922, EPC.

p. 94   "DISSATISFIED LIVERIGHT CONTRACT": T. S. Eliot to John Quinn, June 22, 1922, JQC.

p. 95   "[Liveright] is vulgarity": John Quinn to Ezra Pound, July 5, 1922, JQC.

p. 95   "The sons of": Ezra Pound to John Quinn, July 27, 1922, JQC.

p. 95   "YOU DON'T HAVE": John Quinn to T. S. Eliot, no date, JQC.

p. 96   "I'm disappointed that": HBL to Ezra Pound, November 1, 1922, Rainey, "The Price of Modernism," p. 97.

p. 97   "God bless you": HBL to Ezra Pound, February 5, 1923, Rainey, "The Price of Modernism, p. 107

p. 97   "I am interested": T. S. Eliot to John Quinn, March 12, 1923, JQC.

p. 99   "My book will": Edward de Grazia, *Girls Lean Back Everywhere: The Law of Obscenity and the Assault on Genius,* p. 20.

p. 99   "I think Joyce": ibid., p. 12.

p. 100 "[Liveright] ought to": John Quinn to James Joyce, May 11, 1922, JQC.

p. 101 "Do you suppose": HBL to Ezra Pound, April 5, 1923, EPC.

p. 101 "Liveright has mistrusted": Ezra Pound to Wyndham Lewis, *Pound / Lewis Letters,* p. 163.

p. 102 "HOWEVER, Liveright is": ibid.

p. 102 "What do you": HBL to Ezra Pound, October 16, 1927, EPC.

p. 103 "Why in the": HBL to Ezra Pound, October 10, 1928, EPC.

p. 103 "NOVEL, indeed": Ezra Pound to HBL, January 9, 1929, EPC.

p. 103 "Liveright has been": Ezra Pound to Ford Madox Ford, *Pound / Ford Letters,* p. 63.

p. 105 "The American public": HBL to Ezra Pound, September 20, 1920, EPC.

p. 106 "Here I am": HBL to LL, no date, LWC.

p. 107 "Anyone can write": Constance Babington Smith, *Rose Macaulay,* p. 117.

p. 107 "Rose Macaulay, Mrs.": ibid.

p. 107 "Would you think": HBL to Rose Macaulay, January 18, 1928, HLC.

p. 108 "WOULD FEEL ALMOST": HBL to Rose Macaulay, November 17, 1928, HLC.

p. 108 "As you know": Rose Macaulay to HBL, February 12, 1930, HLC.

p. 109 "Is Wells' mistress": HBL to LL, January 8, 1922, LWC.

p. 109 "He was most": ibid.

p. 109 "Seen Liveright Several": Sinclair Lewis to Alfred Harcourt, 1927, Sinclair Lewis, *From Main Street to Stockholm.*

p. 109   "Please don't think": HBL to LL, February 20, 1922, LWC.

p. 110   "I've wanted you": HBL to LL, January 20, 1922, LWC.

p. 110   "never lost my": HBL to LL, January 20, 1922, LWC.

p. 110   "Julie Lasden": HBL to LL, January 8, 1922, LWC.

p. 110   "And I'd give": HBL to LL, January 20, 1922, LWC.

p. 111   "SAILING AQUITANIA TWENTY": HBL to LL, January 15, 1922, LWC.

p. 111   "There is one": HBL to LL, May 11, 1918, LWC.

p. 111   "Ada [Horace's sister]": HBL to LL, no date, LWC.

p. 111   "I hope, dear": ibid.

p. 112   "You could come": HBL to LL, no date, LWC.

p. 112   "Mr. Hath [illegible]": LL to HBL, September 14, 1919, LWC.

p. 113   "Did he come": HBL to LL, September 4, 1919, LWC.

p. 113   "made me very": HBL to LL, September 3, 1919, LWC.

p. 114   "But you *must*": ibid.

Chapter 6: First Success

p. 115   "What are you": W. A. Swanberg, *Dreiser,* p. 450.

p. 118   "TELL EDWARD STOP": Sigmund Freud to Eli Bernays, Edward L. Bernays, *Biography of an Idea: Memoirs of Public Relations Counsel Edward L. Bernays,* p. 254.

p. 118   "it is the": ibid., p. 268.

p. 119   "natural and desirable": Author's interview with Bernays, June 1992.

p. 119   "Books were handled": Bernays, *Biography of an Idea,* p. 277.

p. 120   "When Leon [Fleischman]": ibid.

p. 121   "In the crucible": ibid., p. 280.

p. 121   "on the loom": ibid.

p. 121   "Love is life": ibid.

p. 122   "would not support": ibid., p. 286.

p. 124   "A Limey . . . snapping": Joseph Blotner, *Faulkner: A Biography* vol. 1, p. 729.

p. 124   "rag-time outfit": Michael S. Howard, *Jonathan Cape, Publisher,* p. 117.

p. 127   "wrote for people": Komroff, "The Liveright Story," p. 41.

p. 128   "Let's shoot the": ibid.

p. 129   "My dream . . .": George Moore to HBL, November 5, 1928, GMC.

p. 130   "I live in": HBL to George Moore, May 14, 1919, GMC.

p. 131   "I suggested that": HBL to George Moore, July 29, 1921, GMC.

p. 132   "This is not": George Moore to HBL, February 23, 1922, GMC.

p. 132   "If you would": George Moore to HBL, February 23, 1923, GMC.

Chapter 7: The House on Forty-eighth Street

p. 133   "A job with": Lillian Hellman, *An Unfinished Woman: A Memoir*, p. 33.

p. 133   "Boni & Liveright": Louis Kronenberger, *No Whippings, No Gold Watches*, p. 5.

p. 134   "take no taffy": Komroff, "The Liveright Story," p. 75.

p. 136   "placed on a": Edward Weeks, *My Green Age*, pp. 183–84.

p. 137   "You two ought": Komroff, "The Liveright Story," p. 48.

p. 138   "a job with": Hellman, *Unfinished Woman*, p. 33.

p. 138   "even the stenographers": ibid., p. 38.

p. 138   "Some days no": ibid.

p. 139   "sometimes one of": ibid.

p. 139   "All the men": ibid.

p. 139   "There was a": Kronenberger, *No Whippings*, p. 17.

p. 140   "a glass of": Hellman, *Unfinished Woman*, p. 39.

p. 140   "tell that ninny": ibid., p. 40.

p. 140   "So now we": ibid., pp. 41–42.

p. 143   "It was the": interview with Donald Klopfer, 1967, p. 17, CU.

p. 143   "Most people I": Burton Rascoe, *We Were Interrupted*, p. 163.

p. 144   "Although the doings": Kronenberger, *No Whippings*, p. 21.

p. 144   "Many other ladies": ibid., p. 20.

p. 144   "Boni & Liveright": ibid.

p. 146   "impromptu; they started": Rascoe, *We Were Interrupted*, p. 242

p. 147   "a four piece": ibid., p. 307.

p. 147   "[Liveright] insisted on": Bertrand Russell to Dora Russell, October 11, 1927, BRC.

p. 147   "In spite of": ibid.

p. 149   "I'll never forget": Cerf, *At Random*, p. 32.

p. 149   "of Hart Crane": Kronenberger, *No Whippings*, p. 21.

p. 150   "Anybody you'd see": Cerf, *At Random*, p. 33.

Chapter 8: Firebrand at Work

p. 153   "No woman was": Paul S. Boyer, *Purity in Print*, p. 118.

p. 154   "[It] . . . must bring": ibid., p. 117.

p. 159   "I suppose I": Komroff, "The Liveright Story," p. 54.

p. 159   "In two weeks": ibid.

p. 159   "the mere existence": Charles Oberwager, "Decision . . . Dismissing the Complaint of the New York Society for the Suppression of Vice," p. 11.

p. 160   "The works of": ibid., p. 12.

p. 160   "To suppress the": ibid., p. 17.

p. 161   "[The Clean Books": Boyer, *Purity in Print*, p. 104.

p. 162   "If that book": ibid.

p. 164   "Some of the": Komroff, "The Liveright Story," p. 213.

p. 165   "the love tradition": Boyer, *Purity in Print,* p. 111.

p. 165   "asphyxiated in the": ibid.

p. 165   "on the grounds": ibid., p. 115.

p. 166   "the absurdity of": Horace Liveright, "The Absurdity of Censorship," p. 192.

p. 166   "A censorship over": ibid., p. 193.

p. 167   "what harm does": Gilmer, *Horace Liveright,* p. 77.

p. 168   "Promptly at ten": Komroff, "The Liveright Story," pp. 223–24.

p. 168   "There is not": Gilmer, *Horace Liveright,* p. 78.

p. 169   "It is one": ibid., p. 79.

p. 170   "After the speeches": Bernays, *Biography of an Idea,* p. 285.

p. 170   "Certainly we cannot": Maxwell Perkins to F. Scott Fitzgerald, *Correspondence of F. Scott Fitzgerald,* p. 147.

p. 171   "What! *this man?*": Waldo Frank, *Time Exposures,* p. 111.

p. 171   "HBL can sponsor": ibid.

p. 174   "I'm not going": Gilmer, *Horace Liveright,* p. 157.

Chapter 9: The Voice of Love: Sherwood Anderson

p. 176   "Yet there were": Irving Howe, *Sherwood Anderson,* p. 256.

p. 178   "cockney Englishman . . . who": Sherwood Anderson, *Sherwood Anderson's Memoirs: A Critical Edition,* p. 490.

p. 178   "It is beyond": Otto Liveright to Sherwood Anderson, October 27, 1924, SAC.

p. 178   "What I would": HBL to Sherwood Anderson, November 18, 1924, SAC.

p. 179   "The truth is": Sherwood Anderson to HBL, no date, SAC.

p. 179   "I am heart-broken": HBL to Sherwood Anderson, November 24, 1924, SAC.

p. 180   "So one day": Anderson, *Memoirs,* p. 491.

p. 180   "took [his] breath": ibid.

p. 181   "I feel you": Sherwood Anderson to HBL, April 28, 1925, SAC.

p. 181   "I'll have to": Anderson, *Memoirs,* p. 491.

p. 181   "Since you were": Sherwood Anderson to HBL, April 18, 1925, SAC.

p. 182   "Sherwood, you've written": HBL to Sherwood Anderson, June 2, 1925, SAC.

p. 182   "But please believe": ibid.

p. 182   "I'll keep you": HBL to Sherwood Anderson, September 11, 1925, SAC.

p. 184   "Something happened and": Raymond Carver, *No Heroics Please*, p. 198.

p. 186   "I had to": Anderson, *Memoirs*, p. 495.

p. 186   "You are what": Sherwood Anderson to HBL, August 1929, SAC.

p. 186   "When you went": Anderson, *Memoirs*, p. 317.

p. 187   "And there was": ibid.

p. 188   "Have you gone": Sherwood Anderson to HBL, March 3, 1929, SAC.

p. 188   "I quite agree": HBL to Sherwood Anderson, March 7, 1929, SAC.

p. 188   "If I were": Sherwood Anderson to HBL, March 8, 1929, SAC.

p. 189   "elephantine kind of": Joseph Blotner, *Faulkner: A Biography*, vol. 1, p. 416.

p. 190   "The exact word": William Faulkner, *Essays, Speeches and Public Letters*, p. 5.

p. 190   "I am pretty": Howe, *Sherwood Anderson*, p. 236.

p. 191   "I am feeling": Sherwood Anderson to HBL, no date, SAC.

p. 191   "When you go": Sherwood Anderson to HBL, August 9, 1929, SAC.

p. 191   "Your bedtime suggestion": HBL to Sherwood Anderson, August 12, 1929, SAC.

p. 191   "I may have": Sherwood Anderson to HBL, December 27, 1929, SAC.

p. 192   "AM SORRY BUT": Sherwood Anderson to HBL, December 29, 1929, SAC.

p. 192   "DEAR SHERWOOD IT'S": HBL to Sherwood Anderson, December 30, 1929, SAC.

p. 192   "I wish it": Townsend, *Sherwood Anderson*, p. 243.

p. 192   "Lots of times": Sherwood Anderson to [name and date unknown,] Kim Townsend, *Sherwood Anderson: A Biography*, p. 243.

p. 192   "he found himself": Faulkner, *Essays*, p. 6.

p. 193   "It's an awful": HBL to Sherwood Anderson, June 2, 1930, SAC.

p. 193   "The omnibus volume": ibid.

p. 193   "I knew that": Faulkner, *Essays*, p. 10.

Chapter 10: A Cup of Coffee

p. 194   "If I can't": HBL to TD, W. A. Swanberg, *Dreiser*, p. 257.

p. 195   "that I get": TD to HBL, date unknown, HLC.

p. 195   "I cross my": HBL to TD, March 29, 1923, HLC.

p. 196   "I have read": HBL to TD, August 2, 1923, HLC.

p. 196   "I am going": ibid.

p. 198   "Well, you're too": Swanberg, *Dreiser*, p. 287.

p. 200   "take care of me": Dreiser to HBL, March 23, 1926, HLC.

p. 200   "taken care of him": ibid.

p. 200   "You're a liar": ibid.

p. 201   "set-up": HBL to TD, March 26, 1926, HLC.

p. 201   "set-up": HBL to TD, ibid.

p. 201   "I may have": HBL to TD, ibid.

p. 201   "five minute talk": ibid.

p. 202   "You are proud": HBL to TD, April 2, 1926, HLC.

p. 203   "Hell, what's fifty": Gilmer, *Horace Liveright,* p. 135.

p. 204   "You have now": TD to HBL, February 15, 1929, HLC.

p. 204   "[Dreiser] was essentially": Mencken, *My Life as Author and Editor,* p. 394.

p. 205   "The corporation has": Confidential report by Robert R. Rucker for TD, February 20, 1929, HLC.

p. 206   "It would be": ibid.

p. 208   "Since Horace Liveright": TD to Leon Shimkin, no date, *Letters of Theodore Dreiser,* vol. 3, p. 859.

Chapter 11: Parade of the Vice Presidents

p. 209   "I pray to": Arthur Garfield Hays, *City Lawyer,* p. 238.

p. 209   "Liveright was head": Donald Friede, *The Mechanical Angel,* p. 25.

p. 211   "Horace, you've got": Edith Stern, "The Man Who Was Unafraid," p. 15.

p. 211   "an unpleasant personality": Klopfer interview, 1967, CU.

p. 215   "You're always moaning": Cerf, *At Random,* p. 27.

p. 216   "You can go": ibid.

p. 217   "wide-eyed boy": ibid., p. 33.

p. 219   "at least 45": Cerf-Liveright contract of 1923.

p. 219   "What must you": Cerf, *At Random,* p. 39.

p. 220   "She looked at": ibid.

p. 220   "lack of integrity": Klopfer interview, 1967, CU.

p. 221   "by some kind": Cerf, *At Random,* p. 38.

p. 221   "It was his": Ben Hecht, *A Jew in Love,* p. 300.

p. 222   "He did not know": Thomas Wolfe, *The Web and the Rock,* pp. 512–13.

p. 223   "[It] is so": David Herbert Donald, *Look Homeward: A Life of Thomas Wolfe,* p. 174.

p. 223   "They all seem": Cerf, *At Random,* p. 51.

p. 224   "The Boni and": Edith Stern, "The Man Who Was Unafraid," p. 14.

p. 226   "[It] strikes me": Norman Douglas to HBL, March 18, 1924, BC.

p. 226   "I feel that": HBL to Norman Douglas, April 18, 1924, BC.

p. 226   "I am determined": HBL to Norman Douglas, September 12, 1924, BC.

p. 227   "Your letter of": HBL to Norman Douglas, October 23, 1924, BC.

p. 228   "And so I'm": Bennett Cerf, Journal, May 20, 1925, Cerf Collection, CU.

p. 228   "Oh, how I'd": Cerf, *At Random*, p. 44.

p. 228   "What will you": ibid.

p. 229   "Well, you're my": Hays, *City Lawyer*, p. 45.

p. 230   "About nine or": Cerf, *At Random*, p. 60.

p. 232   "He [Komroff] continues": Friede, *Mechanical Angel*, p. 17.

p. 233   "So when I": ibid., p. 16.

p. 236   "fits of giggles": Francis Meynell, *My Lives*, p. 86.

p. 236   "Speak! Irene! Wife!": Friede, *Mechanical Angel*, pp. 30–1.

p. 237   "Too bad, Donald": ibid., p. 61.

p. 237   "There seems to": HBL to Donald Friede, June 20, 1927, HLC.

p. 237   "prove that none": Donald Friede to HBL, June 21, 1927, HLC.

p. 238   "I read a": Donald Friede to HBL, July 5, 1927, HLC.

p. 238   "I must repudiate": Tommy Smith to HBL, July 6, 1927, HLC.

p. 238   "I think we": HBL to Donald Friede, July 11, 1927, HLC.

p. 239   "UNANIMOUSLY REJECT ALL": HBL to Donald Friede, May 25, 1927, HLC.

p. 239   "The only thing": HBL to Arthur Garfield Hays, July 14, 1947, HLC.

p. 241   "What shall I": HBL to Ezra Pound, October 25, 1928, EPC.

Chapter 12: Two That Got Away: Faulkner and Hemingway

p. 242   "About Faulkner: he's": HBL to Sherwood Anderson, April 26, 1926, SAC.

p. 242   "If this is": Faulkner, *Essays*, p. 10.

p. 242   "Sherwood says he'll": ibid.

p. 242   "nasty": Sherwood Anderson to HBL, April 18, 1926, SAC.

p. 242 – 43   "read Bill Falkner's": Sherwood Anderson to HBL, June 12, 1925, SAC.

p. 243   "I am glad": Sherwood Anderson to HBL, August 28, 1925, SAC.

p. 243   "I hope you": Sherwood Anderson to HBL, June 12, 1926, SAC.

p. 245   "This doesn't mean": HBL to Sherwood Anderson, April 24, 1926, SAC.

p. 245   "Lost some money": William Faulkner to HBL, "late July" 1927, William Faulkner, *Selected Letters*, pp. 36–7.

p. 247   "Will you please": William Faulkner to HBL, March 11, 1927, WWN.

p. 247   "I remember we": Kronenberger, *No Whippings,* p. 25.

p. 248   "It is with": HBL to William Faulkner, c. November 1927, Blotner, *Faulkner,* vol. 1, pp. 559–600.

p. 248   "little improvement in": ibid.

p. 249   "Every day or": William Faulkner to Mrs. Walter McLean, "probably spring 1928," Faulkner, *Selected Letters,* pp. 40–41.

p. 250   "should have been": Blotner, *Faulkner,* vol. 1, p. 585.

p. 251   "I'm going to": William Faulkner to Mrs. Walter McLean, "probably October 1928," Faulkner, *Selected Letters,* p. 41.

p. 251   "If Liveright had": Ernest Hemingway to Gertrude Stein, ca. May 13, 1924, Ernest Hemingway, *Selected Letters,* p. 118.

p. 251   "pearl among publishers": Ezra Pound to John Quinn, June 20, 1920, JQC.

p. 252   "I thought it": Harold Loeb, *The Way It Was,* pp. 285–86.

p. 253   "I squirmed, I": ibid., p. 227.

p. 253   "low-down kike": ibid.

p. 253   "Just the three": ibid., p. 236.

p. 254   "DELIGHTED. ACCEPT.": Ernest Hemingway to HBL, March 5, 1925, EHC.

p. 254   "I certainly do": Ernest Hemingway to Sherwood Anderson, May 23, 1925, Hemingway, *Selected Letters,* p. 162.

p. 255   "The book is": HBL to Ernest Hemingway, May 1, 1925, EHC.

p. 255   "I do not": Ernest Hemingway to HBL, March 21, 1925, Hemingway, *Selected Letters,* p. 155.

p. 255   "We could have": ibid., p. 163.

p. 255   *"inaccrochable"*: Ernest Hemingway, *A Moveable Feast,* p. 15.

p. 255   "like a picture": ibid.

p. 255   "I'm sorry to": HBL to Ernest Hemingway, May 1, 1925, EHC.

p. 258   "The humor is": Ernest Hemingway to HBL, December 7, 1925, Hemingway, *Selected Letters,* p. 173.

p. 258   "The only reason": ibid.

p. 258   "It might interest": F. Scott Fitzgerald to HBL, "before December 1925," Fitzgerald, *Correspondence,* p. 183.

p. 258   "Frankly I hope": ibid.

p. 259   "I did not": Ernest Hemingway to Charles Poore, January 23, 1953, Hemingway, *Selected Letters,* p. 799.

p. 259   "not like him": ibid.

p. 259   "a model of": Gilmer, *Horace Liveright,* p. 124.

p. 259   "There are too": ibid.

p. 259   "To get back": HBL to Ernest Hemingway, December 30, 1925, Gilmer, p. 124.

p. 260   "[The American public]": HBL to Ernest Hemingway, December 30, 1925, EHC.

p. 260   "REJECTING TORRENTS OF": HBL to Ernest Hemingway, December 30, 1925, Hemingway, *Selected Letters*, p. 183.

p. 260   "Mr. Liveright or": Ernest Hemingway to Louis Bromfield, c. March 8, 1926, Hemingway, *Selected Letters*, p. 194.

p. 261   "God it feels": Ernest Hemingway to F. Scott Fitzgerald, January 1, 1926, ibid., p. 185.

Chapter 13: Winning and Losing

p. 262   ". . . we can't continue": HBL to LL, c. 1925, LWC.

p. 262   "Do you, or": HBL to Bertrand Russell, December 20, 1925, HLC.

p. 263   "I, I believe": HBL to Bertrand Russell, February 9, 1926, HLC.

p. 264   "What a fool": HBL to LL, 1925, LWC.

p. 266   "Today is Lucille's": HBL to Alfred Wallerstein, July 23, 1926, HLC.

p. 266   "could be at": Kronenberger, *No Whippings*, p. 21.

p. 267   "mastodon hangovers": Tom Dardis, *The Thirsty Muse: Alcohol and the American Writer*, p. 183.

p. 268   "rummies are rummies": ibid., p. 157.

p. 268   "At 11:50 you": Waldo Frank to HBL, March 17, 1928, HLC.

p. 269   "certain members of": Kronenberger, *No Whippings*, p. 9.

p. 269   "In walked Mr.": ibid.

Chapter 14: "I Am . . . Dracula"

p. 278   "I SAW WITH": John D. Williams to HBL, September 14, 1929, APC.

p. 280   "light, airy, golden": Edwin Justus Mayer, *A Preface to Life*, p. 183.

p. 281   "You really amuse": HBL to Mildred Gilman, December 4, 1929, HLC.

p. 282   "Since I saw": HBL to Alfred Wallerstein, August 3, 1927, HLC.

p. 282   "of course, the": ibid.

p. 284   "The hero of": Frank, *Time Exposures*, p. 116.

p. 285   "DEAR ALFRED TOMORROW": HBL to Alfred Wallerstein, March 17, 1927, HLC.

p. 286   "I'LL ADMIT I": HBL to Alfred Wallerstein, November 18, 1927, HLC.

p. 286   "Although it was": David J. Skal, *Hollywood Gothic*, p. 78.

p. 286   "A censor-proof way": ibid., p. 79.

p. 286   "flashy American . . . [who]": ibid.

p. 287   "Ye who have": ibid., p. 85.

p. 287   "The count . . . in": ibid.

p. 290   "bluer skies somewhere": F. Scott Fitzgerald, *Correspondence,* p. 494.

Chapter 15: On the Edge

p. 291   "God it's terribly": HBL to Julie Lasden, July 7, 1927, HLC.

p. 291   "dark curly hair": Komroff, "The Liveright Story," p. 200.

p. 292   "minister without portfolio": Kronenberger, *No Whippings,* p. 18.

p. 292   "I think she's": HBL to Julie Lasden, July 7, 1927, HLC.

p. 292   "a very weak": ibid., HLC.

p. 293   "the great love": Author's interview with Herman Liveright, June 1992.

p. 293   "I saw that": HBL to Alfred Wallerstein, July 26, 1928, HLC.

p. 294   "Now for a": ibid.

p. 294   "I have really": HBL to Alfred Wallerstein, August 3, 1927, HLC.

p. 295   "And in spite": HBL to Betsy Wallerstein, May 10, 1929, HLC.

p. 296   "WORKING TERRIBLY HARD": HBL to Alfred Wallerstein, July 2, 1929, HLC.

p. 296   "The stock market": HBL to T. R. Smith, April 5, 1926, HLC.

p. 297   "a rather big": HBL to Leonard Amster, August 29, 1929, HLC.

p. 299   "You can't fire": Maurice Hanline, *The Years of Indiscretion,* pp. 198–99.

p. 300   "I'm pretty badly": HBL to Alfred Wallerstein, June 5, 1929, HLC.

p. 302   "Dear Horace, you": Mike Gold to HBL, July 1929, HLC.

p. 304   "the delicious book": Bertrand Russell to HBL, February 3, 1930, BRC.

p. 306   "brought up on": Bertrand Russell to HBL, January 25, 1925, BRC.

p. 306   "I would be": HBL to Bertrand Russell, September 15, 1925, BRC.

p. 307   "I do not": Bertrand Russell to HBL, June 24, 1929, BRC.

p. 308   "You will find": Bertrand Russell to HBL, July 20, 1929, BRC.

p. 309   "I don't know": HBL to Bertrand Russell, July 7, 1930, BRC.

p. 309   "Certainly not": memo, HBL to Julian Messner, April 10, 1929, HLC.

p. 309   "I cannot understand": HBL to Hart Crane, August 25, 1929, HLC.

p. 310   "However I have": ibid.

p. 310   "Let me tell": HBL to Hart Crane, September 5, 1929, HLC.

p. 312   "The stock market": HBL to Leonard Amster, August 29, 1929, HLC.

p. 313   "I, personally, don't": Fred Hummel to HBL, April 4, 1930, HLC.

p. 314   "Dick had the": Charles Gordon to HBL, June 13, 1930, HLC.

p. 316   "It will interest": HBL to Bertrand Russell, July 7, 1930, HLC.

p. 316   "hadn't sold myself": HBL to Eugene O'Neill, July 25, 1930, HLC.

p. 317 "I am to": ibid.

p. 317 "Of course the": ibid.

Chapter 16: Eisenstein and Hollywood

p. 318 "EVERYTHING HERE IS": HBL to Arthur Pell, August 14, 1930, APC.

p. 321 "I cannot find": Cecil B. DeMille, *Autobiography,* p. 290.

p. 324 "It makes no": Sergei Eisenstein, *Immoral Memories: An Autobiography,* p. 141.

p. 325 "Today on the": HBL to Dorothy Peterson, autumn 1930, TY, p. 142.

p. 325 "[In 1931] the": Hellman, *Unfinished Woman,* p. 48.

p. 326 "was one of": TY, p. 133.

p. 327 "heavenly California sunshine": TY, p. 135.

p. 327 "drink an occasional": ibid.

p. 328 "Gentlemen, it is": Ivor Montagu, *With Eisenstein in Hollywood,* p. 175.

p. 328 "cut-throat Red dog": Marie Seton, *Sergei M. Eisenstein,* p. 167.

p. 328 "Moscow Jew, Eisenstein": ibid., p. 175.

p. 328 "It was for": David O. Selznick, *Memo from David O. Selznick,* pp. 26–27.

p. 329 "NO—Lew": Paramount Pictures personnel files.

p. 329 "Well, Liveright . . . I": Charles Rogers to HBL, TY, p. 138.

p. 330 "I was put": TY, p. 137.

p. 330 "I know all": ibid.

p. 331 "Poor, poor deluded": HBL to Tommy Smith, March 19, 1931, APC.

p. 331 "As a matter": ibid.

p. 333 "commencing to feel": HBL to Julian Messner and Tommy Smith, May 26, 1921, APC.

p. 333 "she termed my": TY, 146.

p. 334 "my love for": ibid., p. 149.

p. 334 "Mr. Liveright . . . when": ibid.

p. 335 "stultifying": TY, 148.

p. 335 "Some of the": Hellman, *Unfinished Woman,* p. 48.

p. 336 "IN THE WORDS": HBL to Julian Messner, May 31, 1931, APC.

p. 337 "Dorothy and Eddie": TY, p. 150.

Chapter 17: The Light Fades

p. 338 "As you stay": Louis-Ferdinand Céline, *Journey to the End of the Night,* p. 273.

p. 338 "[HBL] could be": Cerf, *At Random,* p. 80.

p. 338 "Horace could scarcely": Kronenberger, *No Whippings,* p. 37.

p. 340   "Mostly Horace has": Helen Woodward to E. J. Mayer, December 9, 1931, Theatre Collection, New York Public Library.

p. 341   "Tommy Smith and": ibid.

p. 341   "the party for": ibid.

p. 341   "Beautiful and clear": Hellman, *Unfinished Woman*, p. 49.

p. 341   "a great many": Kronenberger, *No Whippings*, p. 37.

p. 341 – 42   "She's a bitch": Komroff, "The Liveright Story," p. 249.

p. 342   "No, wait for": Hellman, *Unfinished Woman*, p. 49.

p. 342   "I think I": ibid.

p. 342   "Lilly, were you": ibid.

p. 342   "I've been resting": ibid., p. 50.

p. 342   "It's a little": E. J. Mayer to Helen Woodward, March 1932, Theatre Collection, New York Public Library.

p. 343   "I gave it": ibid.

p. 343   "When I arrived": ibid.

p. 343   "I wish him": ibid.

p. 344   "GOLDSMITH HANLINE AGREE": HBL to E. J. Mayer, April 23, 1932, Theatre Collection, New York Public Library.

p. 346   "Don't you love": Komroff, "The Liveright Story," p. 264.

p. 346   "He told me": ibid.

p. 347   In 1933 Frank: Author's interview with Frank Heller, June 1992.

p. 348   "All summer long": Komroff, "The Liveright Story," p. 239.

p. 349   "There was the": ibid.

p. 350   "Why have I": TY, pp. 65–66.

p. 352   "He arose and": Anderson, *Memoirs*, p. 519.

p. 352   "I'll just be": ibid.

p. 352   "Horace, I don't": Kronenberger, *No Whippings*, p. 37.

p. 353   "There is nothing": Komroff, "The Liveright Story," p. 267.

p. 353   "It was pneumonia": HBL to E. J. Mayer, September 21, 1933, Theatre Collection, New York Public Library.

p. 354   "He had raised": James Boswell, *Boswell's Life of Johnson*, vol. 2, p. 281.

Index

About the Author

TOM DARDIS is Professor Emeritus at John Jay College of Criminal Justice in New York City. He obtained his doctorate at Columbia University in 1980. Prior to teaching, he was in the book publishing industry for nearly twenty years, mainly as associate editor at Avon Books and editor in chief of Berkley Books. His previous books include biographies of Buster Keaton and Harold Lloyd, as well as *Some Time in the Sun,* a study of American writers in Hollywood, and *The Thirsty Muse,* about the alcoholism of several American writers. He is married and lives in Riverdale, New York.

About the Type

This book was set in Perpetua, a typeface designed by the English artist Eric Gill, and cut by The Monotype Corporation between 1928 and 1930. Perpetua is a contemporary face of original design, without any direct historical antecedents. The shapes of the roman letters are derived from the techniques of stonecutting. The larger display sizes are extremely elegant and form a most distinguished series of inscriptional letters.